Colin Chapman

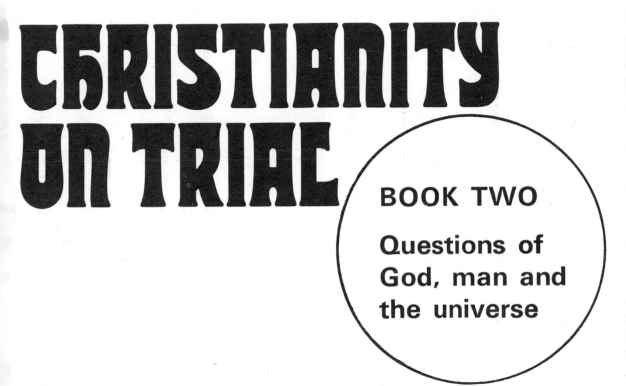

CHRISTIANITY ON TRIAL

BOOK TWO

Questions of God, man and the universe

Lion Publishing

EXPLANATION OF SYMBOLS

 Introducing each of the seven questions dealt with
in the three books

 A road intersection sign then shows the various
possible answers

 Each answer is then introduced by this route sign

Two further symbols appear within the answer sections:

 A one-way sign points out the effect or consequences of
a particular answer

A hazard sign shows the problems or questions arising
out of the answer

LION PUBLISHING
P O Box 50, Berkhamsted, Herts

First edition 1974
ISBN 0 85648 015 0
Copyright © 1974 Lion Publishing

Printed in Great Britain by Compton Printing Ltd., Aylesbury

CONTENTS

BOOK ONE
Question One: How can we know if Christianity is true?

BOOK TWO
Question Two: Who or what is God? Does he exist?   9
—and diagram of answers   10
Answer 1: BIBLICAL CHRISTIANITY   11
    2: PRIMAL RELIGION AND JUDAISM, ISLAM
       AND DEISM   19
    3: AGNOSTICISM AND MYSTICISM   25
    4: ATHEISM   30
    5: PANTHEISM AND SOME MODERN THEOLOGIANS   33
Back to Answer One: Problems and Questions   42

Question Three: What is man?   48
—and diagram of answers   52
Answer 1: BIBLICAL CHRISTIANITY   53
    2: PRIMAL RELIGION AND JUDAISM, ISLAM
       AND DEISM   66
    3: HUMANISM, EXISTENTIALISM, COMMUNISM AND
       EASTERN RELIGIONS   75
Back to Answer One: Problems and Questions   107

Question Four: What kind of universe do we live in?   116
—and diagram of answers   117
Answer 1: BIBLICAL CHRISTIANITY   118
    2: PRIMAL RELIGION AND JUDAISM, ISLAM
       AND DEISM   123
    3: HINDUISM, EUROPEAN THINKERS AND
       SOME MODERN THEOLOGIANS   127
Back to Answer One: Problems and Questions   135
References   138
Index   143

BOOK THREE
Question Five: How was Jesus related to God?
Question Six: What is the meaning of the death of Jesus?
Question Seven: Did Jesus rise from the dead?

ILLUSTRATIONS

9 Member of the Hari-Krishna movement
12/13 Night sky
16 Reconstruction of the Tabernacle
20 Glastonbury gathering. Woman in a trance
21 Voodoo in Haiti
23 Moslem worshipper facing Mecca to pray
26 Head of Buddha at Kamakura, Japan
27 Crossroads in Haight-Ashbury, hippie Mecca
28 Scene from the rock musical *Hair*
34 Pilgrims on the banks of the Ganges
35 Statue of monkey-god Marutti
37 Paul Tillich
40 Hindu holy man reading from the scriptures
45 Relief of the crowning of Homer. Egyptian Papyrus of Ani
48 Tolstoy
49 Somerset Maugham
51 Survivor of an Italian earthquake
56/7 Mother Teresa of Calcutta
61 Japanese child suffering the effects of pollution. Thalidomide victim. Polluted river
62 After an earthquake in Turkey
68 Pilgrims camping outside Mecca
72 A Samaritan
73 John Locke
76 Julian Huxley
78 Karl Marx. Church in the USSR
79 Yin Yang sign
84 Hippie couple in conversation with Allen Ginsberg
86 Rebecca West
90 Materials-testing nuclear reactor at Dounreay
91 Atomic test in the Nevada desert
92 Jed Stone cartoon
93 Tibetan wheel of the Law
96 Nazi storm troopers in Vienna
102 Jean-Paul Sartre. Barrault's Mère Ubu, from *Jarry sur la Butte*
104 Colin Wilson
105 The Trial ; *Alice in Wonderland*
106 Magistrates' court in session
108 Graph machine recording brain waves
114 Charles Darwin
120 Egg of a Noctuid moth seen through a microscope. Marine diatom seen through a microscope
121 Detail of the eye of a moth. Sea sponges
122 H. R. Rookmaaker
126 Spider
133 Sir Henry Moore
136 'Messier 13' in the constellation 'Hercules'

Acknowledgements

British Museum, picture on page 45 ; *British Museum* (*Natural History*), pages 120, 121 ; *Camera Press,* pages 9, 12, 20, 21, 23, 26, 27, 28, 34, 35, 37, 40, 48, 49, 51, 56, 61, 62, 68, 72, 76, 78, 84, 86, 90, 91, 102, 104, 106, 108, 114, 133, 136 ; *Fox Photos,* page 122 ; *Jean-Luc Ray,* page 126 ; *Jed Stone,* page 92 ; *Jon Willcocks,* page 122 ; *National Portrait Gallery,* page 73.

GENERAL INTRODUCTION

**'I could tell you my adventures – beginning from this morning,'
said Alice a little timidly: 'but it's no use going back to yesterday,
because I was a different person then.'
'Explain all that,' said the Mock Turtle.
'No, no! The adventures first,' said the Gryphon in an
impatient tone: 'explanations take such a dreadful time.'**

Explanations take such a dreadful time. But
if we omit them, we are likely to meet with
this reaction:

'What *is* the use of repeating all that stuff,' the
Mock Turtle interrupted, 'if you don't explain it
as you go on? It's by far the most confusing
thing *I* ever heard!'

Is Christianity *true* or is it not?

How can we possibly *know* whether it is
true or not?

These are the basic questions before us in
putting Christianity on trial. We are dealing
primarily with Christian beliefs about God
and Jesus Christ, about man and the universe.
We are asking whether they tell us 'the truth'
about ourselves and about the universe in
which we live.

But how can Christian beliefs be put on
trial?

Questions about Jesus Christ

There was a time when it seemed very simple
to prove the truth of Christianity. A Christian
could stage a trial which ended like this:

Judge: Gentlemen of the Jury, I have laid before

you the Substance of what has been said on
both Sides. You are now to consider of it,
and give your Verdict.

Foreman: My Lord, we are ready to give our
Verdict.

Judge: Are you all agreed?

Jury: Yes.

Judge: Who shall speak for you?

Jury: Our Foreman.
Judge: What say you? Are the Apostles guilty of giving false Evidence in the Case of the Resurrection of Jesus, or not guilty?
Foreman: Not guilty.

This happened in England in 1729.

Recently a similar trial was staged in a youth club in Scotland, but with significant differences. This time a Christian was put on trial, and the charges against him were these:
1. that your faith is based on a myth – the resurrection;
2. that your faith is irrelevant to life in the twentieth century.
All who took part in this trial were speaking for themselves and expressing their own beliefs; they were not acting a part. A few were Christians, but most were not. The audience were the jury, but there was no vote at the end. The judge in his summing up simply explained that each person must decide for himself whether or not he thought the Christian was guilty on these two charges.

If the idea of this second trial appeals to you, or at least makes some sense to you, you may want to go straight to the third book in this series, which deals with the evidence for Jesus Christ, the meaning of his death and the question of his resurrection.

Questions about God, man and the universe

To many, however, this second trial will sound just as strange or absurd as the first. If you cannot understand or accept Christian beliefs about Jesus, it may be because you do not accept some of the most fundamental Christian assumptions about God and man and the universe, and not simply because you are not convinced by the evidence about Jesus.

Bishop Butler, writing in 1736:

It has come, I know not how, to be taken for granted, by many persons, that Christianity is not so much a subject for enquiry but that it is, now at length, discovered to be fictitious. And accordingly they treat it as if in the present age this were an agreed point among all people of discernment, and nothing remained, but to set it up as a principal subject of mirth and ridicule,

as it were by way of reprisals, for its having so long interrupted the pleasures of the world.

J. S. Mill:

I am . . . one of the very few examples, in this country, of one who has not thrown off religious belief, but never had it: I grew up in a negative state with regard to it. I looked upon the modern exactly as I did upon the ancient religion, as something which in no way concerned me.

Nietzsche, writing in 1865 at the age of 21:

If Christianity means belief in a historical person or event, I have nothing to do with it. But if it means the need for salvation, then I can treasure it.

Mahatma Ghandi:

I may say that I have never been interested in an historical Jesus. I should not care if it was proved by someone that the man called Jesus never lived, and that what was narrated in the Gospels was a figment of the writer's imagination. For the Sermon on the Mount would still be true for me.

Colin Wilson:

The need for God I could understand, and the need for religion; I could even sympathize with the devotees like Suso or St. Francis, who weave fantasies around the Cross, the nails and all the other traditional symbols. But ultimately I could not accept the need for redemption by a Saviour. To pin down the idea of salvation to one point in time seemed to me a naive kind of anthropomorphism.

If, therefore, your questions and objections about Christianity are about fundamental assumptions about God, man and the universe, there will be little point in making Jesus the starting-point of the discussion. You ought to begin with one or more of the questions in the second book in this series. Who or what is 'God'? Does 'he' exist? What is man? Who am I? What kind of universe do we live in?

Questions about definition and truth

But what if you are not sure what Christianity is?

James Mitchell:

I used to be a convinced Christian: I am no longer a convinced Christian: I am no longer convinced. In fact like many others of my generation I am profoundly uncertain as to what 'being a Christian' actually means any more.

C. E. M. Joad:

If you will forgive me for mixing my metaphors, to criticize Christianity is like assaulting a feather bed with the consistency of a jelly and the colours of a chameleon.

And what if the idea of putting *any* ideas or beliefs on trial sounds absurd?

The hero in Henri Barbusse's novel L'Enfer:

As to philosophical discussions, they seem to me altogether meaningless. *Nothing can be tested, nothing verified*. Truth – what do they mean by it?

Michael Harrington:

The contemporary spiritual crisis is the result of this simultaneous loss of faith and anti-faith ... Its unique characteristic is that no one really seems to believe in anything.

C. E. M. Joad writing about the war of 1914–18:

Then came the war ... When it came to the point, the ethics of Christianity were, it seemed, as incapable of practical application as its history and biology of scientific verification. The whole religion as it is taught and preached today thus came to seem a gigantic swindle ...

Margaret Cole:

It is partly because I care for verification that I cannot believe in any 'revealed religion' ... When the question of the *truth* of Christianity was raised in my mind ... I perceived almost immediately that it was not true, and that it could not possibly be proved to be true; and the burden of religious belief fell from my back as easily as did the burden of Christian in *The Pilgrim's Progress*, and has never shown any sign of returning to its perch.

If you share these feelings, or have a strong sympathy with those who feel this way, you will probably have to begin with the questions about definition and truth in the first book in this series.

The method and material used

Each of the main sections (in the case of

Book One, the whole book) has an introduction outlining the general approach and defining the question being tackled.

Then the 'road intersection' shows the possible answers to the question.

Each answer is then examined in detail.

Much of the book consists of quotations from different writers, because it is important that we should try to feel the full force of what they are saying. Where there is merely a summary of a person's position, the summary is in most cases taken from a writer who has no particular axe to grind or does not share the outlook of this book (for this reason much use has been made of, for example, Paul Hazard's books *The European Mind 1680–1715* and *European Thought in the Eighteenth Century*). Where italics have been used they are the italics of the original author.

Quotations have been chosen from the philosophers, tracing the history and progression of their thought; from the arts, because often this is the area where beliefs can be worked out and carried to their logical conclusions; from other religions, because East and West are becoming more aware of each other's ways of thinking and no approach to Christianity should leave them out of account; and from modern theology which has been profoundly affected by the history of ideas.

Finally, some problems and questions about the Christian answers are dealt with.

The starting-point

What is 'Christianity'? There are so many definitions that it is necessary, before we begin, to say something about the starting-point of this book.

There are three possible ways of answering the question:

Try to find the lowest common denominator in all the different definitions of Christianity that are offered; limit the definition to include only those items which all Christians or the vast majority of Christians would accept without question.

Refuse to define Christianity at all. Allow each person to have his own understanding of Christianity, and show the maximum tolerance towards anything which is described as 'Christian'.

State your own understanding of what Christianity is, at least as a starting-point; further discussion will show to what extent it is consistent with the mind of Christ.

This third approach is the one I have adopted. I shall take as my starting-point what is generally called Biblical Christianity; *i.e.* dependent solely on what we know of God and Christ from the basic documents of the Bible, both Old and New Testaments. This understanding of Christianity is not that of any one church or denomination.

No discussion is held from a purely 'neutral' position. Therefore the aim in stating my own position is not to be sectarian and doctrinaire, but simply to declare the book's starting-point openly and clearly.

The position of this book, then, is basically a committed one. But its method is open. It is for the reader to start where he will, at the point where he is. He can examine the options, follow up which he wants in the order he wants. It may mean going back to an earlier question to be settled first.

Then it is for the reader to make up his own mind, to follow up the evidence – and act accordingly.

Living with your beliefs

It is not enough simply to outline different answers and consider them coldly as possible theories for discussion. We have to ask: *what does it feel like* to live with a belief about God, to go through life with a particular understanding of man, or to live in one kind of universe?

For this reason the quotations (including those from the Bible) are intended, not simply to convey the answers in a theoretical way, but to help us enter into the experience of those who hold these particular beliefs.

We follow up the different answers to see where they lead, applying the 'simple but profound test of fact': i.e. '*does this concept really work; do its consequences fit our experience?*' (Bronowski, see BOOK ONE, p. 21). In each case we need to ask questions such as these:

— what would happen if we were to be thoroughly consistent and take this belief to its logical conclusion?

— what would happen if we were to live as if this belief were really true?

And for '*what would happen if . . . ?*' we can usually substitute '*what has happened when . . . ?*'—because there have always been people who have tried to be consistent in their search for the truth, and have explored all the possible answers and their consequences.

In many cases we shall discover what Francis Schaeffer calls the 'point of tension' between what a person believes and the real world in which he has to live. If a belief leads to disastrous consequences, or if we can only hold it by not being totally consistent, then it is highly likely that our belief is not true. We are then faced with a choice:

either we accept the full consequences of what we believe

or we look for a different belief which stands up better to the test of truth.

A change of mind of this kind is bound to have a profound effect on all our attitudes. If Christianity is true—and if we are prepared to consider this possibility—we have to be willing to change our minds, to open them to the truth which God has revealed, and see where this leads us. This process of change involves the heart and will as much as the intellect. Jesus said: 'Whoever has the will to do the will of God shall know whether my teaching comes from him or is merely my own.'

QUESTION TWO

"Who or what is God?
Does he exist?"

The question about God is a two-part one:

☐ **Who or what is God? (the question of definition)**

☐ **Does he, if we think of him as a personal God, really exist?
(the question of his existence)**

**In practice, however, we cannot discuss the existence of God
without discussing what we mean by the word 'God'.**

BACK TO GODHEAD

There was a time when people in the western world could take it for granted that everyone had basically the same idea of what God is like. But for the vast majority these days are long past.

George Harrison:

When you say the word 'God' people are going to curl up and cringe—they all interpret it in a different way.

Alasdair MacIntyre:

It is not just that many people no longer believe in God. Many people no longer can understand what is meant.

John Robinson:

The word 'God' is so slippery and the reality so intangible that many today are questioning whether they have reference to anything that can usefully or meaningfully be talked about at all.

The traditional arguments for the existence of God are far from convincing (see Book One, pp. 31–39). We must therefore study in outline the different answers to the question about God which are live options in the world today, and test them by seeing how they affect beliefs about truth, man and the universe.

Who or what is God? Does he exist?

"There is a God; but he is rather different from the Bible's description"
PAGE 19

"We can never know whether or not God exists"
PAGE 25

"There is no God"
PAGE 30

"God really exists; he is as the Bible describes him"
PAGE 11

"There is no God; but the word is useful if we redefine its meaning"
PAGE 33

1. THE ANSWER OF BIBLICAL CHRISTIANITY

"God really exists; he is as the Bible describes him"

We can summarize the Bible's understanding of God in the following propositions. These do not exhaust the meaning of God for the Christian, but they do lay down certain fundamental guidelines.

☐ God is personal
☐ God is the Creator of the universe
☐ God is loving
☐ God is one

☐ and God is infinite
☐ and God is the Sustainer of the universe
☐ and God is holy
☐ and God is three 'persons'

The two propositions in each pair must be taken closely together to balance each other.

For example, it is not enough to say that God is the Creator of the universe, because this says nothing about his relationship to the universe now. So the statement that he is Creator must be paired with the statement that he is the Sustainer of the universe. Similarly, when we say that God is personal, we must immediately add that he is infinite. Although he has something in common with man who is conscious of being a person, he is not subject to the limitations of human personality.

All eight propositions must be held together. If we reject or seriously modify even one of them our whole belief about God will be seriously affected. (See further under Answer Two, pp. 19ff.)

God is personal

▷ He is not an impersonal 'It', or a force like energy or electricity. Just as men have personal names, so God in the Old Testament gives himself a personal name, Yahweh (probably meaning something like 'the One who is', 'the One who is there').

God said to Moses, 'I am who I am . . . the Lord (Yahweh) . . . this is my name for ever, and thus I am to be remembered throughout all generations . . .'

▷ He has *mind* and can think: he is not in some realm beyond thought or reason:

For my thoughts are not your thoughts,
 neither are your ways my ways, says the Lord.
For as the heavens are higher than the earth,
 so are my ways higher than your ways
 and my thoughts than your thoughts.

▷ He has *will* and can decide and make free choices: he is not controlled by any higher power like 'Fate':

I know that the Lord is great,
 and that our Lord is above all gods.
Whatever the Lord pleases he does,
 in heaven and on earth,
 in the seas and all deeps.

▷ He has *emotions* and can feel. The prophet Hosea describes God as speaking in this way about himself:

How can I give you up, O Ephraim! . . .

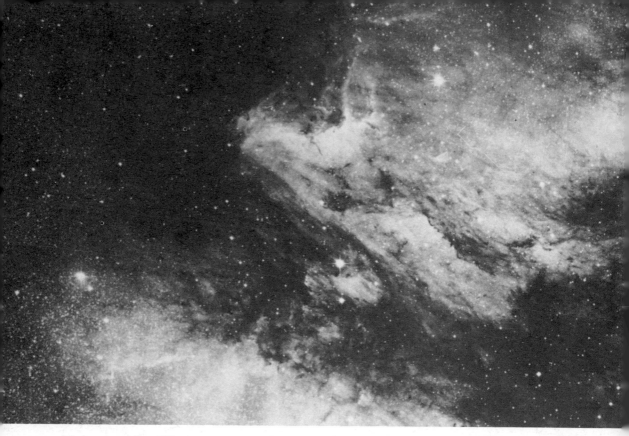

My heart recoils within me, my compassion grows
  warm and tender.

▷ Because he is 'personal', he can communicate truth and reveal himself to men; he can
enter into personal relationships with us, and
we can come to know him in a personal way.

For thus says the high and lofty One
  who inhabits eternity, whose name is Holy:
'I dwell in the high and holy place,
  and also with him who is of a contrite and
    humble spirit,
to revive the spirit of the humble,
  and to revive the heart of the contrite.'

The friendship of the Lord is for those who fear
  him,
  and he makes known to them his covenant.

God is infinite

▷ Although he is personal, he does not have
the limitations of human personality. He himself was not created by someone greater.

'You are my witnesses,' says the Lord,
  'and my servant whom I have chosen,
that you may know and believe me
  and understand that I am He.
Before me no god was formed,
  nor shall there be any after me.'

▷ He has always existed and will always
exist. He is not limited by time, because he
has created both space and time.

Before the mountains were brought forth
  or ever thou hadst formed the earth and the
    world,
  from everlasting to everlasting thou art God.

▷ He is not limited by the universe, because
he is at work throughout it; he is omnipresent.
Nothing in the universe works independently
of him.

Am I a God at hand, says the Lord, and not a
God afar off? Can a man hide himself in secret
places so that I cannot see him? says the Lord.
Do I not fill heaven and earth? says the Lord.

▷ He knows everything; he is omniscient. He
knows everything about each individual
person, and about the future.

O Lord, thou hast searched me and known me!
  Thou knowest when I sit down and when I
    rise up;
  thou discernest my thoughts from afar.

I am God, and there is none like me,
  declaring the end from the beginning.

▷ He can do anything he wants (though he

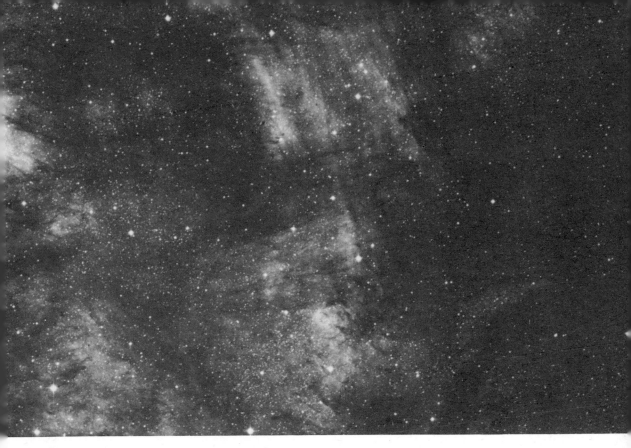

always acts 'in character'); he is omnipotent. There is no Chance or Fate or Luck behind God which works independently of him.

But he is unchangeable and who can turn him?
   what he desires, that he does.
For he will complete what he appoints for me;
   and many such things are in his mind.

▷ In this prayer Habakkuk speaks of God as both personal and infinite:

Art thou not from everlasting,
   O Lord my God, my Holy One?

God is the Creator of the universe

▷ The universe of time and space has been brought into existence by him of his own free choice. He did not *have* to create the universe; he was perfectly complete without it.

In the beginning God created the heavens and
   the earth . . .

Praise him, sun and moon,
   praise him, all you shining stars!
Praise him, you highest heavens,
   and you waters above the heavens!
Let them praise the name of the Lord!
   For he commanded and they were created.

Just some of the millions of stars visible from earth. The North America Nebula in Cygnus.

▷ The universe is completely distinct from God; he is transcendent. The universe is not a part of God or an emanation from God; neither is he a part of it.

By the word of the Lord the heavens were made,
   and all their host by the breath of his mouth.
He gathered the waters of the sea as in a bottle;
   he put the deeps in storehouses.
Let all the earth fear the Lord,
   let all the inhabitants of the world stand in awe
     of him!
For he spoke, and it came to be;
   he commanded, and it stood forth.

▷ God created the universe 'out of nothing'; there was no 'raw material' for God simply to marshal into order.

By faith we understand that the world was created by the word of God, so that what is seen was made out of things which do not appear.

▷ God uses the same great power with which he created the world, to help man in his weakness:

Have you not known? Have you not heard?

The Lord is the everlasting God,
the Creator of the ends of the earth.
He does not faint or grow weary,
his understanding is unsearchable.
He gives power to the faint,
and to him who has no might he increases
strength.
Even youths shall faint and be weary,
and young men shall fall exhausted;
but they who wait for the Lord
shall renew their strength,
they shall mount up with wings like eagles,
they shall run and not be weary,
they shall walk and not faint.

God is the Sustainer of the universe

▷ Not only is the universe created by God,
it is also 'maintained' by him. He is immanent
within the universe, although he is not a part
of it. He is not merely the First Cause. He is
not like the watchmaker who leaves the watch
to run by itself. The universe could not
continue without God.

O Lord my God, thou art very great!
Thou art clothed with honour and majesty,
who coverest thyself with light as with a
garment,
who hast stretched out the heavens like a tent . . .
Thou dost cause grass to grow for the cattle,
and plants for man to cultivate . . .
Thou makest darkness, and it is night . . .

He covers the heavens with clouds,
he prepares rain for the earth,
he makes grass grow upon the hills.
He gives to the beasts their food,
and to the young ravens which cry.

▷ Nehemiah links together the work of God
in creating and sustaining the universe:

Thou art the Lord, thou alone; thou hast made
heaven, the heaven of heavens, with all their host,
the earth and all that is on it, the seas and all that
is in them; and thou preservest all of them.

God is loving

▷ The Old Testament speaks in many different ways of the love of God towards man
whom he has created in his image:

I have loved you with an everlasting love;
therefore I have continued my faithfulness to
you.

As I live, says the Lord God, I have no pleasure

in the death of the wicked, but that the wicked
turn from his way and live . . .

Seek the Lord while he may be found,
call upon him while he is near;
let the wicked forsake his way,
and the unrighteous man his thoughts;
let him return to the Lord, that he may have
mercy on him,
and to our God for he will abundantly pardon.

The steadfast love of the Lord never ceases,
his mercies never come to an end;
they are new every morning;
great is thy faithfulness.

▷ In the New Testament the supreme revelation of the love of God is seen in the coming
of the eternal Son:

For God so loved the world that he gave his only
Son, that whoever believes in him should not
perish but have eternal life.

God shows his love for us in that while we were
yet sinners Christ died for us.

▷ Some passages go further and speak of an
eternal relationship of love between the
Father, the Son and the Spirit. Love is thus
part of the character of God: he did not
become loving after he created man.
Jesus speaks in this way about the Father:

For the Father loves the Son, and shows him all
that he himself is doing . . .

He prays:

Father, I desire that they also, whom thou hast
given me, may be with me where I am, to behold
my glory which thou hast given me in thy love for
me before the foundation of the world.

God is holy

▷ God is morally perfect; he is utterly good.
He is not morally neutral; he is not beyond
good and evil or above morality.

Thou who art of purer eyes than to behold evil
and canst not look on wrong . . .

For thou art not a God who delights in wickedness,
evil may not sojourn with thee.

Thus says the Lord: 'Let not the wise man glory
in his wisdom, let not the mighty man glory in his
might, let not the rich man glory in his riches;
but let him who glories glory in this, that he
understands and knows me, that I am the Lord

who practice kindness, justice, and righteousness in the earth; for in these things I delight, says the Lord.'

▷ The moral laws he has revealed to men are an expression of his character. There is an absolute standard for right and wrong in the character of God himself.

The Lord appeared to Abram, and said to him, 'I am God Almighty; walk before me, and be blameless.'

You shall be holy; for I the Lord your God am holy.

For the Lord is righteous, he loves righteous deeds;
    the upright shall behold his face.

You shall walk before the Lord your God and fear him, and keep his commandments and obey his voice, and you shall serve him and cleave to him . . . You shall purge the evil from the midst of you.

▷ Man's revolt against God is a personal affront to him and a breach of his laws. God cannot simply overlook man's disobedience or behave as if it doesn't matter, or as if it doesn't really exist.

. . . thou who triest the minds and hearts,
    thou righteous God . . .
God is a righteous judge,
    and a God who has indignation every day.

How can I pardon you?
    Your children have forsaken me,
    and have sworn by those who are no gods.
When I fed them to the full,
    they committed adultery
    and trooped to the houses of harlots.
They were well-fed lusty stallions,
    each neighing for his neighbour's wife.
Shall I not punish them for these things? says the Lord;
    and shall I not avenge myself on a nation such as this?

For wicked men are found among my people;
    they lurk like fowlers lying in wait.
They set a trap;
    they catch men.
Like a basket full of birds,
    their houses are full of treachery;
therefore they have become great and rich,
    they have grown fat and sleek.
They know no bounds in deeds of wickedness;
    they judge not with justice
the cause of the fatherless, to make it prosper,
    and they do not defend the rights of the needy.

Shall I not punish them for these things? says the Lord,
    and shall I not avenge myself on a nation such as this?

▷ In this revelation of the character of God given to Moses we have the love of God and the holiness of God held closely together:

The Lord passed before him, and proclaimed, 'The Lord, the Lord, a God merciful and gracious, slow to anger, and abounding in steadfast love and faithfulness, keeping steadfast love for thousands, forgiving iniquity and transgression and sin, but who will by no means clear the guilty.

Isaiah similarly holds together love and holiness:

For a brief moment I forsook you,
    but with great compassion I will gather you.
In overflowing wrath for a moment I hid my face from you,
    but with everlasting love I will have compassion on you,
    says the Lord, your Redeemer.

There is only one God

▷ Other supernatural beings and powers do exist—Satan and the angels; but they are all created beings, and subordinate to God. There are not a number of gods, each controlling different parts of the universe.

The Lord our God is one Lord; and you shall love the Lord your God with all your heart, and with all your soul, and with all your might.

▷ Since there is only one God, all men are bound to acknowledge him:

I am the Lord, and there is no other,
    besides me there is no God.
    I gird you, though you do not know me,
that men may know, from the rising of the sun
    and from the west, that there is none besides me;
I am the Lord, and there is no other.

Turn to me and be saved,
    all the ends of the earth!
    For I am God, and there is no other.
By myself I have sworn,
    from my mouth has gone forth in righteousness
    a word that shall not return:
'To me every knee shall bow,
    every tongue shall swear.'

There are three 'persons' in the one God

The first Christians were orthodox Jews who had been brought up to believe that God is one. They never abandoned their belief that God is one; but they gradually came to understand the oneness of God in a new way, and to distinguish between the Father, the Son and the Spirit. This radical reinterpretation of the oneness of God came about because of three things:

▷ Jesus spoke of himself as 'the Son' who enjoyed an intimate relationship with 'the Father'. This relationship had existed before the creation of the world:

All things have been delivered to me by my Father; and no one knows the Son except the Father, and no one knows the Father except the Son and any one to whom the Son chooses to reveal him.

And now, Father, glorify thou me in thy own presence with the glory which I had with thee before the world was made.

A reconstruction of the Tabernacle. Jewish religion forbids any visual representation of God. The Tabernacle in the desert and later the Temple at Jerusalem, unlike the temples of other religions, therefore contained no figure of God. He was to be worshipped in spirit and in truth.

▷ Jesus spoke about the Holy Spirit as distinct from himself and from the Father:

When the Counsellor comes, whom I shall send to you from the Father, even the Spirit of truth, who proceeds from the Father, he will bear witness to me.

You shall receive power when the Holy Spirit has come upon you; and you shall be my witnesses . . .

▷ The early Christians experienced God working in their lives in a radically new way, and they understood this to be the work of the Holy Spirit.

When the day of Pentecost had come, they were all together in one place. And suddenly a sound came from heaven like the rush of a mighty wind, and it filled all the house where they were sitting. And there appeared to them tongues as of fire, distributed and resting on each one of them. And they were all filled with the Holy Spirit and began to speak in other tongues, as the Spirit gave them utterance.

The fruit of the Spirit is love, joy, peace, patience, kindness, goodness, faithfulness, gentleness, self-control . . .

What kind of response does this God arouse in the believer ?

Worship:

O come, let us worship and bow down,

let us kneel before the Lord, our Maker!

Awe and reverence:

I through the abundance of thy steadfast love
   will enter thy house,
I will worship toward thy holy temple
   in the fear of thee.

Thanksgiving and wonder:

I will give thanks to the Lord with my whole
   heart;
I will tell of all thy wonderful deeds.
I will be glad and exult in thee,
   I will sing praise to thy name, O Most High.

Joy:

How lovely is thy dwelling place,
   O Lord of hosts!
My soul longs, yea, faints
   for the courts of the Lord;
my heart and flesh sing for joy
   to the living God.

Love:

I love thee, O Lord, my strength.

Trust:

The Lord is my strength and my shield;
   in him my heart trusts;
so I am helped, and my heart exults,
   and with my song I give thanks to him.

HOW THIS UNDERSTANDING OF GOD AFFECTS OUR UNDERSTANDING OF TRUTH, MAN AND THE UNIVERSE

TRUTH

If God is personal and has something in common with man,

then there is no reason why God should not be able to communicate truth in different ways to the minds of men. There is no reason why he should not be able to communicate truth in words.

If there are three persons within the Godhead,

then there can be communication between them; and it is not strange to think of this kind of God wanting to communicate also with man whom he has made in his image.

If there are three persons,

then it becomes possible to think of the Son

becoming man in order to reveal God more fully.

See further BOOK ONE, pp. 9–30.

MAN

If man is a creature of God, created by deliberate choice and not the product of a chance process, which could easily have produced something different,

then we have at least a starting-point for understanding and explaining the dignity of man, and finding answers to the questions of man.

See further, pp. 53ff.

THE UNIVERSE

If the universe has been created by God and is even now sustained by God,

then we have a starting-point for understanding its complexity, order and beauty, and for finding answers to the basic questions about the universe.

See further, pp. 118ff.

Problems and Questions arising out of Biblical Christianity's answer to the question 'Who or what is God? Does he exist?' are taken up on pp. 42ff.

2. THE ANSWER OF PRIMAL RELIGION AND JUDAISM, ISLAM AND DEISM

"There is a God; but he is rather different from the Bible's description"

The concept of God in these religions differs from the Christian concept in certain important respects:

Some have no knowledge of certain aspects of the Christian understanding of God; or they ignore or deny them (that God is infinite, for example, or that there are three persons in one God, or that he can be known in a personal way).

Primal religion

In all the primal religions there is a strong awareness of the existence of a personal God. Examples are taken from African religions, which have much in common with primal religions in other continents.

John Mbiti:

African knowledge of God is expressed in proverbs, short statements, songs, prayers, names, myths, stories and religious ceremonies. All these are easy to remember and pass on to other people, since there are no sacred writings in traditional societies. One should not, therefore, expect long dissertations about God. But God is no stranger to African peoples, and in traditional life there are no atheists. This is summarized in an Ashanti proverb that 'No one shows a child the Supreme Being'. That means that everybody knows of God's existence almost by instinct, and even children know Him.

This God, however, has withdrawn himself. He exists, but he is too distant for any man to enjoy communion with him.

John Mbiti:

It is particularly as Spirit that God is incomprehensible. So the Ashanti rightly refer to Him as 'the fathomless Spirit', since no human mind can measure Him, no intellect can comprehend or grasp Him . . . Many people readily admit that they do not know what God is like, and that they do not possess the words of God—since words are vehicles of someone's thoughts and to a certain degree they give a portrait of the speaker. Some even say that God's proper name is unknown; or give Him a name like that of the Lunda, which means or signifies 'the God of the Unknown', or that of the Ngombe which means 'the Unexplainable', or of the Maasai which means 'the Unknown'. A person's name in African societies generally has a meaning descriptive of His personality and being. In the case of God, people might know some of His activities and manifestations, but of His essential nature they know nothing. It is a paradox that they 'know' Him, and yet they do not 'know' Him; He is not a Stranger to them, and yet they are strangers to Him; He knows them, but they do not know Him. So God confronts men as the mysterious and incomprehensible, as indescribable and beyond human vocabulary. This is part of the essential nature of God.

The remoteness and unknowableness of God also calls for different kinds of mediators to put man in touch with the power which controls the universe. In this way the spirits of the ancestors and witchdoctors come to play an important role in man's quest for health, happiness and security.

It was once thought that primite religion as practised by many tribes all over the world is the nearest thing one can find to the original

religion of man. But the evidence is more easily explained by the assumption that this form of religion has developed (or degenerated) from an original worship of the one Creator-God.

Robert Brow:

Led by Fr. Wilhelm Schmidt of Vienna, anthropologists have shown that the religion of the hundreds of isolated tribes in the world today is not primitive in the sense of being original. The tribes have a memory of a 'High God', a benign Creator-Father-God, who is no longer worshipped because he is not feared. Instead of offering sacrifice to him, they concern themselves with the pressing problems of how to appease the vicious spirits of the jungle. The threats of the witch-doctor are more strident than the still, small voice of the Father-God.

We see, then, that the evolution of religion from a primitive Animatism can no longer be assumed as axiomatic and that some anthropologists now suggest that Monotheism may be more naturally primitive as a world-view than Animism. Their research suggests that tribes are not animistic because they have continued unchanged since the dawn of history. Rather, the evidence indicates degeneration from a true knowledge of God. Isolation from prophets and religious books has ensnared them into sacrificial bribery to placate the spirits instead of joyous sacrificial meals in the presence of the Creator.

Judaism

The understanding of God in Judaism is based on the Old Testament, and thus has a great deal in common with the Christian understanding.

Roy A. Stewart:

Jew and Christian agree on certain essential characteristics of God . . . A working basis for the doctrine of God, acceptable at least in outline to either faith, may be posited as follows. *God is One and unique, eternally existing, endowed with limitless power and knowledge, present throughout His creation, throned in unimaginable transcendent splendour, yet close to every creature, supreme in His decrees, righteous, just, holy and merciful.*

Top left: *The revival of the old religions in England. The rock/religious festival held on the midsummer solstice at Glastonbury, a place where cosmic forces are said to be strongly felt.*
Bottom left: *During spirit worship dancers often go into a trance.*
Right: *The symbolic markings used in a voodoo rite.*

The only one of the eight propositions which Judaism denies is that there are three 'Persons' in the one God. But this denial has a profound effect on the interpretation of the other beliefs about God.

Islam

The Qur'an lays great emphasis on the oneness of God, his transcendence and power, and his lordship over the whole universe.

Allah: there is no god but Him, the Living, the Eternal One. Neither slumber nor sleep overtakes Him. His is what the heavens and the earth contain. Who can intercede with Him except by His permission? He knows what is before and behind men. They can grasp only that part of His knowledge which He wills. His throne is as vast as the heavens and the earth, and the preservation of both does not weary Him. He is the Exalted, the Immense One.

He is Allah, besides whom there is no other god. He is the Sovereign Lord, the Holy One, the Giver of Peace, the Keeper of Faith; the Guardian, the Mighty One, the All-powerful, the Most High! Exalted be He above their idols! He is Allah, the Creator, the Originator, the Modeller. His are the most gracious names. All that is in heaven and earth gives glory to Him. He is the Mighty, the Wise One.

One result of this emphasis on the sovereignty of God is that it is very difficult to establish any point of contact between God and man, and God can hardly be known.

Al-Junayd, the ninth-century mystic:

No one knows God save God Himself Most High, and therefore even to the best of His creatures He has only revealed His names in which He hides himself.

This kind of agnosticism about the nature of God has led many Moslems to move towards the mystical faith of the Sufis. Much of the teaching of Sufism, instead of being rejected as heretical, has been accepted into the mainstream of Islamic thought.

Reynold Nicholson, writing about the Qur'an:

Are there any germs of mysticism to be found there (in the Koran)? The Koran . . . starts with the notion of Allah, the One, Eternal, and Almighty God, far above human feelings and aspirations—the Lord of His slaves, not the Father of His children; a judge meting out stern justice to sinners, and extending His mercy only to those who avert His wrath by repentance, humility, and unceasing works of devotion; a God of fear rather than of love. This is one side, and certainly the most prominent side, of Mohammed's teaching; but while he set an impassible gulf between the world and Allah, his deeper instinct craved a direct revelation from God to the soul. There are no contradictions in the logic of feeling. Mohammed, who had in him something of the mystic, felt God both as far and near, both as transcendent and immanent. In the latter aspect, Allah is the light of the heavens and the earth, a Being who worked in the world and in the soul of man.

Writing about the development of Islamic theology, he says:

The champions of orthodoxy had set about constructing a system of scholastic philosophy that reduced God's nature to a purely formal, changeless, and absolute unity, a bare will devoid of all affections and emotions, a tremendous and incalculable power with which no human creature could have any communion or personal intercourse whatsoever. That is the God of Mohammedan theology. That was the alternative to Sufism. Therefore, 'all thinking, religious Moslems are mystics,' as Professor D. B. Macdonald, one of our best authorities on the subject, has remarked. And he adds: 'All, too, are pantheists, but some do not know it.'

Another consequence of the Islamic belief about God is that God's attitude towards man tends to be defined in terms of compassion and mercy, rather than of love. These, for example, are some of the Ninety Nine Names of God:

The Merciful; the Compassionate, the Forgiver, the Forgiving; the Clement, the Generous, the Affectionate, the Kind.

If the Moslem ever speaks about the love of God, he thinks not so much of God's love for man, as man's love for God, as the response which is aroused by contemplating the attributes of God.

Ahmad Galwash, a contemporary apologist:

Rightly to understand the love of God is so difficult a matter that one sect of philosophers have altogether denied that man can love a being who is not of his own species, and they have defined the love of God as consisting merely in obedience to Him. But this is not true . . . The following

prayer was taught by the Arabian Prophet to his followers: '*O God, grant me to love Thee and to love those who love Thee, and whatsoever brings me nearer to Thy love, and make Thy love dearer to me than cold water to the thirsty traveller in the desert.*' . . .

We now come to treat love in its essential nature, according to the spiritual Muslim conception. Love may be defined as an inclination to that which is pleasant.

The Moslem is probably forced to speak of the mercy and compassion of God rather than the love of God because love sounds too human a word to apply to God. One could also say that if God is one in the sense that the Moslem understands, it does not make sense, logically, to speak of love as being part of the character of God. Love by definition demands an object, unless it is to become self-love. And if there is no Trinity which allows a relationship of love between the three persons of the godhead, then the only possible object of the love of God can be the universe and man. But this makes it difficult to think of God as sufficient in himself and not dependent on the existence of the universe.

Deism

The Deists of the eighteenth century did not deny the existence of God. They simply

A Moslem worshipper in the Pakistan desert faces Mecca to pray.

denied or ignored certain aspects of the traditional Christian teaching about God. Gradually, however, the idea of God was so emptied of content that hardly anything could be said about him.

Joseph Joubert:

God has withdrawn within himself and hidden within the bosom of his own being; withdrawn even as the sun, when it hides behind a cloud. The sun of the spirit is visible to them no more . . . With nothing now to wake them to ecstasy, nothing to excite their lofty contemplation, able no more to gaze upon God, they busy themselves with the world.

Voltaire:

I shall always be convinced that a watch proves a watch-maker, and that a universe proves a God.

I believe in God, not the God of the mystics and the theologians, but the God of nature, the great geometrician, the architect of the universe, the prime mover, unalterable, transcendental, everlasting.

Paul Hazard, writing about the God of the Deists:

God was to remain, but a God so remote, so

watered down, so pallid that his presence imposed no constraint on the City of Men. He would neither visit them with his wrath, nor bedazzle them with his glory . . .

Deism had recourse to a sort of filtering process. If we strain off whatever strikes us as superstitious in the Church of Rome, in the Reformed Church, and in every other church and sect, what remains at the conclusion of the process will be God; a God whom we know not, and whom we cannot know. Hardly anything has been left to him save the bare fact of his existence. Of all the possible adjectives, he was awarded the one which was at once the most honourable and the most vague; he was called the Supreme Being.

HOW THIS UNDERSTANDING OF GOD AFFECTS OUR UNDERSTANDING OF TRUTH, MAN AND THE UNIVERSE

The clearest way of seeing where these different beliefs about God lead—and the problems and questions they raise—is to apply them to the questions of truth (see BOOK ONE, especially pp. 31—59), man (see pp. 69ff.) and the universe (see pp. 125f.).

3. THE ANSWER OF AGNOSTICISM AND MYSTICISM

"We can never know whether or not God exists"

Some of the great European thinkers join with Hinduism and Buddhism in returning a 'don't know' answer to the question of the existence of God. (See also BOOK ONE, pp. 46ff. for further examples and discussion of agnosticism.)

European thinkers

The Deists of the eighteenth century ignored or denied or modified some of the aspects of the biblical understanding of God (see pp. 11ff.). It was not long before some took this scepticism one step further and said: 'God *may* exist; but we just do not know, and we have no way of knowing for sure.' (See BOOK ONE, pp. 47ff.)

Thomas Hobbes' agnosticism is summed up in this way by Basil Willey:

It is, then, the God of deism—first mover and designer of the world-machine—that Hobbes offers as a substitute for Zeus or Jehovah. But even to say that he 'offers' this is an overstatement. For him the word God is really little but a symbol of the philosopher's fatigue. In his quest for truth the investigator at last reaches the limits of human capacity; then, in sheer weariness, he gives over, and says 'God' . . . And it is noticeable that in speaking of God his main endeavour is to empty this conception of all content. Of that which has not reached us through the senses we can have no 'image', thus we can have no 'idea' or 'conception' of God. We can only speak of him in a series of negatives, such as 'infinite', 'immutable', 'incomprehensible', or in terms signifying his remoteness from our mortal state, such as 'omnipotent', 'most high', and the like. All these 'attributes' are really 'pseudo-statements', that is to say, the reality to which they point is just simply our own pious disposition.

Thomas Carlyle, in the nineteenth century:

The name (of God) has become as if obsolete to the most devout of us; and it is, to the huge idly impious million of writing, preaching, and talking people as if the *fact* too had quite ceased to be certain.

Hinduism

Hinduism starts from a profound agnosticism about the nature of God.

Radhakrishnan:

The Hindu never doubted the reality of the one supreme universal spirit, however much the descriptions of it may fall short of its nature. Whatever the doctrinaires may say, the saints of God are anxious to affirm that much is hidden from their sight. God hideth himself. It is a sound religious agnosticism which bids us hold our peace regarding the nature of the supreme spirit. Silence is more significant than speech regarding the depths of the divine. The altars erected to the unknown gods in the Graeco-Roman world were but an expression of man's ignorance of the divine nature. The sense of failure in man's quest for the unseen is symbolized by them. When asked to define the nature of God, the seer of the Upanishad sat silent, and when pressed to answer exclaimed that the Absolute is silence. The mystery of the divine reality eludes the machinery of speech and symbol. The 'Divine Darkness', 'That of which nothing can be said', and such other expressions are used by the devout when they attempt to describe their consciousness of direct communion with God.

See further pp. 33ff. for other Hindu definitions of the word 'God'.

Buddhism

Christmas Humphreys would not use the word 'agnostic' about the Buddhist understanding of God; but his description of the Buddhist position fits more easily into this category than that of the theist or the atheist, and is similar to that of some western mystics like Eckhart:

As between the theist and atheist positions, Buddhism is atheistic, but it would be more correct to say that it analyses the complex of conflicting ideas comprised in the term God with the same dispassionate care as it analyses the so-called soul. Such analysis, which all are pressed to make for themselves, proves, say Buddhists, that the Western ideas are inaccurate and inadequate. The Buddhist teaching on God, in the sense of an ultimate Reality, is neither agnostic, as is sometimes claimed, nor vague, but clear and logical. Whatever Reality may be, it is beyond the conception of the finite intellect; it follows that attempts at description are misleading, unprofitable, and waste of time. For these good reasons the Buddha maintained about Reality 'a noble silence'. If there *is* a Causeless Cause of all Causes, an Ultimate Reality, a Boundless Light, an Eternal Noumenon behind phenomena, it must clearly be infinite, unlimited, unconditioned and without attributes. We, on the other hand, are clearly finite, and limited and conditioned by, and in a sense composed of, innumerable attributes. It follows that we can neither define, describe, nor usefully discuss the nature of THAT which is beyond the comprehension of our finite consciousness. It may be indicated by negatives and described indirectly by analogy and symbols, but otherwise it must ever remain in its truest sense unknown and unexpressed, as being to us in our present state unknowable.

Mysticism

The Mystic generally starts from the same position as the agnostic: he denies the possibility of knowing God with his mind. But he believes that knowledge of God of a different kind *is* possible—and this is a knowledge based purely on the mystical experience of union with God (see BOOK ONE, pp. 74ff.).

Meister Eckhart (?1260–?1327) writes that knowledge of God is only possible through union with him:

Know'st thou of him anything? He is no such

The bronze head of Buddha at Kamakura, Japan.

thing, and in that thou dost know of him anything at all thou art in ignorance, and ignorance leads to the condition of the brute; for in creatures what is ignorant is brutish. If thou wouldst not be brutish then, know nothing of the unuttered God.—'What then shall I do?'—Thou shalt lose thy thy-ness and dissolve in his his-ness; thy thine shall be his mine, so utterly one mine that thou in him shalt know eternalwise his is-ness, free from becoming; his nameless nothingness.

The Cloud of Unknowing (an anonymous work of the fourteenth century) speaks of 'love' as a way of knowing God:

All rational beings, angels and men, possess two faculties, the power of knowing and the power of loving. To the first, to the intellect, God who made them is forever unknowable, but to the second, to love, he is completely knowable, and that by every separate individual. So much so that one loving soul by itself, through its love, may know for itself him who is incomparably more than sufficient to fill all souls that exist.

Whoever hears or reads about all this, and thinks that it is fundamentally an activity of the mind, and proceeds then to work it all out along these lines, is on quite the wrong track . . . Do not attempt to achieve this experience intellectually. I tell you truly that it cannot come this way . . .

By 'darkness' I mean 'a lack of knowing'—just as anything that you do not know or may have forgotten may be said to be 'dark' to you, for you cannot see it with your inward eye. For this reason it is called 'a cloud', not of the sky, of course, but 'of unknowing', a cloud of unknowing between you and your God.

With the Beat movement in America in the 1950's religious mysticism with a Buddhist flavour became the basis for a popular philosophy which is still being worked out in the popular arts.

Jack Kerouac the Beat movement's chronicler, attempted to describe his experience, in the character of Ray Smith, in *The Dharma Bums:*

And then I thought, later, lying on my bag smoking, 'Everything is possible. I am God, I am Buddha, I am imperfect Ray Smith, all at the same time, I am empty space, I am all things. I have all the time in the world from life to life to do what is to do, to do what is done, to do the timeless doing, infinitely perfect within, why cry, why worry, perfect like mind essence and the minds of banana peels' I added laughing remembering my poetic Zen Lunatic Dharma Bum friends of San Francisco whom I was beginning to miss now. And I added a little prayer for Rosie.

Kerouac's advice was reprinted in 1971 in a book of poetry called *Amazing Grace:*

Wait awhile, close your eyes, let your breathing stop three seconds or so, listen to the inside silence in the womb of the world, let the bliss you forgot, the emptiness and essence and ecstasy of ever having been and ever to be the golden eternity. This is the lesson you forgot.

Tom Wolfe wrote about the experience of Ken Kesey and his Merry Pranksters in the early days of Haight-Ashbury in *The Electric Kool-Aid Acid Test:*

Gradually the Prankster attitude began to involve the main things religious mystics have always felt, things common to Hindus, Buddhists, Christians, and for that matter Theosophists and even flying-saucer cultists. Namely, the *experiencing* of an Other World, a higher level of reality. And a perception of the cosmic unity of this higher level. And a feeling of timelessness, the feeling that what we know as time is only the result of a naive faith in causality . . .
There was something so . . . *religious* in the air, in the very atmosphere of the Prankster life, and yet one couldn't put one's finger on it. On the face of it there was just a group of people who had shared an unusual psychological state, the LSD experience—

But exactly! The *experience*—that was the word! and it began to fall into place. In fact, none of the great founded religions, Christianity, Buddhism, Islam, Jainism, Judaism, Zoroastrianism, Hinduism, none of them began with a philosophical framework or even a main idea. They all began with an overwhelming *new experience*, what Joachin Wach called 'the experience of the holy,' and Max Weber, 'possession of the deity,' the sense of being a vessel of the divine, of the All-one.

Crossroads in Haight-Ashbury, focal point of the drug cult in the 60s.

Every vision, every insight of the . . . original . . . circle always came out of the *new experience* . . . the *kairos* . . . and how to tell it! How to get it across to the multitudes who have never had this experience for themselves? *You couldn't put it into words.* You had to create conditions in which they would feel an approximation of *that feeling*, the sublime *kairos.* You had to put them into ecstasy . . . Buddhist monks immersing themselves in cosmic love through fasting and contemplation, Hindus zonked out in Bhakti, which is fervent love in the possession of God, ecstatics flooding themselves with Krishna through sexual orgies or plunging into the dinners of the Bacchanalia, Christians off in Edge City through gnostic onanism or the Heart of Jesus or the Child Jesus with its running sore—or—

THE ACID TESTS

And suddenly Kesey sees that they, the Pranksters, already have the expertise and the machinery to create a mindblown state such as the world has never seen, totally wound up, lit up, amplified and . . . controlled—plus the most efficient key ever devised to open the doors in the mind of the world: namely, Owlsley's LSD.

The Beatles did a lot to draw both the LSD experience and eastern mysticism together and to express it in their music. The first thing to do is to turn off your mind:

Turn off your mind relax and float
down-stream,
it is not dying, it is not dying,
lay down all thought surrender to the void,
it is shining, it is shining.
That you may see the meaning of within,
it is speaking, it is speaking,
that love is all and love is ev'ryone,
it is knowing, it is knowing.

The Tribal Chorus from the rock musical, "Hair".

Without going out of my door.
I can know all things on earth.
Without looking out of my window
I could know the ways of heaven

The Rock musical *Hair* tried to sum up the feeling of moving towards a mystical under-standing for everyone:

Harmony and Understanding,
Sympathy and Trust abounding,
No more falsehoods or derisions.
Golden living dreams of visions,
Mystic crystal revelation,
And the mind's true liberation,
This is the dawning of the Age of Aquarius . . .

PROBLEMS AND QUESTIONS

If we can't know about God, can we be sure we know about anything else?

In most cases, agnosticism about the existence of God or the character of God is closely connected with agnosticism about truth in general.

Albert Camus:

Contemporary unbelief does not rest on science as it did towards the close of the last century. It denies both science and religion. It is no longer the skepticism of reason in the presence of miracle. It is a passionate unbelief.

Sartre's novel *Nausea:*

I am beginning to believe that nothing can ever be proved. These are reasonable hypotheses which take the facts into account: but I am only too well aware that they come from me, that they are simply a way of unifying my own knowledge.

The question of truth is therefore even more fundamental than the question of God's existence.

See further Agnosticism, BOOK ONE, pp. 47–59.

Is anyone really satisfied with pure agnosticism?

It is very hard for most people to be content with the bare answer of agnosticism. Their restlessness has usually led them *beyond* the point of pure agnosticism.

Baron von Hugel, writing in 1916, sums up in some prophetic words how dissatisfaction with agnosticism would lead many to the answer of pantheism:

Agnosticism is going, going, gone. Not it, but Pantheism is now and will long be, the danger of religion.

See further, pp. 33ff.

If we do not know, we must act as if God does NOT exist

The agnostic has to live in practice as if there is no God.

Somerset Maugham:

In religion above all things the only thing of use is an objective truth. The only God that is of use is a being who is personal, supreme, and good, and whose existence is as certain as that two and two makes four. I cannot penetrate the mystery. I remain an agnostic, and the practical outcome of agnosticism is that you act as though God did not exist.

See further Atheism, pp. 30ff. and Question Three, 'What is Man?', pp. 75ff.

4. THE ANSWER OF ATHEISM

"There is no God"

Whereas the agnostic says 'God may exist, but we shall never know' (see pp. 25ff.), the atheist says categorically 'God does not exist; there is no one there'.

Nietzsche, writing in 1882:

Have you not heard of the madman who lit a lamp in broad daylight and ran up and down the market place shouting incessantly, 'I'm looking for God! I'm looking for God!' But, because many of the people who were standing there did not believe in God, he aroused a good deal of mirth. . . But the madman thrust in between them and fixed them with his eyes. 'Where is God?' he shouted. 'I'll tell you! We have killed him— you and I! We are all his murderers! But how have we done it? How could we drink the sea dry? Who gave us the sponge to wipe away the horizon? What did we do when we uncoupled the earth from its sun? Where is the earth moving to now? Where are we moving to? Away from all suns? Are we not running incessantly? Backwards, sideways and forwards, in all directions? Is there still an above and a below? Are we not wandering through an infinite nothing? Is not the void yawning ahead of us? Has it not become colder? Is it not more and more night? Do the lamps not have to be lit during the day? Do we hear nothing of the noise of the gravediggers who are burying God? Do we smell nothing of the decomposition of God? The gods are decomposing! God is dead! God is dead! And we have killed him! . . . I have come too soon! My time has not yet come. This terrible event is still coming.'

Matthew Arnold, writing in 1882, speaks of the widespread rejection of Christian beliefs on the Continent of Europe, while most Englishmen were completely unaware of what was happening:

The partisans of traditional religion in this country do not know, I think, how decisively the whole force of progressive and liberal opinion on the Continent has pronounced against the Christian religion.

Martin Esslin, writing about the implications of Nietzsche's atheism in his book *The Theatre of the Absurd:*

Zarathustra was first published in 1883. The number of people for whom God is dead has greatly increased since Nietzsche's day, and mankind has learned the bitter lesson of the falseness and evil nature of some of the cheap substitutes that have been set up to take his place. And so, after two terrible wars, there are still many who are trying to come to terms with the implications of Zarathustra's message, searching for a way in which they can, with dignity, confront a universe deprived of what was once its centre and its living purpose, a world deprived of a generally accepted integrating principle, which has become disjointed, purposeless—absurd.

The Theatre of the Absurd is one of the expressions of this search.

Arthur Adamov, the playwright, quoted in *The Theatre of the Absurd:*

The name of God should no longer come from the mouth of man. This word that has so long been degraded by usage no longer means anything . . . To use the word God is more than sloth, it is refusal to think, a kind of short cut, a hideous shorthand.

A. J. Ayer:

I do not believe in God. It seems to me that theists of all kinds have largely failed to make their concept of a deity intelligible; and to the extent that they have made it intelligible they have given no reason to think that anything answers to it.

Jean-Paul Sartre, describing the religious atmosphere in which he was brought up and which contributed to his atheism:

My family had been affected by the slow de-christianization which was born in the Voltaire-influenced *haute bourgeoisie* and took a century to spread to every stratum of Society: without this general slackening of faith, Louise Guillemin, a young Catholic lady from the provinces, would have made more fuss about marrying a Lutheran. Naturally, everyone at home believed: for reasons of discretion . . . An atheist was an eccentric, a hot-head whom you did not invite to dinner lest he 'create a scandal', a fanatic burdened with taboos who denied himself the right to kneel in church, to marry his daughters or indulge in tears there, who took it on himself to prove the truth of his doctrine by the purity of his conduct, who injured himself and his happiness to the extent of robbing himself of his means of dying comforted, a man with a phobia about God who saw his absence everywhere and who could not open his mouth without saying His name: in short, a Gentleman with religious convictions. The believer had none: for two thousand years the Christian certainties had had time to prove themselves; they belonged to everyone, and they were required to shine in the priest's glance, in the half-light of a church, and to illumine souls, but no one needed to appropriate them to himself; they were the common patrimony. Polite society believed in God so that it need not talk of Him. How tolerant religion seemed! How convenient it was: the Christian could abandon Mass and yet marry his children in church, smile at the religious 'art' of the Place Saint-Sulpice and shed tears as he listened to the Wedding March from Lohengrin; he was not obliged to lead an exemp-

lary life or to die in despair, or even to have himself cremated. In our circle, in my family, faith was nothing but an official name for sweet French liberty; I had been baptized, like so many others, to preserve my independence: in refusing me baptism, they would have been afraid of doing harm to my soul; as a registered Catholic, I was free, I was normal. 'Later on,' they said, 'he can do as he pleases.' It was reckoned, at the time, far harder to acquire faith than to lose it.

Deep down, it all bored me to death; I was led to unbelief not through conflicting dogma but through my grand-parents' indifference. Yet I believed: in my nightshirt, kneeling on my bed, hands folded, I said my daily prayer but thought less and less often about the good God . . . For several years longer, I kept up public relations with the Almighty; in private, I stopped associating with Him. Once only I had the feeling that He existed. I had been playing with matches and had burnt a mat; I was busy covering up my crime when suddenly God saw me. I felt His gaze inside my head and on my hands; I turned round and round in the bathroom, horribly visible, a living target. I was saved by indignation: I grew angry at such a crude lack of tact, and blasphemed, muttering like my grandfather: '*Sacré nom de Dieu de nom de Dieu de nom de Dieu.*' He never looked at me again.

I have just told the story of a missed vocation; I needed God, he was given to me, and I received him without understanding what I was looking for. Unable to take root in my heart, he vegetated in me for a while and then died. Today, when he is mentioned, I say with the amusement and lack of regret of some ageing beau who meets an old flame: 'Fifty years ago, without that misunderstanding, without that mistake, without the accident which separated us, there might have been something between us.'

Nothing happened between us . . .

Atheism is a cruel, long-term business: I believe I have gone through it to the end.

PROBLEMS AND QUESTIONS

⚠ How do you know?

It is usually the Christian who is challenged with this question and asked to give a reasonable basis for his belief in God; and he ought

to be able to give some solid reasons.

But the Christian has every right to challenge the atheist with the same question and ask: how do *you know for certain* that there is no God? Is there a reasonable basis for your atheism? On what grounds do you base your belief? How do you know that your atheism is true?

The atheist will probably give the answer of the Rationalist (see BOOK ONE, pp. 40–46).

But if he shrinks from defending his belief in this way, he will probably have to take refuge in the answer of Agnosticism (see p. 25 and BOOK ONE, pp. 47–59).

⚠ If we don't believe in God, what do we believe about man?

Albert Camus, writing about the significance of Nietzsche's atheism:

We sense the change of position that Nietzsche makes. With him, rebellion begins at 'God is dead' which is assumed as an established fact. . . Contrary to the opinion of certain of his Christian critics, Nietzsche did not form a project to kill God. He found Him dead in the soul of his contemporaries. He was the first to understand the immense importance of the event and to decide that this rebellion among men could not lead to a renaissance unless it were controlled and directed.

Nietzsche believed that atheism opened new horizons:

The most important of more recent events—that 'god is dead', that the belief in the Christian God has become unworthy of belief—already begins to cast its first shadows over Europe . . . In fact, we philosophers and 'free spirits' feel ourselves irradiated as by a new dawn by the report that the 'old God is dead'; our hearts overflow with gratitude, astonishment, presentiment and expectation. At last the horizon seems open once more, granting even that it is not bright; our ships can at last put out to sea in face of every danger; every hazard is again permitted to the discerner; the sea, *our* sea, again lies open before us; perhaps never before did such an 'open sea' exist.

Michael Harrington writes of those who have passed beyond this exhilaration to a profound pessimism:

After God died, Man, who was supposed to replace Him, grew sick of himself. This resulted in a crisis of belief and disbelief which made the twentieth century spiritually empty.

God died in the nineteenth century. Nietzsche announced the event as a fact, not as an argument, and his report has been taken as the starting point of most serious theology ever since . . .

But since God did not have any heir, the funeral has been going on for over a hundred years. The nineteenth century predicted often enough that the modern world would dispel faith. It did not, however, expect that it would subvert anti-faith as well.

Jean-Paul Sartre:

And when we speak of 'abandonment'—a favourite word of Heidegger—we only mean to say that God does not exist, and that it is necessary to draw the consequences of his absence right to the end.

The discussion must therefore move from the question of *God* to the question of *man*. See further, Question Three, 'What is Man?', pp. 48ff.

5. THE ANSWER OF PANTHEISM AND SOME MODERN THEOLOGIANS

"There is no God; but the word is useful if we redefine its meaning"

Certain conclusions seem to follow from thoroughgoing atheism or agnosticism:

☐ **What we have in the universe is all there is; there is nothing beyond what we can see or touch—no unseen supernatural world.**

☐ **Death is the end of the individual; there is no life beyond.**

But not everyone is prepared to accept these conclusions as inevitable, to live with the idea that there is nothing beyond appearances, nothing but the present.

Although many are consistent and build their philosophies on these assumptions— e.g. Communism, Existentialism and Humanism (see Man, pp. 75ff.)—others are only too conscious of the vacuum created by the 'death' of God and the supernatural. They are anxious to find some belief which will account for their sense of awe and mystery as they look at the universe, and give it some meaning.

Those who take this course tend to retain the word 'God' and words such as 'divinity' and 'transcendence', but they give them different meanings. This position has many different forms of expression, but they all have certain features in common:

▷ 'God' does not mean a Personal Being who is distinct from the universe and was there 'before' the universe was created.

▷ 'God' is identified in some way with the universe as a whole or with some part or aspect of it (e.g. the spirit or consciousness of man, the 'personal' aspect of the universe).

Hindu Pantheism

Hinduism, as we now understand it, sprang from a reaction against the debased poly-theistic religion which developed in India before the eighth century BC.

Robert Brow, writing about the religion which the Aryan invaders took with them to India in the second millennium BC:

If we could look down on the ancient world abou 1500 BC we would see ordinary men and women still offering animal sacrifices as their normal way of approaching God or the gods. The earliest literature of India, the Sanskrit *Vedas*, picture the nomadic Aryan tribes who fought their way eastwards across the Indus and Ganges plains. The head of the family offered animal sacrifice with the same simplicity as Abraham. When they settled in India the Aryans developed a regular priesthood, and the *Vedas* are the hymns which the priests chanted as the sacrificial smoke ascended to God. The hymns address God under various names such as 'The Sun', 'The Heavenly One' and 'The Storm', but the interesting thing is that, whatever name they give to God, they worshipped him as the Supreme Ruler of the universe. This practice is called *Henotheism*. God has several names, just as Christians today have several names for God, but the names do not indicate different gods. They are different facets of the one God. Henotheism changes into Polytheism when the names of God are so personified that various gods are separated, and they begin to disagree and fight among themselves. The later Vedic literature has certainly become polytheistic by, say, 1000 BC, but the earliest Aryans must have been Monotheists.

Then, after believing in the existence of many gods, someone took the step of identifying 'God' more closely with the universe and saying 'God is *not different* from or distinct from the universe. God *is* everything there is, and everything there is *is* God.'

It is important to realize, however, that not all forms of Pantheism are quite as simple and crude as this. *Robert Brow* distinguishes four variations or refinements on this basic theme:

1. 'Everything there is is God.' (Absolute Pantheism)
2. 'God is the reality or principle behind nature.' (Modified Pantheism)
3. 'God is to nature as soul is to body.' (Modified Monism)
4. 'Only God is reality. All else is imagination.' (Absolute Monism).

The nearest word to 'God' in Hinduism is 'Brahman', the Universal Spirit. In the *Upanishads* he is described as the one Divine Being . . .

hidden in all beings, all-pervading, the self within all beings, watching over all works, dwelling in all beings, the witness, the perceiver, the only one, free from all qualities. He is the one ruler of many who (seem to act, but really) do not act; he makes the one seed manifold.

In the *Bhagavad Gita*, the Brahman 'speaks' to Arjuna through Krishna in these words:

Listen and I shall reveal to thee some manifestations of my divine glory . . .

I am the soul, prince victorious, which dwells in the heart of all things. I am the beginning, the middle, and the end of all that lives . . .

Among the sons of light I am Vishnu, and of luminaries the radiant sun. I am the lord of the winds and storms, and of the lights in the night I am the moon.

Of the Vedas I am the Veda of songs, and I am Indra, the chief of the gods. Above man's senses I am the mind, and in all living beings I am the light of consciousness.

Crowds of pilgrims gather to bathe in the sacred River Ganges at sunrise.

Among the terrible powers I am the god of destruction . . .

I am time, never-ending time. I am the Creator who sees all. I am death that carries off all things, and I am the source of things to come.

And know, Arjuna, that I am the seed of all things that are; and that no being that moves or moves not can ever be without me . . .

Know thou that whatever is beautiful and good, whatever has glory and power is only a portion of my own radiance.

But of what help is it to thee to know this diversity? Know that with one single fraction of my Being I pervade and support the Universe, and know that I AM.

In the many traditions of Hindu philosophy, 'God' may be *either* personal *or* impersonal: or 'God' may be *both* personal *and* impersonal.

H. D. Lewis:

All that can be said is that the scriptures provide grist for the mills of both theistic and monistic interpretations which come later in Hindu story, with more grist, perhaps, for the monist than for the theist.

This different understanding of the meaning of 'God' means that Hinduism and Christianity are not even starting from the same premises.

A bronze statue of the monkey-god Marutti, part of the Hindu pantheon.

Professor Zaehner, writing out of a Hindu background:

To maintain that all religions are paths leading to the same goal, as is so frequently done today, is to maintain something that is not true.

Not only on the dogmatic, but also on the mystical plane, too, there is no agreement.

It is then only too true that the basic principles of Eastern and Western, which in practice means Indian and Semitic, thought are, I will not say irreconcilably opposed; they are simply not starting from the same premises. The only common ground is that the function of religion is to provide release; there is no agreement at all as to what it is that man must be released from. The great religions are talking at cross purposes.

European thinkers

Spinoza's position, summarized by Paul Hazard:

The *Ethic*, which appeared posthumously in 1667, introduced us to a sort of palace, a palace wrought of concepts so aspiring they seem like a vaulted roof soaring up as though to mingle with the heavens. Geometrical, no doubt, but tremulous throughout with the breath of life itself, the *Ethic* is woven of tissues both human and divine, making the two a single category, and over its portals are engraven the words, God is All and All is God . . . All that is, is in God, and nothing can be, or be conceived, apart from God. God is thought; God is extension, and man, body, and soul, is a mode of Being.

Hegel:

We define God when we say, that He distinguishes Himself from Himself, and is an object for Himself, but that in this distinction He is purely identical with Himself, is in fact Spirit. This notion or conception is now realised, consciousness knows this content and knows that it is itself absolutely interwoven with this content; in the Notion which is the process of God, it is itself a moment. Finite consciousness knows God only to the extent to which God knows Himself in it; thus God is Spirit, the Spirit of His Church in fact, i.e. of those who worship Him. This is the perfect religion, the Notion become objective to itself. Here it is revealed what God is; He is no longer a Being above and beyond this world, and Unknown, for He has told men what He is, and this is not merely in outward history, but in consciousness.

Julian Huxley:

It is a fact that many phenomena are charged with some sort of magic or compulsive power, and do introduce us to a realm beyond our ordinary experience. Such events and such experiences merit a special designation. For want of a better, I use the term *divine*, though this quality of divinity is not truly supernatural but *trans-natural*—it grows out of ordinary nature, but transcends it. The divine is what man finds worthy of adoration, that which compels his awe.

From the specifically religious point of view, the desirable direction of evolution might be defined as the divinization of existence—but for this to have operative significance, we must frame a new definition of 'the divine' free from all connotation of external supernatural beings.

Religion today is imprisoned in a theistic frame of ideas, compelled to operate in the unrealities of the dualistic world. In the unitary Humanist frame it acquires a new look and new freedom. With the aid of our new vision it has the opportunity of escaping from the theistic impasses and of playing its proper role in the real world of unitary existence.

Some modern theologians

Some of these writers would maintain that they are not *departing from* the historic Christian understanding of God, but are merely *reinterpreting* the traditional ideas in a form that is more intelligible and acceptable today. These restatements, however, seem to come much closer to this general answer than to the biblical answer (pp. 11ff); or else they present an uneasy compromise between the two.

Paul Tillich describes God as 'Being Itself' rather than 'A Being':

The God who is *a* being is transcended by the God who is Being itself, the ground and abyss of every being. And the God who is *a* person is transcended by the God who is the Personal—Itself, the ground and abyss of every person.

God does not exist, He is being-itself beyond essence and existence. Therefore, to argue that God exists is to deny him.

This is how Tillich explains his concept of God in a more popular form:

The name of this infinite and inexhaustible depth and ground of all being is *God*. That depth is what the word *God* means. And if that word has not much meaning for you, translate it, and speak of the depths of your life, of the source of your being, of your ultimate concern, of what you take seriously without any reservation. Perhaps, in order to do so, you must forget everything traditional that you have learned about God, perhaps even that word itself. For if you know that God means depth, you know much about him. You cannot then call yourself an atheist or unbeliever. For you cannot think or say: Life has no depth! Life is shallow. Being itself is surface only. If you could say this in complete seriousness, you would be an atheist; but otherwise you are not. He who knows about depth knows about God.

Teilhard de Chardin:

As early as in St. Paul and St. John we read that to create, to fulfil and to purify the world is, for God, to unify it by uniting it organically with himself. How does he unify it? By partially immersing himself in things, by becoming 'element', and then, from this point of vantage in the heart of matter, assuming the control and leadership of what we now call evolution. Christ, principle of universal vitality because sprung up as a man among men, put himself in the position (maintained ever since) to subdue under himself, to purify, to direct and super-animate the general ascent of consciousness into which he inserted himself. By a perennial act of communion and sublimation, he aggregates to himself the total psychism of the earth. And when he has gathered everything together and transformed everything, he will close in upon himself and his conquests, thereby rejoining, in a final gesture, the divine focus he has never left. Then, as St. Paul tells us, *God shall be in all*. This is indeed a superior form of 'pantheism' without trace of the poison of adulteration or annihilation: the expectation of perfect unity, steeped in which each element will reach its consummation at the same time as the universe.

The universe fulfilling itself in a synthesis of centres in perfect conformity with the laws of union. God, the centre of centres.

He describes his position as 'a superior form of "pantheism" '. But he identifies God so closely with the universe that it is difficult for him to maintain at the same time that God is transcendent and distinct from the universe:

To put an end once and for all to the fears of 'pantheism', as regards evolution, how can we

Dr Paul Tillich, West German protestant theologian.

fail to see that, in the case of a *converging universe* . . . the universal centre of unification . . . must be conceived as pre-existing and transcendent. A very real 'pantheism' if you like (in the etymological meaning of the word) but an absolutely legitimate pantheism—for if, in the last resort, the reflective centres of the world are effectively 'one with God', this state is obtained not by identification (God becoming all) but by the differentiating and communicating action of love (God all *in everyone*). And that is essentially orthodox and Christian.

John Robinson seeks to go beyond a mere 'restating of traditional orthodoxy':

I believe we are being called, over the years ahead, to far more than a restating of traditional orthodoxy in modern terms. Indeed, if our defence of the Faith is limited to this, we shall find in all likelihood that we have lost out to all but a tiny religious remnant. A much more radical recasting, I would judge, is demanded, in the process of which the most fundamental categories of our theology—of God, of the supernatural, and of religion itself—must go into the melting.

Like Tillich, he rejects the idea of God as 'a Being'. In doing so he is not merely rejecting certain caricatures of God (as in Deism), but vital elements of historic Christian belief:

The conception of God as *a* Being, a Person—

like ourselves but supremely above and beyond ourselves—will, I believe, come to be seen as a human projection.

I believe, with Tillich, that we should give up speaking of 'the existence' of God. For it belongs to a way of thinking that is rapidly ceasing to be ours.

Unless we can represent him (God) in functional rather than ontological terms, he will rapidly lose all reality. As a Being he has no future.

He agrees with some words written by *Julian Huxley* in his book *Religion without Revelation:*

The sense of spiritual relief which comes from rejecting the idea of God as a superhuman being is enormous.

He vigorously rejects the accusation that he is propounding pantheism. He describes his position by the word 'panentheism'. Writing about his earlier book *Honest to God* he says:

I was concerned not to abolish transcendence (for without transcendence God becomes indistinguishable from the world, and so superfluous), but to find a way of *expressing* transcendence which would not tie God's reality to a supernaturalistic or mythological world-view which, if not actually falsifying, was largely meaningless for twentieth century man.

If one had to find a label to replace that of traditional 'theism' I would fall back on one that has a respectable pedigree but has never quite succeeded in establishing itself in orthodox Christian circles—namely, 'panentheism'. This is defined by *The Oxford Dictionary of the Christian Church* as 'the belief that the Being of God includes and penetrates the whole universe, so that every part of it exists in him, but (as against pantheism), that his Being is more than, and is not exhausted by, the universe.' It is the view that God is in everything and everything is in God.

He explains his beliefs in their simplest form by saying that the starting-point of his belief is:

. . . the awareness of the world as 'Thou'—and . . . the meeting through it of 'the Eternal Thou'.

. . . the overmastering, yet elusive, conviction of the 'Thou' at the heart of everything.

This seems to amount to saying: 'The universe is not impersonal. There is a kind of personal x, a personal quality in the universe over and above matter.' He uses the word 'God' as a kind of pointer to this feeling that the universe is personal:

To use the famous image of Lao Tzu, it is the hole in the middle that makes the wheel. The word 'God' is useful not because it fills in what is in the middle, but precisely because it witnesses to that which can never be filled in. In itself the word is expendable, it 'says' nothing. But *something like it* is an indispensable necessity if we are to refer to the hole at all. Since there is in fact nothing quite like it—no word that can replace it as a direct substitute—I am convinced that we must be able to go on using it, if only as shorthand. And this means that we must try to redeem it.

To assert that '*God* is love' is to believe that in love one comes into touch with the most fundamental reality in the universe, that Being itself ultimately has this character.

To affirm that 'the Lord is my rock' is to affirm that there is a bottom, an utterly reliable and unshakable basis to living.

God-language does not describe a Thing-in-Itself or even a Person-in-Himself . . . It points to an ultimate relatedness in the very structure of our being from which we cannot get away. It is a way of keeping guard over the irreducible, ineffable mystery at the heart of all experience.

John Wren-Lewis:

The first essential step in convincing people that Christianity can be true in spite of Freud is to assert outright that belief based on the projection-mechanism he describes is false, however much it may say 'Lord, Lord.' It is not enough to describe such beliefs as childish or primitive, for this implies that the truth is *something* like them, even though much more 'refined' or 'enlightened', whereas in reality *nothing like* the 'God' and 'Christ' I was brought up to believe in can be true. It is not merely that the Old Man in the Sky is only a mythological symbol for the Infinite Mind behind the scenes, nor yet that this Being is benevolent rather than fearful: the truth is that this whole way of thinking is wrong, and if such a Being did exist, he would be the very devil.

F. C. Happold:

The Something, within and beyond the polarities of human perception, which simply *is* has been called by many names with various shades of meaning. In general terms it is spoken of as Ultimate Reality or Ultimate Truth. Some philosophers call it the Absolute. For the religious it is God. Chinese metaphysicians call it Tao, Plotinus the One. For Hinduism it is the Everlasting Spirit.

For others Ultimate Reality is conceived as Mind, though in a much wider sense than our finite minds. Scientists use the concept of Energy, which cannot be known in itself, but only through its effects.

This Something which is the Is-ness of everything, is, however, in its completeness, concealed from human perception. It is the *Unknowable*, the *Inexpressible*, the *Unconditioned*. It is the *Mystery* which can only be known, at least intellectually, as an *image*, a *model*, an *approximation*.

The 'Death of God' theologies

This theology is not pure atheism. The following are the main points of this school.

▷ For many, the traditional language about God has become meaningless.

T. J. J. Altizer:

The man who chooses to live in our destiny can neither know the reality of God's presence nor understand the world as his creation; or, at least, he can no longer respond, either interiorly or cognitively, to the classical Christian images of the Creator and the creation.

William Hamilton:

When we speak of the death of God, we do not speak only of the death of the idols or the falsely objectivized being in the sky; we speak as well of the death in us of any power to affirm any of the traditional images of God . . . and wonder whether God himself has gone.

God is dead. We are not talking about the absence of the experience of God, but about the experience of the absence of God. Yet the death of God theologians claim to be theologians, to be Christians, to be speaking out of a community to a community. They do not grant that their view is really a complicated sort of atheism dressed in a new spring bonnet.

▷ This calls for a denial of much that historic Christianity stands for.

T. J. J. Altizer:

In the presence of a vocation of silence, theology must cultivate the silence of death. To be sure, the death to which theology is called is the death of God. Nor will it suffice for theology to merely accept the death of God. If theology is truly to die, it must *will* the death of God, must *will* the death of Christendom, must freely choose the destiny before it, and therefore must cease to be itself. Everything that theology has thus far become must now be negated; and negated not simply because it is dead, but rather because theology cannot be reborn unless it passes through, and freely wills, its own death and dissolution.

▷ The 'Death of God' refers to an actual event which has happened in history: i.e. the God who once existed as a God distinct from the universe actually died at a particular time, and became incarnate in the world.

T. J. J. Altizer:

To confess the death of God is to speak of an actual and real event, not perhaps an event occurring in a single moment of time or history, but notwithstanding this reservation an event that has actually happened both in a cosmic and in a historical sense . . . The radical Christian proclaims that God has actually died in Christ, that this death is both a historical and a cosmic event, and as such, it is a final and irrevocable event, which cannot be reversed by a subsequent religious or cosmic movement.

God has fully and totally become incarnate in Christ . . . a dynamic process of the transcendent's becoming immanent.

Only by accepting and even willing the death of God in our experience can we be liberated from a transcendent beyond, an alien beyond which has been emptied and darkened by God's self-annihilation in Christ.

▷ The 'Death of God' theologies continue to use the word 'God', as expressing a wistful longing and hope that the death of the supernatural God of Christianity will lead to the rebirth of faith, to a new revelation of 'God'.

William Hamilton:

There is an element of expectation, even hope, that removes my position from classical atheisms and that even removes from it a large amount of anguish and gloom.

Thus we wait, we try out new words, we pray for God to return, and we seem to be willing to descend into the darkness of unfaith and doubt that something may emerge on the other side. . .

But we do more than play the waiting game. We concentrate our energy and passion on the specific, the concrete, the personal. We turn from the problems of faith to the reality of love.

PROBLEMS AND QUESTIONS

Why not call a spade a spade and admit that this view is atheistic?

Why keep the name 'God'? If there is no personal Being called God, why not dispense with the name altogether? If we still need some name to describe the mystery of the universe, why not find a new and less confusing one?

Peter Dumitriu describes a kind of mystical experience in which he sees that the sense and meaning of the universe is 'love'. He then wonders what *words* he should use:

What name was I to use? 'God', I murmured, 'God'. How else should I address Him. O Universe? O Heap? O Whole? As 'Father'? or Mother'? I might as well call Him 'Uncle''.

As 'Lord'? I might as well say, 'Dear Sir', or 'Dear Comrade'. How could I say 'Lord' to the air I breathed and my own lungs which breathed the air? 'My child'? But he contained me, preceded me, created me. 'Thou' is His name, to which 'God' may be added. For 'I' and 'me' are no more than a pause between the immensity of the universe which is Him and the very depth of our self, which is also Him.

Dumitriu thinks it is obvious that he should use the name of 'God'. But is it so obvious and self-evident? Would not words like 'O Universe' 'O Heap' and 'O Whole' be very much more consistent? Is there anything more than convention and sentiment to justify choosing 'God'?

Y. Takeuchi, a Japanese Buddhist philosopher, suggests what he sees as the logical conclusion of the desire of many theologians to go beyond the idea of a personal God:

If we were to transcend the personal God (trinity of God) it would not be toward Being-itself, but rather towards Absolute Nothingness.

Walter Kaufmann similarly asks the question, why the name 'God'?

The atheist can agree with Tillich in his denial of the 'existence' of God and the affirmation of 'being-itself'—only why name it God?

All these answers, therefore, contain an element of linguistic cheating. There is bound to be an element of deception in continuing to use the word 'God'—which most people associate with a personal Being—while denying that any such Being exists. Humanists and Christians are not slow to point this out.

Julian Huxley:

(Robinson) is surely wrong in making such statements as that 'God is ultimate reality'. God is a hypothesis constructed by man to help him understand what existence is all about. The God hypothesis asserts the existence of some sort of supernatural person or supernatural being, exerting some kind of purposeful power over the universe and its destiny. To say that God is ultimate reality is just semantic cheating, as well as being so vague as to become effectively meaningless (and when Dr. Robinson continues by saying 'and ultimate reality must exist', he is surely running round a philosophically very vicious circle.)

  Dr. Robinson, like Dr. Tillich and many other modernist theologians, seems to me, and indeed to any humanist, to be trying to ride two horses at once, to keep his cake and eat it. He wants to be modern and meet the challenge of our new knowledge by stripping the image of God of virtually all its spatial, material, mythological, Freudian, and anthropomorphic aspects. But he still persists in retaining the term *God*, in spite of all its implication of supernatural power and personality; and it is these implications, not the modernists' fine-spun arguments, which consciously or unconsciously affect the ordinary man and woman. Heads I win, tails you lose: humanists dislike this elaborate double-talk.

A Hindu Sadhu (holy man) reading from the sacred scriptures at a festival for the worship of Shiva, god of destruction in the Hindu trinity.

Alasdair MacIntyre, writing about John Robinson's *Honest to God:*

What is striking about Dr. Robinson's book is first and foremost that he is an atheist . . . Yet . . . he is unwilling to abandon the word 'God' and a great many kindred theological words. Yet I think that we might well be puzzled by this strong desire for a theological vocabulary; for the only reason given for preserving the name 'God' is that 'our being has depths which naturalism whether evolutionary, mechanistic, dialectical or humanistic, cannot or will not recognize'. But this is to say that all atheists to date have described 'our being' inadequately . . . His book testifies to the existence of a whole group of theologies which have retained a theistic vocabulary but acquired an atheistic substance.

He points out that while the new theologies disown historic Christianity, they still depend on all the associations which surround the traditional language:

The formulas of the new theology seem to me to derive both such sense and such emotional power as they have by reason of their derivation from and association with the much more substantial faith of the past. Without that derivation and association these formulas, far from providing modern man with a faith rewritten in terms that he can understand, would be even more unintelligible than the theology they seek to correct.

Thus the new theologians are in a fundamentally false position. They in fact depend on the traditionalism which they proclaim that they discard.

Writing about Paul Tillich:

Belief in God has been evacuated of all its traditional content. It consists now in moral seriousness and nothing more.

Barbara Wooton:

The disappearance of a personal deity does not . . . dispose of the riddle of the universe and of man's place therein. Nor can this riddle be solved by such verbal tricks as those which the Bishop of Woolwich proceeds to employ. According to him, 'God is by definition ultimate reality. And one cannot argue whether ultimate reality *exists*. One can only ask what ultimate reality is like.' Such statements, I submit, are purely semantic exercises, which, strictly interpreted, are devoid of all meaning. If God and ultimate reality are identical, then the statement that God is ultimate reality amounts to neither more nor less than an assertion that ultimate reality is ultimate reality.

Altizer, writing about Teilhard de Chardin:

It is true that Teilhard occasionally and inconsistently introduces traditional Christian language into the pages of *The Phenomenon of Man*; but this fact scarcely obviates the truth that virtually the whole body of Christian belief either disappears or is transformed in Teilhard's evolutionary vision of the cosmos.

Professor Peter Beyerhaus expresses his fears about the transformation of Christian theology:

Personally I am most worried by the teaching of theologians who adapt the traditional Christian concepts to the expectations and desires of the new generation.

Here the language, in contrast to both the old fashioned liberalism and Bultmannian demythologization, sounds more and more orthodox. The doctrine of the Trinity, the two natures of Christ, the redemptive character of his cross, the reality of his resurrection and second coming are re-affirmed. But their authentic content has secretly been changed and replaced by evolutionist concepts. That which euphemistically is called a 'theology related to society' or 'political theology' is, in its deepest analysis, a camouflaged atheistic humanism, in which the names of God and Christ are simply cyphers for the real nature and destiny of man.

 In what sense can this answer be true?

This answer is usually based on a particular understanding of truth, and many who give this answer have to a greater or lesser extent accepted the Hindu answer.

Radhakrishnan:

Hinduism developed an attitude of comprehensive charity instead of fanatic faith in an inflexible creed. It accepted the multiplicity of aboriginal gods and others which originated, most of them, outside the Aryan tradition, and justified them all. It brought together into one whole all believers in God. Many sects professing many different beliefs live within the Hindu fold.

Arnold Toynbee:

Since I do not believe in a personal god, I don't

have a vested interest in any one religion . . . Although, of course, I can't get away from my Judaeo-Christian background, temperamentally I am a Hindu. As a Hindu, I don't have any difficulty in believing in many gods simultaneously, or thinking that a syncretist faith may be the answer for our age. To Hindus, it's of no consequence which road, Siva or Vishnu, one travels— all roads lead to heaven.

In this case, therefore, the discussion must shift from the question about *God* to the question about *truth*. See further the different answers to the question of truth in BOOK ONE: 'We can never know for certain' (pp. 47ff.); 'We can know only by a leap of faith' (pp. 60ff.); 'We can know only through mystical experience' (pp. 74ff.).

How does this understanding of God affect our view of man?

Sooner or later all our 'God-talk' must be related to *man*, and it is here that the profound implications of this concept of God become

even more apparent.
See Question Three: 'What is Man?', pp. 75ff.

BACK TO ANSWER ONE

"God really exists; he is as the Bible describes him"

PROBLEMS AND QUESTIONS

Having examined other possible answers to the question 'Who or what is God? Does he exist?', we return to option one, the Biblical Christian answer, for a closer look at some of the questions and objections raised.

What sort of mental image of God does the Bible give? Are we supposed to know what he looks like?

▷ The Old Testament emphasizes the fact that no one can see God as he really is, in all his glory. When we read of certain individuals who 'saw' God, their description of what they saw is hardly adequate to convey a clear mental image of what God 'looks like'. But it at least conveys the conviction that there really is Someone there and points to certain aspects of his character.

Moses:

Moses said, 'I pray thee, show me thy glory.' And he (God) said, 'I will make all my goodness pass before you, and will proclaim before you my name "The Lord" . . . But . . . you cannot see my face; for man shall not see me and live . . . Behold, there is a place by me where you shall stand upon the rock; and while my glory passes by I will put you in a cleft of the rock, and I will cover you with my hand until I have passed by; then I will take away my hand, and you shall see my back; but my face shall not be seen.' . . .

And the Lord descended in the cloud and stood with him there, and proclaimed the name of the Lord. The Lord passed before him, and proclaimed, 'The Lord, the Lord, a God merciful and gracious, slow to anger, and abounding in steadfast love and faithfulness, keeping steadfast love for thousands, forgiving iniquity and transgression and sin, but who will by no means clear the guilty . . .'

Isaiah:

In the year that King Uzziah died I saw the Lord sitting upon a throne, high and lifted up; and his train filled the temple. Above him stood the seraphim; each had six wings: with two he covered his face, and with two he covered his feet, and with two he flew. And one called to another and said:

'Holy, holy, holy is the Lord of hosts; the whole earth is full of his glory.'

And the foundations of the thresholds shook at the voice of him who called, and the house was filled with smoke. And I said: 'Woe is me! For I am lost; for I am a man of unclean lips, and I dwell in the midst of a people of unclean lips; for my eyes have seen the King, the Lord of hosts!'

Ezekiel:

Above the firmament over their heads there was the likeness of a throne, in appearance like sapphire; and seated above the likeness of a throne was a likeness as it were of a human form. And upward from what had the appearance of his loins I saw as it were gleaming bronze, like the appearance of fire enclosed round about; and downward from what had the appearance of his loins I saw as it were the appearance of fire . . . Such was the appearance of the likeness of the glory of the Lord.

▷ To have a clear idea of the *character* of God is far more important, and this can be known through the action of God in history and through revelation in words.

Jeremiah:

Thus says the Lord: 'Let not the wise man glory in his wisdom, let not the mighty man glory in his might, let not the rich man glory in his riches; but let him who glories glory in this, that he understands and knows me, that I am the Lord who practice kindness, justice, and righteousness in the earth; for in these things I delight, says the Lord.'

▷ When we come to the New Testament, the character of Jesus gives us the clearest picture we have of what God is like.

John writes:

No one has ever seen God; the only Son, who is in the bosom of the Father, he has made him known.

He records the following conversation with Philip:

Philip said to him, 'Lord, show us the Father, and we shall be satisfied.' Jesus said to him, 'Have I been with you so long, and yet you do not know me, Philip? He who has seen me has seen the Father; how can you say, "Show us the Father"? Do you not believe that I am in the Father and the Father in me?'

Towards the end of his life John records a vision of the living Christ in heaven:

Then I turned to see the voice that was speaking to me, and on turning I saw seven golden lampstands, and in the midst of the lampstands one like a son of man, clothed with a long robe and with a golden girdle round his breast; his head and his hair were white as white wool, white as snow; his eyes were like a flame of fire, his feet were like burnished bronze, refined as in a furnace, and his voice was like the sound of many waters; in his right hand he held seven stars, from his mouth issued a sharp two-edged sword, and his face was like the sun shining in full strength. When I saw him, I fell at his feet as though dead.

To see Christ as he is and to know his character is to know what God is like.

▷ People who have never seen Jesus but believe in him on the basis of the apostles' testimony can share the same kind of knowledge, the same certainty and joy:

Peter writes:

Without having seen him you love him; though you do not now see him you believe in him and rejoice with unutterable and exalted joy.

⚠ Isn't the idea of 'God' simply a projection of the human mind?

Thomas Merton:

Our ideas of God tell us much more about ourselves than they do about God.

James Mitchell writes about collecting a series of essays for a book entitled 'The god I want' (note the 'god' with a small *g*), and about the conclusion he reached:

The question running through the whole book is: was man created in god's image? Or god in man's?

What kind of a god, if any, would you create if you had the chance?

This whole exercise has forever destroyed for me the possibility that I might again find certitude in religious belief.

Aldous Huxley:

It is, I take it, generally agreed, that the origin of religion is to be found in the savage's fear of the unknown. All around him the savage sees the operation of forces, thunder and lightning, earthquakes and floods, which he cannot understand, or can understand only if he personifies them. And so he personifies them . . . And being human inventions they bear the stamp of their creators all too visibly on them. Literally they

are made in man's image. As man is, so too are his gods, or rather his God, for . . . in the course of time the multitudinous deities of the savage world are unified into a single personage, and Jehovah appears upon the scene.

Albert Einstein:

I cannot imagine a God who rewards and punishes the object of his creation, whose purposes are modelled after our own—a God, in short, who is but a reflection of human frailty.

▷ This objection does not take into account the vast *differences* between the ideas of God in the different religions. The ancient Greeks would have acknowledged quite unashamedly that their gods were very much like themselves. They have human virtues and vices, and have the advantage that they are not subject to as many limitations as human beings.

Ernst Cassirer describes the religion of ancient Greece and Rome in this way:

What man portrays in his gods is himself, in all his variety and multiformity, his turn of mind, his temperament, even his idiosyncracies. But it is not, as in Roman religion, the practical side of his nature that man projects upon the deity. The Homeric gods represent no moral ideals, but they express very characteristic mental ideals. They are not those functional and anonymous deities that have to watch over a special activity of man: they are interested in and favour individual men. Every god and goddess has his favourites who are appreciated, loved, and assisted, not on the ground of a mere personal predilection but by virtue of a kind of mental relationship that connects the god and the man. Mortals and immortals are the embodiments not of moral ideals but of special mental gifts and tendencies.

There is good evidence to believe that this kind of belief developed from a degenerate form of monotheism.

▷ It is not as easy as Huxley suggests to see precisely *how* such indulgent and 'human' gods of this kind could be transformed into the righteous and loving God of the Old Testament. It is much easier to trace the possible process of development if we begin with the assumption that men originally worshipped *one* Creator God, and that this belief degenerated into belief in many different gods. (See the quotations from Robert Brow on pp. 21 and 33.)

The uncomfortable thing about the God of the Bible is that he so often cuts across our personal desires and wishes. He does not allow us to be selfish, and always confronts us with an uncompromisingly high standard. This is *not* the kind of God man creates when he sets out to make a god in his own image.

▷ Even if we had a full scientific explanation of the *process* by which a person comes to hold certain beliefs about God, we would still be no nearer to discovering whether or not those beliefs were *true*. The most exact description of the mechanism of the brain when it believes the law of gravity, can not help us to know whether the law of gravity is in fact true.

To take another example, a child's ideas of God are built up largely through what he hears from others and through his own experience. He may be told 'God is like a father; he loves you, cares for you and provides for your needs like a father does.' And he may be taught to pray 'Our Father...' He therefore naturally attaches to his image of God the qualities which he observes in his father. If he experiences little love and kindness from his father, this will inevitably affect his understanding of God. Now although this kind of explanation may tell us a great deal about *how* a person comes to believe, it still does not tell us whether *what* he believes is true or false.

▷ Agnosticism about God often goes hand in hand with agnosticism or scepticism about the possibility of *any* kind of knowledge. If we say that the idea of God must be the product of the imagination, then the idea of 'beauty' may equally be the product of the human mind; there is no objective beauty in what we see—it is simply the name we attach to things that happen to please us. Similarly, we could say that the idea of Cause and Effect, or the laws of science are nothing more than the product of the human mind. They do not tell us the truth about what is there in the natural world, but are simply ideas that we find convenient for describing what we see. This is not mere theorizing. Ever since David Hume challenged the idea of Cause and Effect, others have taken this kind of scepticism quite seriously. And if we are prepared to go all the way with this scepticism, we must eventually conclude, with Sartre's Roquentin, that:

these are reasonable hypotheses which take the facts into account: but I am only too well aware that they come from me, that they are simply a way of unifying my own knowledge.

(See further BOOK ONE, pp. 47–59.)

⚠ Surely some of these beliefs about God are contradictory

How can God be both personal *and* infinite? How can he be both loving *and* holy? How can he be one *and* three?

Ronald Hepburn:

Recent philosophical studies have not been so much concerned with evidence for or against God's existence, as with the question of the coherence or incoherence of the concept of God. If the concept is ultimately incoherent, that is because theism tries to pack into it a wealth of sublime but incompatible elements—God is personal but infinite, is in causal contact with the

world but not in space and time, is impenetrably mysterious yet known beyond doubt in the Christian revelation. This is a downfall through excessive riches.

▷ Some pairs of words are obviously *mutually exclusive:* e.g. black and white (if something is black it cannot also be white), personal and impersonal (if God is personal he cannot also be impersonal—except in the thinking of Hinduism, which allows the laws of logic to be set aside—see BOOK ONE, pp. 50–53).

▷ In the four pairs of statements about God (p. 11), the words in each pair do not *exclude* each other, but merely help to *define* or *qualify.* When we say, for example, that God is one, but that there are three persons within that oneness, we are simply defining the kind of unity or oneness we mean. It is not the mathematical or physical oneness of something that is indivisible, but a oneness that is nearer to the unity of the atom; a oneness which is a complex unity holding together the Father, the Son and the Spirit, who share the same nature and enjoy a living relationship.

▷ Similarly with the other pairs: God's love is a holy love and his holiness is a loving holiness. His infinity is not a philosophical abstraction: he is personal, but without most of the limitations that we see in human beings.

 ## How can we talk about the 'God of the Bible'? Surely the Bible contains many different ideas of God

▷ If we see a father being angry with his children one day and kind to them the next, we may think him inconsistent, or we may go away with two quite different impressions of his character. But as we get to know him better, we may discover that he had every reason to be angry: it is *because he cares* for his children that he must sometimes discipline them.

The same holds good in the relationship between God and man. The many different pictures of God in the Bible may seem inconsistent, until we realize their underlying unity. Each is an expression of the same holy and loving God in his relationship with men in many different situations.

To take the analogy one stage further: a father may often scold his children, but only occasionally tell them that he loves them. If he really loves his children it will show in action more than in words. Similarly, God does not have to keep saying he loves us: sooner or later we come to realize that everything he says and does springs from his holy love.

▷ The Bible claims to record a *progressive* revelation of God. It is vital to notice that according to the biblical account, one of the results of the Fall was banishment from the presence of God, and therefore, we must assume, an increasing ignorance about him. Thus Cain says:

'Behold, thou hast driven me this day away from the ground; and from thy face I shall be hidden; and I shall be a fugitive and a wanderer on the earth . . .' . . . Then Cain went away from the presence of the Lord.

This is how the writer of Genesis describes the condition of man before the Flood:

The Lord saw that the wickedness of man was great in the earth, and that every imagination of the thoughts of his heart was only evil continually.

If this is a true account of the state of alienation which man had reached as a result of his rebellion, God would have to begin by revealing himself gradually. Therefore, in studying the course of this progressive revelation, we must ask ourselves: does this new revelation *complement* and *add to* what has already been revealed, or does it *contradict* it? If we understand truth as the writers of the Bible understood it, we can see how the apparently different pictures of God complement each other, taking their place in the context of the whole revelation.

▷ We can see how this principle works out by taking one specific objection which is often raised: how can we reconcile the God of love in the New Testament with the God of wrath in the Old? Surely the earlier revelation of God in the Old Testament as one who is wrathful and seeking vengeance must be superseded by the God of love revealed in the life and teaching of Jesus.

▷ This objection rests partly on a misunderstanding of phrases like 'the wrath of God'. The Bible does not use expressions like this to mean that God is losing his temper; there is no suggestion that his wrath is petty or selfish or vindictive in the way that human anger often is. These expressions are used simply to describe God's opposition to sin and evil. They emphasize that God is not morally neutral, and that he cannot allow sin to have a permanent place in his universe. Thus the writer of Proverbs says:

There are six things which the Lord hates,
   seven which are an abomination to him:
haughty eyes, a lying tongue,
   and hands that shed innocent blood,
a heart that devises wicked plans,
   feet that make haste to run to evil,
a false witness who breathes out lies,
   and a man who sows discord among
      brothers.

Stephen Neill:

The best way to understand the doctrine of the wrath of God is to consider the alternatives. The alternative is not love; since rightly considered, love and wrath are only the obverse and reverse of the same thing . . . The alternative to wrath is neutrality—neutrality in the conflict of the world . . . To live in such a world would be a nightmare. It is only the doctrine of the wrath of God, of his irreconcilable hostility to all evil, which makes human life tolerable in such a world as ours.

▷ This objection is also based on a very selective reading of the Bible. The Old Testament has much to say about the love of God, while the New Testament speaks as much as the Old Testament about the wrath of God— perhaps even more. The following passages are from two of the prophets who are revealing the mind of God.

Jeremiah:

'I have loved you with an everlasting love;
   therefore I have continued my faithfulness
      to you.'

Isaiah:

'For a brief moment I forsook you,
   but with great compassion I will gather you.
In overflowing wrath for a moment I hid my face
      from you,
but with everlasting love I will have compassion
      on you,
   says the Lord, your Redeemer.'

'Can a woman forget her sucking child,
   that she should have no compassion on the
      son of her womb?'
Even these may forget, yet I will not forget you.
Behold, I have graven you on the palms of my
      hands.

Jesus had much to say about the love of God; but he also spoke in the strongest language about the awfulness of the judgement on those who refused to recognize him and follow his teaching:

And when he drew near and saw the city he wept over it, saying, 'Would that even today you knew the things that make for peace! But now they are hid from your eyes. For the days shall come upon you, when your enemies will cast up a bank about you and surround you, and hem you in on every side, and dash you to the ground, you and your children within you, and they will not leave one stone upon another in you; because you did not know the time of your visitation.

Then he (the Son of man) will say to those at his left hand, 'Depart from me, you cursed, into the eternal fire prepared for the devil and his angels; for I was hungry and you gave me no food, I was thirsty and you gave me no drink, I was a stranger and you did not welcome me, naked and you did not clothe me, sick and in prison and you did not visit me.' . . . And they will go away into eternal punishment, but the righteous into eternal life.

Paul saw no difficulty in holding together the wrath of God and the love of God and speaking of them in the same breath:

God shows his love for us in that while we were yet sinners Christ died for us. Since, therefore, we are now justified by his blood, much more shall we be saved by him from the wrath of God.

John, similarly, holds the love and the wrath of God together; the word 'propitiation' contains the idea of turning away wrath:

In this is love, not that we loved God, but that he loved us and sent his Son to be the propitiation for our sins.

One of the most striking expressions of the wrath of God is in the phrase 'the wrath of the Lamb', which is found in the book of Revelation, where John is describing his vision of the day of judgement:

Then the kings of the earth and the great men and the generals and the rich and the strong, and every one, slave and free, hid in the caves and among the rocks of the mountains, calling to the mountains and rocks, 'Fall on us and hide us from the face of him who is seated on the throne, and from the wrath of the Lamb; for the great day of their wrath has come, and who can stand before it?'

The phrase 'the wrath of the Lamb' combines the thought of the love and the wrath of God. In the first place we immediately think of the weakness and gentleness of a young lamb. Then further we are reminded of John's description of Jesus as 'The Lamb of God, who takes away the sins of the world'. The Lamb, therefore, has done all in his power to *save* men from this terrifying judgement, if only they will turn to him. He has a right to our love and trust because of who he is and what he has done; and where his love is rejected, there can be no neutrality, only wrath.

QUESTION THREE

"What is man?"

Certain vital questions are being asked today, and are likely to be asked more and more in the future—questions which focus on the individual, on the meaning and purpose of life, on choice, on relationships, on coming to terms with suffering and evil. The answer we give to the question 'What is man?' directly affects these more specific and personal questions. For this reason each of the three basic answers is outlined in turn and tested for its effect in these five major areas.

THE INDIVIDUAL

Who am I?

Harold Pinter, the dramatist, puts the question into the mouth of one of his characters:

The point is, who are you? Not why or how, not even what. I can see what, perhaps, clearly enough. But who are you? It's no use saying you know who you are just because you tell me you can fit your particular key into a particular slot which will duly receive your particular key because that's not foolproof and certainly not conclusive.

Am I in any sense 'free'? Am I a self or a machine?

Jacob Bronowski:

This is where the fulcrum of our fears lies: that man as a species and we as thinking men, will be shown to be no more than a machinery of atoms. We pay lip service to the vital life of the amoeba and the cheese mite; but what we are defending is the human claim to have a complex of will and thoughts and emotions—to have a mind.

. . . the crisis of confidence . . . springs from each

Leo Tolstoy, Russian novelist and philosopher.

man's wish to be a mind and a person, in the face of the nagging fear that he is a mechanism. The central question I ask is this: Can man be both a machine and a self?

The question of the freedom of the individual is also forced upon us because of the vast concentrations of power in the hands of individuals in government, industry and the mass media.

Thomas Mann:

The whole question of the human being and what we think about him is put to us today with a life-and-death seriousness unknown in times that were not so stern as ours. For everybody, but most particularly for the artist, it is a matter of spiritual life or spiritual death; it is to use the religious terminology, a matter of salvation. I am convinced that that writer is a lost man who betrays the things of the spirit by refusing to face and decide for himself the human problem, put, as it is today, in political terms.

Aldous Huxley:

How can we control the vast impersonal forces that now menace our hard-won freedoms?

MEANING

What do I mean? What is the meaning of my life?

Somerset Maugham:

If . . . one puts aside the existence of God and the possibility of survival as too doubtful to have any effect on one's behaviour, one has to make up one's mind what is the meaning and use of life. If death ends all, if I have neither to hope for good to come nor to fear evil, I must ask myself what I am here for, and how in these circumstances I must conduct myself.

Tolstoy:

What is life for? To die? To kill myself at once? No, I am afraid. To wait for death till it comes? I fear that even more. Then I must live. *But what for?* In order to die? And I could not escape from that circle. I took up the book, read, and forgot myself for a moment, but then again, the same question and the same horror. I lay down and closed my eyes. It was worse still.

Adam Schaff, the Polish Marxist philosopher, asks questions about the meaning and value

W. Somerset Maugham, British novelist.

of man in his book *A Philosophy of Man.* Communism has generally refused to admit that these are genuine questions, and its philosophy has never attempted to include answers. But he insists that they are real questions, and that Communists can no longer pretend that they do not exist:

'Vanity, vanity, all is vanity!' These words, repeated in various forms in all the philosophies of the East, seem to appeal to many who in old age begin to reflect on life and death. It is possible to shrug this off with a compassionate smile as nonsense, and yet the words echo a problem which simply cannot be ignored. Nor can the questions 'Why?', 'What for?', which force their way to the lips of people tired of the adversities and delusions of life. This applies still more to the compulsive questions which come from reflection upon death—why all this effort to stay alive if we are going to die anyway? It is difficult to avoid the feeling that death is senseless—avoidable, accidental death especially. Of course we can ask: senseless from what point of view? From the point of view of the progress of nature death is entirely sensible. But from the point of view of a given individual death is senseless and places in doubt everything that he does . . . Attempts to ridicule this do not help . . .

'What is the meaning of life?' 'What is man's

place in the universe?' It seems difficult to express oneself scientifically on such hazy topics. And yet if one should assert ten times over that these are typical pseudo-problems, problems would remain.

VALUES

How am I to make choices?

Nietzsche:

As soon as . . . no thinker can any longer relieve his conscience with the hypothesis 'God or eternal values', the claim of the lawgiver to determine new values rises to an awfulness which has not yet been experienced.

Arthur Koestler speaks of the moral dilemma which must have faced Scott during his return from the South Pole in 1912; either he must take the sick Owens along with him and accept the risks of delay, or he must leave him behind in the hope of saving his own life and the lives of the other three in the party.

This dilemma . . . symbolises the eternal predicament of man, the tragic conflict inherent in his nature. It is the conflict between expediency and morality . . . This conflict is at the root of our political and social crisis, . . . it contains in a nutshell the challenge of our time . . .
    That both roads end as blind alleys is a dilemma which is inseparable from man's condition; it is not an invention of the philosophers, but a conflict which we face at each step in our daily affairs . . . The more responsible the position you hold, the sharper you feel the horns of the dilemma. When a decision involves the fate of a great number of people, the conflict grows proportionately. The technical progress of our age has enormously increased the range and consequence of man's actions, and has thus amplified his inherent dilemma to gigantic proportions. This, therefore, is the reason for our acute awareness of a crisis. We are like the patient who for the first time hears in a loudspeaker the irregular ticking of his heart.

Albert Camus:

When man submits God to moral judgement, he kills Him in his own heart. And then what is the basis of morality? God is denied in the name of justice but can the idea of justice be understood without the idea of God?

Jean-Paul Sartre:

Any morality which does not present itself explicitly as *impossible today* contributes to the mystification and alienation of man. The moral 'problem' arises from the fact that morals are *for us* both unavoidable and impossible. Action must give itself its ethical norms in this climate of unsurmountable impossibility. It is in this light, for example, that one should consider the problem of violence or that of the relation between the means and the end.

I do not present these contradictions to condemn Christian morals: I am too deeply convinced that *any* morals are both impossible and necessary.

RELATIONSHIPS

What hope is there for communication and love?

John Russell Taylor, in his comments on a play by Harold Pinter, speaks of the doubt about knowing the truth about other people:

The technique of casting doubt upon everything by matching each apparently clear and unequivocal statement with an equally clear and unequivocal statement of its contrary . . . is one which we shall find used constantly in Pinter's plays to create an air of mystery and uncertainty . . . in these ordinary surroundings lurk mysterious terrors and uncertainties—and by extension, the whole external world of everyday realities is thrown into question. Can we ever know the truth about anybody or anything? Is there any absolute truth to be known?

Bertrand Russell, speaking of the obstacles which stand in the way of human progress:

What stands in the way? Not physical or technical obstacles, but only the evil passions in human minds; suspicion, fear, lust for power, intolerance . . .
    The root of the matter is a very simple and old-fashioned thing, a thing so simple that I am almost ashamed to mention it, for fear of the derisive smile with which wise cynics will greet my words. The thing I mean—please forgive me for mentioning it—is love, Christian love, or compassion . . .

Thomas Mann ends his novel *The Magic Mountain* with the question:

Out of this universal feast of death, out of this extremity of fever, kindling the rain-washed evening sky to a fiery glow, may it be that Love one day shall mount?

SUFFERING AND EVIL

How can I live with suffering and evil?

Ionesco:

Shortly after my arrival in my second homeland, I saw a man, still young, big and strong, attack an old man with his fists and kick him with his boots . . . I have no other images of the world except those of evanescence and brutality, vanity and rage, nothingness or hideous, useless hatred. Everything I have since experienced has merely confirmed what I had seen and understood in my childhood: vain and sordid fury, cries suddenly stifled by silence, shadows engulfed forever in the night.

Aldous Huxley:

In the form in which men have posed it, the Riddle of the Universe requires a theological answer. Suffering and enjoying, men want to know why they enjoy and to what end they suffer. They see good things and evil things, beautiful things and ugly, and they want to find a reason—a final and absolute reason—why these things should be as they are.

A survivor from an Italian earthquake.

Adam Schaff:

The fact alone of some agnostics undergoing deathbed conversions gives much food for thought. Philosophy must take the place of religion here. It must tackle a number of diverse questions which have remained from the wreck of the religious view of life—the senselessness of suffering, of broken lives, of death, and many other questions relgatin to the fate of the living, struggling, suffering and dying individuals. Can this be done scientifically, that is in a way that is communicable and subject to some sort of verification?

Albert Camus:

The certainty of the existence of a God who would give meaning to life has a far greater attraction than the knowledge that without him one could do evil without being punished. The choice between these alternatives would not be difficult. But there is no choice, and that is where the bitterness begins.

Confronted with this evil, confronted with death, man from the very depths of his soul cries out for justice.

What is man?

"Man is a creature created by God—but this is not the God of the Bible"

PAGE 66

"Man is a creature created in the image of God—the God of the Bible"

PAGE 53

"Man is not the creation of God because there is no personal Creator"

PAGE 75

1. THE ANSWER OF BIBLICAL CHRISTIANITY

"Man is a creature created in the image of God— the God of the Bible"

The Christian teaching on man can be summarized as follows:

☐ **Man has been created in the image and likeness of God**

☐ **Man is now a rebel against his Creator**

☐ **Man can become a 'son' of God**

MAN IS A CREATURE CREATED IN THE IMAGE OF GOD

▷ The Bible recognizes that man in his physical make-up has a great deal in common with the animals; the writer of Genesis speaks of man being made 'of dust from the ground', like the animals. But the basic difference between man and the animals is that man is in some ways *like* God:

Then God said, 'Let us make man in our image, after our likeness . . .' So God created man in his own image, in the image of God he created him; male and female he created them.

The following passage later in the book of Genesis makes it clear that the 'image and likeness' is to be understood quite naturally as resemblance:

When God created man, he made him in the likeness of God. Male and female he created them, and he blessed them and named them Man and they were created. When Adam had lived a hundred and thirty years, he became the father of a son in his own likeness, after his image.

▷ To say that man is *like* God means that:

Just as God is personal, *so* man is personal.
Just as God has mind and can think and communicate, *so* man has a mind and can think and communicate; he is rational.

Just as God has will and can decide and make free choices, *so* man has a will and can make certain free choices; he is responsible and accountable.
Just as God has emotions and can feel, *so* man has emotions and can feel.

▷ Man, however, is clearly *unlike* God in certain respects:

God is infinite, unlimited by space and time: man is not.
God is Spirit and has no body: man has a physical body with all its limitations.
God has absolute knowledge and absolute power: man does not.

▷ As he was originally created man 'was perfect:

And God saw everything that he had made, and behold, it was very good.

▷ Although man is no longer perfect, he is still God's creation, bearing his image. The likeness has been spoiled, but not obliterated completely. Man still has something in common with God, and it is this which gives him his greatness and dignity. So however much the writers of the Bible may stress man's fallen state, they never lose sight of the fact that he is the crown of God's creative work in the universe.

When I look at thy heavens, the work of thy
    fingers,
    the moon and the stars which thou hast
      established;
what is man that thou art mindful of him,
    and the son of man that thou dost care for him?
Yet thou hast made him little less than God,
    and dost crown him with glory and honour.
Thou hast given him dominion over the works of
    thy hands,
    thou hast put all things under his feet,
all sheep and oxen, and also the beasts of the field,
the birds of the air, and the fish of the sea,
    whatever passes along the paths of the sea.

▷ I am a created being, and I have to accept that fact. I have to acknowledge my own imperfections and limitations and weaknesses:

Woe to him who strives with his Maker,
    an earthen vessel with the potter!
Does the clay say to him who fashions it, 'What
    are you making'?

or 'Your work has no handles'?
Woe to him who says to a father, 'What are you
      begetting?'
or to a woman, 'With what are you in travail?'

▷ Once I reach this point of acceptance I can have a deep sense of confidence and joy in the one who has made me and knows me so completely:

For thou didst form my inward parts,
    thou didst knit me together in my mother's
      womb.
I praise thee, for thou are fearful and wonderful.
    Wonderful are thy works!
Thou knowest me right well;
    my frame was not hidden from thee,
when I was being made in secret,
    intricately wrought in the depths of the earth.
Thy eyes beheld my unformed substance;
    in thy book were written, every one of them,
the days that were formed for me,
    when as yet there was none of them.
How precious to me are thy thoughts, O God!

Thy hands have made and fashioned me;
    give me understanding that I may learn thy
      commandments.

MAN IS NOW A REBEL AGAINST HIS CREATOR

▷ The human race is now in a state of rebellion against its Creator. Men may recognize that God exists. They may even try to worship him in different ways. But they fail to love him as he deserves. They fail to live up to his standards.

▷ Man was not *created* a rebel; he has *become* a rebel. When Adam was created, he was given a choice: either to depend on God and obey him, or to be independent.

God plainly warned what the consequences of disobedience would be:

You may freely eat of every tree of the garden; but of the tree of the knowledge of good and evil you shall not eat, for in the day that you eat of it you shall die.

▷ The effects of Adam's rebellion and sin were transmitted to the whole human race:

Sin came into the world through one man and death through sin, and so death spread to all men because all men sinned.

▷ Man's rebellion against God at the present

time thus consists in a refusal to live according to God's revealed laws.

John defines sin in terms of lawlessness:

Every one who commits sin is guilty of lawlessness; sin is lawlessness.

Paul defines sin as man's refusal to acknowledge the truth that he knows about God:

The wrath of God is revealed from heaven against all ungodliness and wickedness of men who by their wickedness suppress the truth. For what can be known about God is plain to them, because God has shown it to them. Ever since the creation of the world his invisible nature, namely, his eternal power and deity, has been clearly perceived in the things that have been made. So they are without excuse; for although they knew God they did not honour him as God or give thanks to him, but they became futile in their thinking and their senseless minds were darkened.

▷ Those who have not had the fuller revelation of God through the Bible and through Jesus Christ are in the same state of rebellion against God. *Paul* writes that although they have not had the fuller revelation, they have set certain standards for themselves and others, and have failed to live up to them:

Therefore you have no excuse, O man, whoever you are, when you judge another; for in passing judgement upon him you condemn yourself, because you, the judge, are doing the very same things. We know that the judgement of God rightly falls upon those who do such things. Do you suppose, O man, that when you judge those who do such things and yet do them yourself, you will escape the judgement of God?

This means that men who have never heard the fuller revelation of God recorded in the Bible will be judged on the basis of whether or not they have lived up to the standards they have set for themselves and others. And on this basis, there is no one who is innocent before God.

... all men, both Jews and Greeks, are under the power of sin.

... all have sinned and fall short of the glory of God.

▷ God's reaction to this situation cannot be neutral. He cannot pretend that disobedience does not matter or that it can be passed over or forgiven lightly. The prophets give many examples of situations in which God is compelled to act in judgement:

I was ready to be sought by those who did not ask for me;
I was ready to be found by those who did not seek me.

I said, 'Here am I, here am I,' to a nation that did not call on my name.
I spread out my hands all the day to a rebellious people,
who walk in a way that is not good, following their own devices;
a people who provoke me to my face continually . . .
Behold, it is written before me:
'I will not keep silent, but I will repay,
yea, I will repay into their bosom their iniquities and their fathers' iniquities together, says the Lord.'

The Bible uses the word 'wrath' to describe God's reaction to man's rebellion:

... we all once lived in the passions of our flesh, following the desires of body and mind, and so we were by nature children of wrath . . .

Paul speaks in this way about the final consequences of man's rebellion, if there is no repentance and turning to God:

They shall suffer the punishment of eternal destruction and exclusion from the presence of the Lord and from the glory of his might.

▷ But this punishment is not inevitable. God offers forgiveness, if only rebel man will seek it:

Come now, let us reason together, says the Lord:
Though your sins are like scarlet,
    they shall be as white as snow;
though they are red like crimson,
    they shall become like wool.

MAN CAN BECOME A 'SON' OF GOD

▷ Although man is a rebel by nature and under the judgement of God, God has taken the initiative and done something to restore the broken relationship.

While we were yet helpless, at the right time Christ died for the ungodly. Why, one will hardly die for a righteous man—though perhaps for a good man one will dare even to die. But God shows his love for us in that while we were yet sinners Christ died for us . . . We also rejoice in God through our Lord Jesus Christ, through whom we have now received our reconciliation.

▷ Jesus is the 'Son of God' in a special and unique sense. But those who put their trust in him and accept the reconciliation which is offered on the basis of his death (see BOOK THREE, Question Six, 'What is the meaning of the death of Jesus?'), are born into the family of God to become 'sons':

To all who received him, who believed in his name, he gave power to become children of God; who were born, not of blood nor of the will of the flesh nor of the will of man, but of God.

▷ Peter speaks in this way about the transforming process which can go on in the life of the Christian here and now—even to the point of 'sharing the divine nature':

His divine power has granted to us all things that pertain to life and godliness, through the knowledge of him who called us to his own glory and excellence, by which he has granted to us his precious and very great promises, that through these you may escape from the corruption that is in the world because of passion, and become partakers of the divine nature.

THE ANSWER THIS APPROACH GIVES TO THE BASIC QUESTIONS ABOUT MAN

THE INDIVIDUAL

Job has a frightening sense of God's awareness of every individual. In his suffering he even wishes that God were *less* concerned about him:

What is man, that thou dost make so much of him,
   and that thou dost set thy mind upon him,
dost visit him every morning,
   and test him every moment?
How long wilt thou not look away from me
   nor let me alone till I swallow my spittle?
If I sin, what do I do to thee, thou watcher of men?
   Why hast thou made me thy mark?
   Why have I become a burden to thee?
Why dost thou not pardon my transgression
   and take away my iniquity?
For now I shall lie in the earth;
   thou wilt seek me, but I shall not be.

At other times Job takes comfort from the knowledge that God knows him and deals with him as an individual:

But he knows the way that I take;
   when he has tried me, I shall come forth as gold.

Ezekiel emphasizes that every individual is held responsible by God for his own choices, and cannot blame his parents or anyone else:

The word of the Lord came to me again: 'What do you mean by repeating this proverb concerning the land of Israel, "The fathers have eaten sour grapes, and the children's teeth are set on edge"? As I live, says the Lord God, this proverb shall no more be used by you in Israel. Behold, all souls

Mother Teresa of Calcutta feeds a young boy weakened by hunger.

are mine; the soul of the father as well as the soul of the son is mine: the soul that sins shall die . . . The son shall not suffer for the iniquity of the father, nor the father suffer for the iniquity of the son; the righteousness of the righteous shall be upon himself, and the wickedness of the wicked shall be upon himself.

Jesus speaking about the value of the individual to God:

Are not five sparrows sold for two pennies? And not one of them is forgotten before God. Why, even the hairs of your head are all numbered. Fear not; you are of more value than many sparrows.

This belief in the value of the individual provides a compelling reason for fighting for the rights of the individual.

Leslie Newbiggin:

During World War II, Hitler sent men to the famous Bethel Hospital to inform Pastor Bodel-schwingh, its director, that the State could no longer afford to maintain hundreds of epileptics who were useless to society and only constituted a drain on scarce resources, and that orders were being issued to have them destroyed. Bodel-schwingh confronted them in his room at the entrance to the Hospital and fought a spiritual battle which eventually sent them away without having done what they were sent to do. He had no other weapon for the battle than the simple affirmation that these were men and women made in the image of God and that to destroy them was to commit a sin against God which would surely

be punished. What other argument could he have used?

MEANING

What gives meaning and significance to man's life is the fact that God himself seeks to enter into a relationship with him:

'... I am the Lord ... and I will take you for my people, and I will be your God; and you shall know that I am the Lord your God ...'

The individual can know that God has a plan and purpose for his life. God says to *Jeremiah* the prophet:

Before I formed you in the womb I knew you,
and before you were born I consecrated you;
I appointed you a prophet to the nations.

Paul writes in this way about the plan of God which embraces the whole of our universe:

Blessed be the God and Father of our Lord Jesus Christ, who has blessed us in Christ with every spiritual blessing in the heavenly places, even as he chose us in him before the foundation of the world, that we should be holy and blameless before him. He destined us in love to be his sons through Jesus Christ, according to the purpose of his will, to the praise of his glorious grace which he freely bestowed on us in the Beloved. In him we have redemption through his blood, the forgiveness of our trespasses, according to the riches of his grace which he lavished upon us. For he has made known to us in all wisdom and insight the mystery of his will, according to his purpose which he set forth in Christ as a plan for the fullness of time, to unite all things in him, things in heaven and things on earth.

The simplest and clearest description of the meaning of man's existence is given in the words of the *Westminster Shorter Catechism:*

Man's chief end is to glorify God, and to enjoy him for ever.

VALUES

The ultimate standard of what is right and good is the character of God himself. What is in accordance with his character is right and what is contrary to his character is wrong.

... the Lord appeared to Abram, and said to him, 'I am God Almighty; walk before me, and be blameless ...'

... as he who called you is holy, be holy yourselves in all your conduct; since it is written, 'You shall be holy, for I am holy.'

The *Ten Commandments* revealed to Moses give an outline of the standards which God sets for men:

You shall have no other gods before me ...
You shall not make yourself a graven image ...
    you shall not bow down to them or serve
    them ...
You shall not take the name of the Lord your
    God in vain ...
Remember the sabbath day, to keep it holy ...
Honour your father and your mother ...
You shall not kill.
You shall not commit adultery.
You shall not steal.
You shall not bear false witness against your
    neighbour.
You shall not covet ...

The prophets were constantly exposing injustice and corruption in personal and public life, applying the commandments in particular situations:

For I the Lord love justice,
    I hate robbery and wrong ...

Then I will draw near to you for judgement; I will be a swift witness against the sorcerers, against the adulterers, against those who swear falsely, against those who oppress the hireling in his wages, the widow and the orphan, against those who thrust aside the sojourner, and do not fear me, says the Lord of hosts.

Jesus extended some of these commandments to cover the thought life as well as outward actions, and he gave his own summary of the Law of the Old Testament by bringing together two verses from different books:

You shall love the Lord your God with all your heart, and with all your soul, and with all your mind. This is the great and first commandment. And a second is like it, You shall love your neighbour as yourself. On these two commandments depend all the law and the prophets.

In the New Testament the meaning of love for others is revealed much more clearly in the example of the love of Christ. The character and teaching of Jesus thus becomes the clearest demonstration of what Christian values are supposed to be:

Put to death . . . what is earthly in you: immorality, impurity, passion, evil desire, and covetousness, which is idolatry. On account of these the wrath of God is coming. In these you once walked, when you lived in them. But now put them all away: anger, wrath, malice, slander, and foul talk from your mouth. Do not lie to one another, seeing that you have put off the old nature with its practices and have put on the new nature, which is being renewed in knowledge after the image of its creator. . . . Put on then, as God's chosen ones, holy and beloved, compassion, kindness, lowliness, meekness, and patience, forbearing one another . . . forgiving each other; as the Lord has forgiven you, so you also must forgive. And above all these put on love, which binds everything together in perfect harmony . . .

While the Christian, therefore, does not have ready-made solutions to all moral problems, he at least has a firm starting-point. And where there is doubt in particular situations, he can rely on the leading of the Holy Spirit who can make his conscience sensitive to the mind of Christ.

. . . try to learn what is pleasing to the Lord . . . do not be foolish, but understand what the will of the Lord is. And do not get drunk with wine, for that is debauchery; but be filled with the Spirit . . .

RELATIONSHIPS

There is a possibility of real communication between men because man still bears the image of the three-in-one God.

The Bible recognizes the deep *untruthfulness* in fallen human nature, and reminds us that no deception can be hidden from God:

The heart is deceitful above all things,
  and desperately corrupt;
  who can understand it?
'I the Lord search the mind and try the heart,
to give to every man according to his ways,
  according to the fruit of his doings.'

O Lord, thou hast searched me and known me!
Thou knowest when I sit down and when I rise up;
  thou discernest my thoughts from afar.
Thou searchest out my path and my lying down,
  and art acquainted with all my ways.
Even before a word is on my tongue,
  lo, O Lord, thou knowest it altogether.

Living in the light of God's presence and being a member in the 'body' of those who believe are real incentives to truthfulness:

If we walk in the light, as he is in the light, we have fellowship with one another, and the blood of Jesus his Son cleanses us from all sin.

Therefore, putting away falsehood, let every one speak the truth with his neighbour, for we are members one of another.

Similarly, there is the possibility of love between people because man is made in the image of the God who *is* love, in his very nature. Thus all relationships can be restored and guided by the love that Christ has shown in practice:

Let all bitterness and wrath and anger and clamour and slander be put away from you, with all malice, and be kind to one another, tenderhearted, forgiving one another, as God in Christ forgave you. Therefore be imitators of God, as beloved children. And walk in love, as Christ loved us and gave himself up for us.

Paul goes on to say in the same letter that within the marriage relationship there can be a deep belonging and loving, not only because man and woman become 'one flesh', but because the Christian has, in the sacrificial and self-giving love of Christ, a pattern of what love can be in marriage:

Wives, be subject to your husbands, as to the Lord . . . Husbands, love your wives, as Christ loved the church and gave himself up for her.

Within this relationship there can be a deep sense of mutual belonging:

I am my beloved's and my beloved is mine.

SUFFERING AND EVIL

The Christian is bound to feel this problem intensely. His belief in the goodness of God is bound to accentuate the question of '*why* suffering and evil?'

My God, my God, why hast thou forsaken me?
  why art thou so far from helping me, from the
    words of my groaning?
O my God, I cry by day, but thou dost not answer;
  and by night, but find no rest.

Thou who art of purer eyes than to behold evil
  and canst not look on wrong,
why dost thou look on faithless men,
  and art silent when the wicked swallows up the
    man more righteous than he?

Righteous art thou, O Lord, when I complain
    to thee;
  yet I would plead my case before thee.
Why does the way of the wicked prosper?
    Why do all who are treacherous thrive?
Thou plantest them, and they take root;
    they grow and bring forth fruit . . .

The Bible does not present a complete and
systematic explanation of suffering and evil;
but it does at least give some clues to this
great mystery.

The origin of suffering and evil

At the start, everything in the universe was
good:

And God saw everything that he had made, and
behold, it was very good.

Evil and suffering as we now know them
are described as an intrusion as far as the
human race is concerned. Man disobeyed
God at the suggestion of the Serpent, who in
other parts of the Bible is interpreted as the
mouthpiece of Satan—a created supernatural
being, less powerful than God, who has
rebelled against him and is doing his utmost
to spoil God's universe. Human suffering is
very closely connected with man's rebellion;
for God says to the woman after her disobedience:

I will greatly multiply your pain in child-
    bearing;
  in pain you shall bring forth children . . .

And to the man:

In the sweat of your face you shall eat bread till
you return to the ground, for out of it you were
taken; you are dust, and to dust you shall return.

Jesus saw the activity of Satan behind much
suffering. For example, he describes a woman
who has been paralysed for eighteen years as
one 'whom Satan bound'.

The Bible makes a distinction between
suffering where there is an element of human
responsibility, and suffering where the sufferer
is in no sense responsible.

**Suffering where there is an element of human
responsibility.** If man is free to do good, he is
also free to do evil. This is part of the real
freedom God has given to man. *Moses* here
reminds the children of Israel about the laws
of God for their national life; he tells them
that, as a general principle, disobedience will
bring suffering:

All these blessings shall come upon you and over-
take you, if you obey the voice of the Lord your
God. Blessed shall you be in the city, and blessed
shall you be in the field. Blessed shall be the fruit
of your body, and of your ground, and the fruit
of your beasts.

But on the other hand:

If you are not careful to do all the words of this
law which are written in this book, that you may
fear this glorious and awful name, the Lord your
God, then the Lord will bring upon you and your
offspring extraordinary afflictions, afflictions
severe and lasting, and sickness grievous and
lasting.

Jesus on one occasion suggested a possible
connection between a man's suffering and his
sin. The man had been ill for thirty-eight
years, and after Jesus had healed him, he said:

See, you are well! Sin no more, that nothing
worse befall you.

There are times when we realize we have
brought suffering on ourselves; the blame is
ours. Then we may be able to say with the
Psalmist:

It is good for me that I was afflicted,
    that I might learn thy statutes. . .
I know, O Lord, that thy judgements are right,
    and that in faithfulness thou hast afflicted me.
Let thy steadfast love be ready to comfort me
    according to thy promise to thy servant.

**Suffering where the sufferer has no responsi-
bility.** The book of *Job* deals with the problem
of the suffering of the innocent. Job is portrayed as a God-fearing man (though not
perfect or sinless), who suffers bereavement,
the loss of his possessions and finally an
intensely painful and unpleasant illness. The
prologue of the book makes it clear that Job's

Top left: *A Japanese child suffering from
Mimimata, a disease caused by pollution and
over-crowding.*
Top right: *Factory pollution of a river in Britain.*
Bottom: *A Thalidomide child learns to use
specially developed artificial limbs.*
Page 62: *After the earthquake in Turkey.*

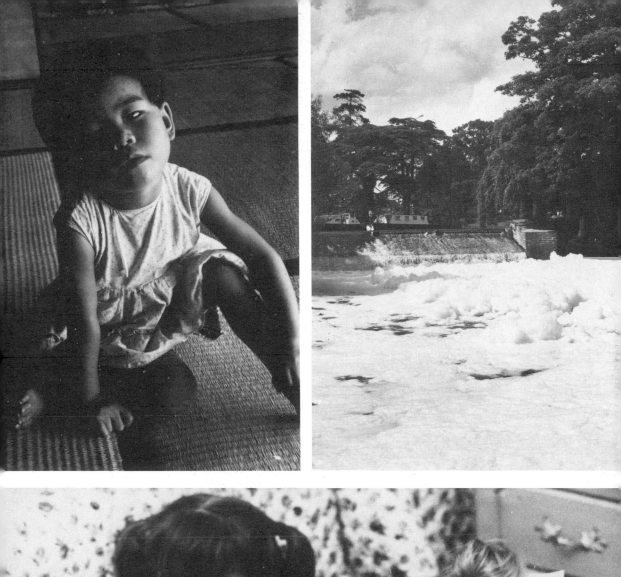

suffering is not in any way connected with any sin or disobedience, but is brought about by the malicious activity of Satan. Job's friends do not know what has happened 'behind the scenes' in heaven, and they argue that Job's suffering is a direct result of his sin, or that it comes from God to teach him some lesson. But Job is naturally impatient with these half-truths which do not meet his need or explain his particular suffering.

At the end of the book, God breaks into the discussion and speaks to Job as the Sovereign Creator and Sustainer of the universe. What he says to Job in effect is this: 'I am the Creator of the universe and you are a creature. I am infinite, and know the answers to the questions about your suffering; but you are finite and cannot expect to know all the answers. If you did, you would be God. But look around you at the universe which I have created and which I still control. Can't you see enough evidence there to convince you that I am still in control? Can't you go on *trusting* me as Creator, even though you do not understand the reason for your suffering?' After this Job reaches the point of surrendering himself to God in trust and humility:

I know that thou canst do all things,
    and that no purpose of thine can be thwarted . . .
Therefore I have uttered what I did not under-
    stand,
    things too wonderful for me, which I did not
    know . . .
I had heard of thee by the hearing of the ear,
    but now my eye sees thee;
therefore I despise myself,
    and repent in dust and ashes.

At the conclusion of the book we are told that Job's reaction to his suffering—with all its despair and angry questioning—is much nearer to the truth about his suffering than the inadequate half-truths which his comforters have expressed:

After the Lord had spoken these words to Job, the Lord said to Eliphaz the Temanite: 'My wrath is kindled against you and against your two friends; for you have not spoken of me what is right, as my servant Job has . . .'

Jesus' attitude to suffering and evil

His mission included relieving suffering and fighting evil. At the beginning of his public ministry Jesus applied some words of Isaiah to himself—words which have been described as the 'Nazareth Manifesto':

The Spirit of the Lord is upon me,
    because he has anointed me to preach good
    news to the poor.
    He has sent me to proclaim release to the
    captives
    and recovering of sight to the blind,
    to set at liberty those who are oppressed,
    to proclaim the acceptable year of the Lord.

He described himself as the one who is stronger than Satan, and has come to undo the ravages of Satan:

. . . if it is by the finger of God that I cast out demons, then the kingdom of God has come upon you. When a strong man, fully armed, guards his own palace, his goods are in peace; but when one stronger than he assails him and overcomes him, he takes away his armour in which he trusted, and divides his spoil.

When he stood before the grave of Lazarus his friend, we read:

When Jesus saw (Mary) weeping, and the Jews who came with her also weeping, he was deeply moved in spirit and troubled . . .

The word that is used here suggests that Jesus was moved not only with sorrow, but also with indignation—indignation over the terrible power of death. When he raised Lazarus from death, he was showing his determination and his power to overcome death and break its power.

There is something worse than physical suffering. Alongside this determination to fight suffering and evil, there is the reminder that there is something very much worse than physical suffering in this life:

There were some present at that very time who told him of the Galileans whose blood Pilate had mingled with their sacrifices. And he answered them, 'Do you think that these Galileans were worse sinners than all the other Galileans, because they suffered thus? I tell you, No; but unless you repent you will all likewise perish. Or those eighteen upon whom the tower of Siloam fell and killed them, do you think that they were worse offenders than all the others who dwelt in Jerusalem? I tell you, No; but unless you repent you will all likewise perish.'

I tell you, my friends, do not fear those who kill the body, and after that have no more that they can do. But I will warn you whom to fear: fear him who, after he has killed, has power to cast into hell; yes, I tell you, fear him!

The meaning of his own suffering. Jesus endured suffering himself, and fully identified himself with suffering humanity. After recording some of his healing miracles, Matthew says of Jesus:

This was to fulfil what was spoken by the prophet Isaiah,
'He took our infirmities and bore our diseases.'

The writer of the letter to the Hebrews speaks of the significance of the suffering of Jesus in this way:

The children of a family share the same flesh and blood; and so he too shared ours, so that through death he might break the power of him who had death at his command, that is, the devil; and might liberate those who, through fear of death, had all their lifetime been in servitude . . . And therefore he had to be made like these brothers of his in every way, so that he might be merciful and faithful as their high priest before God, to expiate the sins of the people. For since he himself has passed through the test of suffering, he is able to help those who are meeting their test now.

Thus when Jesus the eternal Son suffered and died a cruel death which he did not deserve, it was as if he was saying to men: 'I know what it means to suffer and I am prepared to share the worst human suffering. But your greatest problem is not suffering, it is sin and evil. And I am going through suffering and death now in order to break their power.'

The certainty of an end to suffering and evil

One of the basic convictions of the Old Testament writers is that God will one day judge the world, right wrongs and act in such a way that justice is done and seen to be done.

Let the heavens be glad, and let the earth rejoice;
    let the sea roar, and all that fills it;
    let the field exult, and everything in it!
Then shall all the trees of the wood sing for joy
    before the Lord, for he comes,
    for he comes to judge the earth.
He will judge the world with righteousness,
    and the peoples with his truth.

This 'coming' has been partially fulfilled in the coming of the Son among men. One of the 'Servant Songs' in Isaiah emphasizes that the coming of God's Servant must lead to the establishing of justice 'in the earth':

Behold my servant, whom I uphold,
    my chosen, in whom my soul delights . . .
He will not fail or be discouraged
    till he has established justice in the earth.

If this bringing of justice has begun in the coming of Jesus, the disciples of Jesus bear a heavy responsibility to see that it is worked out in practice in society. These words of Isaiah emphasize the priority of justice even over 'religious' duties:

Is not this the fast that I choose:
    to loose the bonds of wickedness,
    to undo the thongs of the yoke,
to let the oppressed go free,
    and to break every yoke?
Is it not to share your bread with the hungry,
    and bring the homeless poor into your
        house . . .?

The book of the Revelation speaks of the judgement of God on evil beginning to be worked out in history. But the final goal is the new heaven and the new earth:

Then I saw a new heaven and a new earth; for the first heaven and the first earth had passed away, and the sea was no more. And I saw the holy city, new Jerusalem, coming down out of heaven from God, prepared as a bride adorned for her husband; and I heard a great voice from the throne saying, 'Behold the dwelling of God is with men. He will dwell with them, and they shall be his people, and God himself will be with them; he will wipe away every tear from their eyes, and death shall be no more, neither shall there be mourning nor crying nor pain any more, for the former things have passed away.'

▷ The Christian answer to the problem of suffering and evil has something to say to the *sufferer himself*.

Michel Quoist:

'It is not I, your God, who has willed suffering, it is men . . . Sin is disorder, and disorder hurts . . . But I came, and I took all your sufferings upon me, as I took all your sins. I took them and suffered them before you.'

▷ It also has something to say to *those who are thinking about* the problem.

C. E. M. Joad describes how the Christian

answer to the problem of evil brought him to Christian faith. In his book *Recovery of Belief* he writes:

What I have to record is a changed view of the nature of man, which in due course led to a changed view of the nature of the world . . .

This view of human evil (that evil is merely the product of heredity and environment and can be eradicated through progress) which I adopted unthinkingly as a young man I have come fundamentally to disbelieve. Plausible, perhaps, during the first fourteen years of this century when . . . the state of mankind seemed to be improving—though even then the most cursory reading of human history should have been sufficient to dispose of it—it has been rendered utterly unplausible by the events of the last forty years. To me, at any rate, the view of evil implied by Marxism, expressed by Shaw and maintained by modern psychotherapy, a view which regards evil as a by-product of circumstances, which circumstances can, therefore, alter and even eliminate, has come to seem intolerably shallow and the contrary view of it as endemic in man, more particularly in its Christian form, the doctrine of original sin, to express a deep and essential insight into human nature.

▷ It provides *a strong motive for fighting suffering and evil* here and now. They are seen to be intruders in God's universe. Jesus committed himself to fighting them. And our present struggle against them will contribute to their final overthrow.

Stephen Neill:

It is only the doctrine of the wrath of God, of his irreconcilable hostility to all evil, which makes life tolerable in such a world as ours.

Problems and Questions arising out of Biblical Christianity's answer to the question 'What is man ?' are taken up on p. 107.

2. THE ANSWER OF PRIMAL RELIGION AND JUDAISM, ISLAM AND DEISM

"Man is a creature created by God—but this is not the God of the Bible"

The concepts of man in the different religions have a certain amount in common with the Christian concept. But the differences are significant and have far-reaching consequences. Adopting the three main points of the Christian answer (p. 53), we can pin-point some of the major points of difference:

☐ **Man the creature:** all these religions think of man as God's creation. Judaism (and to some extent Islam) teaches that man has been made in the image of God. But since the concept of God is different, this is bound to be understood in a different way.

☐ **Man the rebel:** the non-Christian religions do not have the same sense of the serious consequences of man's disobedience towards God, and of the deep corruption of human nature.

☐ **Man the son:** if man is ever thought of as a son of God, it is usually in the general sense, meaning little more than 'God's creature'.

Primal religion

In the different tribal religions of Africa, for example, man feels himself to be a creature of God. But at the same time he is very aware of many other supernatural powers which are at work in the universe and affect his everyday life.

Leopold Senghor, writing about the way in which the African tends to think of man and his place in the universe:

Let us . . . consider the Negro African as he faces the object to be known, as he faces the Other: God, man, animal, tree or pebble, natural or social phenomenon. In contrast to the classic European, the Negro African does not draw a line between himself and the object; he does not hold it at a distance, nor does he merely look at it and analyze it. After holding it at a distance,

after scanning it at a distance without analyzing it, he takes it vibrant in his hands, careful not to kill or fix it. He touches it, feels it, *smells* it . . . Thus the Negro African *sympathizes*, abandons his personality to become identified with the Other, dies to be reborn in the Other. He does not assimilate; he is assimilated. He lives a common life with the Other; he lives in a symbiosis. To use Paul Claudel's expression, he 'knows the Other'. Subject and object are dialectically face to face in the very act of knowledge. It is a long caress in the night, an embrace of joined bodies, the act of love . . . The Negro African could say, 'I feel, I dance the Other; I am.' To dance is to discover and to recreate, especially when it is a dance of love. In any event it is the best way to know. Just as knowledge is at once discovery and creation—I mean, re-creation and recreation, after the model of God.

Writing about the African's unique way of

looking at man, he says:

The Negro will have contributed, with other peoples, to reforging the unity of man and the world: linking flesh to the spirit, man to fellow men, the pebble to God.

Judaism

Judaism tends to have a more optimistic estimate of man's present condition than Christianity and denies the Christian belief that the individual inherits a sinful nature.

Dr. Isidore Epstein:

The divine relationship with man is indestructible. It can be strained or marred but cannot be severed entirely and broken beyond repair, not even by transgression and sin . . . If by erring from the right path man yields to temptation and lapses into sin, regret and penitence can repair the ravages of his sin and restore perfect harmony to this relationship.

Judaism rejects the idea of human proneness to sin. A natural tendency to evil would be a contradiction to the fundamental command of holiness, a contradiction to the holiness of God which man is called upon to reproduce in himself . . . Sin lieth at the door, not within man himself, and this is followed by 'and thou shalt rule over him'.

Dr. Hertz outlines the Jewish 'doctrine of salvation' in this way:

Note that the initiative in atonement is with the sinner. He cleanses himself on the Day of Atonement by fearless self-examination, open confession, and the resolve not to repeat the transgressions of the past year. When our Heavenly Father sees the abasement of the penitent sinner, He sprinkles, as it were, the clean waters of pardon and forgiveness upon him.

On the Day of Atonement the Israelites resemble the angels, without human wants, without sins, linked together in love and peace. It is the only day of the year on which the accuser Satan is silenced before the throne of Glory, and even becomes the defender of Israel . . . The closing prayer begins: 'Thou givest a hand to transgressors, and Thy right hand is stretched out to receive the penitent. Thou hast taught us to make confession unto Thee of all our sins, in order that we may cease from the violence of our hands and may return unto Thee who delightest in the repentance of the wicked.' These words contain what has been called 'the Jewish doctrine of salvation'.

Islam

The Qur'an has much to say about the dignity of man as God's creature:

Your Lord said to the angels: 'I am creating man from clay. When I have fashioned him and breathed of My Spirit into him, kneel down and prostrate yourselves before him.

The angels all prostrated themselves except Satan, who was too proud, for he was an unbeliever.

'Satan,' said Allah, 'why do you not bow to him whom My own hands have made? Are you too proud, or do you think he is beneath you?'

Satan replied: 'I am nobler than he. You created me from fire, but him from clay.'

. . . your Lord said to the angels: 'I am placing on the earth one that shall rule as My deputy' . . .

But in Islamic theology, the emphasis on the 'otherness' of God has tended to create a qualitative difference between God and man.

H. A. R. Gibb:

In . . . setting man as it were face to face with God, without any mediating spiritual or personal elements, Islam necessarily emphasised the contrast between them. In spite of the passages of mystical intuition in the Koran, the dogmatic derived from it could not but start from the postulate of the opposition between God and man, and (as a necessary corollary) the equality of all men in their creaturely relation to God. In this stark contrast lies the original tension of Islam.

C. C. Adams, writing about the attitude of Mohammad Abduh, the nineteenth-century apologist, to the attributes of God:

The orthodox position . . . is reaffirmed: although they may be similar in name to attributes and qualities ascribed to human beings, they are in reality not the same in nature. 'God does not resemble any of His creatures, and there is no relation between them and Him, except that He is the one who brought them into existence, and they belong to Him and will return to Him.'

The Qur'an has a different emphasis from the Bible's in its story of Adam and his sin:

'Adam,' we said, 'Satan is an enemy to you and to your wife. Let him not turn you out of Paradise and plunge you into affliction. Here you shall not hunger or be naked; you shall not thirst, or feel the scorching heat.'

But Satan whispered to him, saying: 'Shall I show you the Tree of Immortality and an everlasting kingdom?'

They both ate of its fruit, so that they beheld their nakedness and began to cover themselves with leaves. Thus Adam disobeyed his Lord and went astray.

Then his Lord had mercy on him; He relented towards him and rightly guided him.

Deism

Deism ignores or denies certain aspects of the Christian understanding of man.

Carl Becker, summarizing typical beliefs about man in the eighteenth century:

1. Man is not natively depraved;
2. The end of life is life itself, the good life on earth instead of the beatific life after death;
3. Man is capable, guided solely by the light of reason and experience, of perfecting the good life on earth; and
4. The first essential condition of the good life on earth is the freeing of men's minds from the bonds of ignorance and superstition, and of their bodies from the arbitrary oppression of the constituted social authorities.

The Deists of this period were often well aware of the end to which a more complete denial of Christian beliefs about God and man could go.

Paul Hazard:

The Deism which we meet with in the writings of the period attenuates the idea of God, but does not annihilate it. It makes God the object of a belief vaguely defined, perhaps, yet positive none the less, and intentionally so. It sufficed at all events to endow its adherents with a sense of superiority over their godless brethren; it enabled them to pray and to worship; it prevented them from feeling that they were alone in the world, lost and fatherless . . . It is no easy matter to be an Atheist and brutally to crush out belief in the divine; it is incomparably easier to be a Deist . . . 'A Deist', Bonald will one day be telling us, 'is simply a man who hasn't had time to become an Atheist.' 'A man who doesn't want to be an Atheist', would be much nearer the mark.

Pilgrims camping outside Mecca, birthplace of the prophet Mohammed. To visit the city is a life-long ambition for Moslems.

THE ANSWER THIS APPROACH GIVES TO THE BASIC QUESTIONS ABOUT MAN

The quotations in this section are selective: we have not attempted to give the answer of EVERY religion to EVERY question.

THE INDIVIDUAL

Belief in any kind of personal God is likely to give the individual some feeling of uniqueness and significance in his relationship with his Creator. But in some cases the sense of individuality may be called in question or severely modified.

Islam

The problem for the individual is that the greatness and sovereignty of God can be stressed to the point where the individual no longer feels that he has any freedom, because all his actions have already been determined by God.

This is an admonition to all men: to those among you that have the will to be upright. Yet you cannot will except by the will of Allah, the Lord of the Creation.

Mohammad Abduh outlines the orthodox teaching in this way:

All .. Muslim sects believe that they have a share of free choice in their actions which they call 'acquisition' (*kasb*), and this is the basis of reward and punishment in the opinion of all of them.

At the same time he admits that, in practice, this balance has not always been held:

We do not deny that in the thought of the common people in Muslim lands this article has been contaminated with traces of the belief in compulsion, and this perhaps has been the cause of some of the misfortunes that have befallen them in past generations.

The Qur'an stresses that the individual stands alone before God:

There is none in the heavens or the earth but shall return to Him in utter submission. He has kept strict count of all His creatures, and one by one they shall approach Him on the Day of Resurrection. Invoke no other god with Allah. There is no god but He. All things shall perish except Himself. His is the judgement, and to Him you shall return.

However, the emphasis on the sovereignty of God is such that there is always the danger of the individual being swallowed up in the presence of the all-powerful God. And in some forms of Sufi mysticism, the sense of the individual is in danger of being lost completely.

Nicholson:

Does personality survive in the ultimate union with God? If personality means a conscious existence distinct, though not separate, from God, the majority of advanced Moslem mystics say 'No!' As the rain-drop absorbed in the ocean is not annihilated but ceases to exist individually, so the disembodied soul becomes indistinguishable from the universal Deity.

Deism

The Deist's God has made the universe work according to its own fixed laws. But if the universe as a whole seems to work according to these laws, then man also must work in the same way. He cannot think that he is exempt from the working of these mechanical laws.

Norman Hampson describes how this problem was felt in the eighteenth century:

The general direction of scientific thought combined . . . with a more pessimistic view of Providence to drive mid-century writers towards an unwilling choice between complete scepticism and rigorous determinism.
The great mass of the population of western Europe continued to accept the literal truth of

the Bible and the existence of a Christian order. But those in the forefront of the new scientific and intellectual movements had come to recognize that Moses was an unreliable historian. Alienated from a Church that insisted on the literal truth of Revelation, natural religion no longer afforded them acceptable proof of a providential order. Only two attitudes seemed to remain: to follow Hume in denying man's access to objective knowledge of any kind, or to accept d'Holbach's conception of a universe of matter in motion, in which everything happened of necessity and the answer to every question was 'because it cannot be otherwise'.

Charles Darwin, who came to call himself an agnostic, expresses the dilemma of the Deist who feels the difficulty of holding on to the significance of the individual:

Believing as I do that man in the distant future will be a far more perfect creature than he now is, it is an intolerable thought that he and all other sentient beings are doomed to complete annihilation after such long-continued progress.

MEANING

Primal religion

John Mbiti describes the African world-view of man and his ultimate hopes of the future:

According to African religions and philosophy, the grave is the seal of everything, even if a person survives and continues to exist in the next world. There is an accelerated rhythm from death through the state of personal immortality (as the living-dead) to the state of collective immortality (as ordinary spirits). This final 'beat' of the rhythm may or may not have an end. There is, however, nothing to hope for, since this is the destiny of everybody; though older people do not seem to fear, and may even long for, the 'departure' from this to the next world. There is no resurrection for either the individual or mankind at large . . . The departed do not grow spiritually towards or like God, though some may act as intermediaries between men and God and may have more power and knowledge than human beings. Such is the anthropocentric view of the destiny of man, and as far as traditional African concepts are concerned, death is death and the beginning of a permanent ontological departure of the individual from mankind to spirithood. Beyond that point, African religions and philosophy are absolutely silent, or at most extremely vague. Nothing can reverse or halt that process, and death is the end of real and complete man.

African religions have their own mythology about the origins of the human race; but they can hold out little hope for the individual as he faces death:

Yet behind these fleeting glimpses of the original state and bliss of man, whether they are rich or shadowy, there lie the tantalizing and unattained gift of the resurrection, the loss of human immortality and the monster death. Here African religions and philosophy must admit a defeat: they have supplied no solution. This remains the most serious cul-de-sac in the otherwise rich thought and sensitive feeling of our peoples.

Islam

The Qur'an emphatically agrees with Christianity that 'man's chief end is to glorify God . . .':

'I created mankind and the jinn in order that they might worship Me.'

Many passages speak of the hope of Paradise which is held out to believers:

For the unbelievers We have prepared fetters and chains, and a blazing fire. But the righteous shall drink of a cup tempered at the Camphor Fountain, a gushing spring at which the servants of Allah will refresh themselves: they who keep their vows and dread the far-spread terrors of Judgement-day; who for love of Allah give sustenance to the poor man, the orphan, and the captive, saying: 'We feed you for Allah's sake only; we seek of you neither recompense nor thanks: for we fear from Him a day of anguish and of woe.'
    Allah will deliver them from the evil of that day and make their countenance shine with joy. He will reward them for their steadfastness with robes of silk and the delights of Paradise. Reclining there upon soft couches, they shall feel neither the scorching heat nor the biting cold. Trees will spread their shade around them, and fruits will hang in clusters over them . . .
    They shall be arrayed in garments of fine green silk and rich brocade, and adorned with bracelets of silver. Their Lord will give them a pure beverage to drink.
    Thus you shall be rewarded; your high endeavours are gratifying to Allah.

Many Moslems would not interpret passages such as these in a literal way. But when every allowance has been made for metaphor and symbol, the Moslem cannot hold out the hope of enjoying a personal relationship with God. He may point to the mystic's hope of union with God, but this has to be understood in terms of absorption into God. So that although he can speak of man's goal as being 'to glorify God', he cannot consistently add with the Christian, 'and to enjoy him for ever.'

Deism

The God of Deism offers little consolation to man in his search for meaning.

Diderot:

O God, I do not know if you exist . . . I ask nothing in this world, for the course of events is determined by its own necessity if you do not exist, or by your decree if you do . . . Here I stand, as I am, a necessarily organized part of eternal and necessary matter—or perhaps your own creation.

Martin Esslin, quoting and explaining some words from Samuel Beckett's *Waiting for Godot:*

'Given the existence . . . of a personal God . . . outside time without extension who from the heights of divine apathia divine athambia divine aphasia loves us dearly with some exceptions for reasons unknown . . . and suffers . . . with those who for reasons unknown are plunged in torment . . .' Here again we have the personal God, with his divine apathy, his speechlessness (aphasis), and his lack of the capacity for terror or amazement (athambia), who loves us dearly—with some exceptions, who will be plunged into the torments of hell. In other words, God, who does not communicate with us, cannot feel for us, and condemns us for reasons unknown.

VALUES

Primal religion

God tends to have little to do with the standards or values adopted by any society.

John Mbiti, writing about African religions:

Even if . . . God is thought to be the ultimate upholder of the moral order, people do not consider Him to be immediately involved in the keeping of it. Instead, it is the patriarchs, living-dead, elders, priests, or even divinities and spirits who are the daily guardians or police of human morality. Social regulations of a moral nature are directed towards the immediate contact between individuals, between man and the living-dead and the spirits. Therefore, these regulations are on the man-to-man level, rather than the God-to-man plane of morality.

Judaism

The moral values of Judaism are derived, with varying strictness, from the Old Testament law. In many cases they differ from Christian values because they are affected by Judaism's more optimistic diagnosis of man's present condition.

Roy Stewart:

The Christian view of sin and atonement is sterner, more realistic, and more inward than the Jewish one. Its outward rules are fewer, less related to specific circumstance, centred in greater measure in the intangible realm of the human heart—which makes its canons loftier and more difficult for the observer. Much of what the Christian regards as sin might be redefined as insufficiency of love, God-ward or manward . . . It follows from this that a Jew may sometimes feel a satisfaction with his life and conduct which is impossible for the Christian . . . If ever a Jew looks for some divine reward for his virtues, a Christian can look only for divine pardon for his sins.

Herbert Danby, writing about an article by Ahad ha-Am (Asher Ginzberg):

The Christian 'golden rule' is 'Do unto others what you would that men should do unto you.' Judaism has the same, or what seems to be the same rule in the negative form: 'What is hateful to thyself, do not do unto thy neighbour.' And Ahad ha-Am believes that in these two forms lies the ethical difference in the two religions: egotism is the mark of Jewish ethics; but Christian altruism, he insists, is merely inverted egotism, the substitution of *other* for *self*.

Ahad ha-Am is not content to leave the matter at that. To make an apparently abstruse point clear as daylight he quotes the following case from the Talmud:

Imagine two men travelling in the desert; only one of them has a bottle of water; if both drink they will both die before their journey's end; if only one drinks he will reach safety, but his companion will certainly die. What should the man with the bottle of water do? Rabbi Akiba decided (and Ahad ha-Am fully agrees that the decision counts as a fundamental principle of Jewish morality)—R. Akiba decided that the man with the water should keep it and drink it all himself; because *both* of them could not survive, it is more *just*, more in accord with God's righteousness, that a man should save himself rather than that he should save his neighbour and so lose his own life. Other things being equal, says Jewish morality, you have no right to assume that your neighbour's affairs are of more worth in God's eyes than your own affairs. Certainly Judaism approves of the laying down of life to fulfil a religious ideal (sanctification of the name of God, martyrdom); but it condemns the man who will suppress himself for the sake of his fellow. Christianity, on the contrary, teaches: 'Greater love hath no man than this, that a man lay down his life for his friends.'

Ahad ha-Am maintains that this, the basic difference between Jewish and Christian ethics, shows the superiority of Jewish ethics, in that it replaces the illogical Christian doctrine of self-sacrifice, self-renunciation, by the *absolute rule of justice*.

Islam

The word 'holy' is applied to God, but it occurs only once in the Qur'an:

He is Allah, besides whom there is no other god. He is the Sovereign Lord, the Holy One, the Giver of Peace, the Keeper of Faith, the Guardian, the Mighty One, the All-Powerful, the Most High! Exalted be He above their idols!

This holiness, however, is not defined in terms of moral purity or perfection, but in terms of transcendence:

Beidhawi, the great Moslem commentator on the Qur'an of the thirteenth century writes:

Holy means the complete absence of anything that would make Him less than He is.

Al-Ghazzali writes in this way about the justice of God:

Allah's justice is not to be compared with the justice of men. For a man may be supposed to act unjustly by invading the possession of another, but no injustice can be conceived on the part of God. It is in His power to pour down upon men torments, and if He were to do it, His justice could not be arraigned. Yet he rewards those that worship Him for their obedience on account of His promise and beneficence, not of their merit or of necessity, since there is nothing which He can be tied to perform; nor can any injustice be supposed in Him nor can He be under any obligation to any person whatsoever.

A Samaritan, one of the dwindling community which still worships God on Mount Gerizim today.

Thus, since God is not holy in the biblical sense, the moral law for man cannot be based on the character of God—what he *is* by nature. It has to be based on the commands or decrees of God. And the Five Pillars of Islam express the most important things in the life of the Moslem: Recital of the Creed, Prayer, Fasting, Almsgiving, Pilgrimage.

J. N. D. Anderson:

It is these Five Pillars, and particularly the profession of the Creed and the performance of prayer and fasting, which chiefly make up the practice of Islam to the average Muslim. He who acknowledges the Unity and Transcendence of God, pays Him His due in prayer and fast, and accepts Muhammed as the last and greatest of the Prophets, may well, indeed, have to taste the Fire, but hopes that he will not, like the infidel, remain in it for ever—through the timely intercession of the Prophet. The most heinous sins are polytheism, apostasy, scepticism and impiety, besides which social sins and all subtler forms of evil pale into comparative insignificance.

Deism

The eighteenth-century Deists believed that Nature and Reason pointed to certain basic values and truths which were self-evident. Any reasonable person therefore should be able instinctively to recognize these values for himself.

John Locke:

The state of Nature has a law of Nature to govern it, which obliges every one, and reason, which is that law, teaches all mankind who will but consult it, that being all equal and independent, no one ought to harm another in his life, health, liberty or possessions.

Hooke:

There is in all men a general benevolence and freely given goodness . . . Thus there is no duty that is not commended to us, not only by reason, but even by appetite.

This attitude to Reason and Nature, however, eventually led many towards a profound moral scepticism, as soon as they realized the impossibility of establishing agreed values on this basis.

Basil Willey writing about William Wordsworth:

By the summer of 1795 the effort to rise superior to 'infirmities of nature, time and place' had landed him in moral scepticism, and he reached 'the crisis of that strong disease' in which he 'yielded up moral questions in despair' . . . His own experience had taught him that the process of dragging all precepts to the bar of reason led to moral chaos.

RELATIONSHIPS

Two basic questions we need to ask are these:

☐ Do these religions supply a compelling reason for truthfulness and love in personal relationships?

☐ If one cannot speak of God as being 'love' in his very nature, does it make sense to speak of the 'love of God' as a guide in our understanding of human love?

Primal religion

John Mbiti writes about the closely-knit tribal society:

John Locke, Deist philosopher.

Within this tightly knit corporate society where personal relationships are so intense and so wide, one finds perhaps the most paradoxical areas of African life. This corporate type of life makes every member of the community dangerously naked in the sight of other members. It is paradoxically the centre of love and hatred, of friendship and enmity, of trust and suspicion, of joy and sorrow, of generous tenderness and bitter jealousies. It is paradoxically the heart of security and insecurity, of building and destroying the individual and the community. Everybody knows everybody else: a person cannot be individualistic, but only corporate. Every form of pain, misfortune, sorrow or suffering; every illness and sickness; every death whether of an old man or of the infant child; every failure of the crop in the fields, of hunting in the wilderness or of fishing in the waters; every bad omen or dream: these and all the other manifestations of evil that man experiences are blamed on somebody in the corporate society.

The love of God is taken for granted, but is seldom made explicit:

As for the love of God, there are practically no

'direct sayings that God loves. This is something reflected also in the daily lives of African peoples, in which it is rare to hear people talking about love. A person shows his love for another more through action than through words. So, in the same way, people experience the love of God in concrete acts and blessings; and they assume that He loves them, otherwise He would not have created them.

Islam

The following are some of the passages of the Qur'an which speak about the obligation to love:

Such is Allah's promise to true believers who do good works. Say: 'For this I demand of you no recompense. I ask you only to love your kindred. He that does a good deed shall be repaid many times over. Allah is forgiving and bounteous in His rewards.'

By one of His signs He created you from dust; you became men and multiplied throughout the earth. By another sign He gave you wives from among yourselves that you might live in joy with them, and planted love and kindness in your hearts. Surely there are signs in this for thinking men.

It may well be that Allah will put good will between you and those with whom you have hitherto been at enmity. Allah is mighty. He is forgiving and merciful.

   Allah does not forbid you to be kind and equitable to those who have neither made war on your religion nor driven you from your homes. Allah loves the equitable. But he forbids you to make friends with those who have fought against you on account of your religion and driven you from your homes or abetted others to do so. Those that make friends with them are wrong-doers.

SUFFERING AND EVIL

Primal religion

John Mbiti describes how suffering and evil are understood in African tribal society:

By this ('natural evil') I mean those experiences in human life which involve suffering, misfortune, diseases, calamity, accidents and various forms of pain. In every African society these are well known. Most of them are explainable through 'natural' causes. But . . . for African peoples nothing sorrowful happens by 'accident' or 'chance': it must all be 'caused' by some agent (either human or spiritual) . . . In some societies it is thought that a person suffers because he has

contravened some regulation, and God or the spirits, therefore, punish the offender. In that case, the person concerned is actually the cause of his own suffering . . . But in most cases, different forms of suffering are believed to be caused by human agents who are almost exclusively witches, sorcerers and workers of evil magic . . . They are . . . 'responsible' for 'causing' what would be 'natural evil', by using incantations, mystical power, medicines, by sending secondary agents like flies and animals, by using their 'evil eye', by wishing evil against their fellow man, by hating or feeling jealous, and by means of other 'secret' methods . . . In the experience of evil, African peoples see certain individuals as being intricately involved, but wickedly, in the otherwise smooth running of the natural universe.

In African villages, disease and misfortune are religious experiences, and it requires a religious approach to deal with them. The medicine-men are aware of this, and make attempts to meet the need in a religious (or quasi-religious) manner— whether or not that turns out to be genuine or false or a mixture of both . . .

Suffering, misfortune, disease and accident, are all 'caused' mystically, as far as African peoples are concerned. To combat the misfortune or ailment the cause must also be found, and either counteracted, uprooted or punished. This is where the value of the traditional medicine-man comes into the picture. So long as people see sickness and misfortune as 'religious' experiences, the traditional medicine-man will continue to exist and thrive.

Islam

Everything, both good and evil, is determined by the Will of God, although man is not completely absolved from his responsibility.

Allah does not change a people's lot unless they change what is in their hearts. If he seeks to afflict them with a misfortune, none can ward it off. Besides Him, they have no protector.

Whatever good befalls you, man, it is from Allah: and whatever ill from yourself.

While the problem of suffering and evil must remain an inscrutable mystery, the Qur'an on the one hand emphasizes the need to create a just society here and now, and on the other points forward to the day of judgement when evil will be overcome. The crucial difference between this and the Christian answer is that Islam has no place for Jesus as the suffering Saviour who defeated evil by experiencing its full horrors and going through death.

3. THE ANSWER OF HUMANISM, EXISTENTIALISM, COMMUNISM AND EASTERN RELIGIONS

"Man is not the creation of God because there is no personal Creator"

After many centuries of Christian theism, the 'Western mind' has rejected the Creator and the supernatural, and proclaimed the autonomy of man. In consequence:

☐ Man is now 'forlorn', he is on his own.

☐ The question 'What is man?' becomes almost unanswerable. We can no longer hope to explain what we are.

☐ The autonomy of man's thinking about himself has brought him to a 'complete anarchy of thought'.

Albert Camus:

Up till now, man derived his coherence from his Creator. But from the moment that he consecrates his rupture with Him, he finds himself delivered over to the fleeting moment, to the passing days, and to wasted sensibility. Therefore he must take himself in hand..

Jean-Paul Sartre:

If God does not exist . . . man is in consequence forlorn, for he cannot find anything to depend upon, either within or outside himself.

Christopher Dawson:

The Western mind has turned away from the contemplation of the absolute and eternal to the knowledge of the particular and the contingent. It has made man the measure of all things and has sought to emancipate human life from its dependence on the supernatural. Instead of the whole intellectual and social order being subordinated to spiritual principles, every activity has declared its independence, and we see politics, economics, science, and art organizing themselves as autonomous kingdoms which owe no allegiance to any higher power.

Hannah Arendt:

The problem of human nature . . . seems unanswerable in both its individual psychological sense and its general philosophical sense. It is highly unlikely that we, who can know, determine, and define the natural essences of all things surrounding us, which we are not, should ever be able to do the same for ourselves . . . The conditions of human existence—life itself, natality and mortality, worldliness, plurality, and the earth— can never 'explain what we are' . . .

Ernst Cassirer, writing about the legacy of thinkers like Nietzsche, Freud and Marx:

Owing to this development our modern theory of man lost its intellectual centre. We acquired instead a complete anarchy of thought . . . An established authority to which one might appeal no longer existed. Theologians, scientists, politicians, sociologists, biologists, psychologists, ethnologists, economists all approached the problem from their own viewpoints . . . Every author seems in the last count to be led by his own conception and evaluation of human life.

He quotes *Max Scheler:*

In no other period of human knowledge has man become more problematical to himself than in our own days . . . We no longer possess any clear and consistent idea of man.

Humanism

Humanism is defined in *The Glossary of Humanism* as follows:

In broad terms contemporary Humanism subscribes to a view of life that is centred on man and his capacity to build a worthwhile life for himself and his fellows here and now. The emphasis is placed on man's own intellectual and moral resources, and the notion of supernatural religion is rejected.

One of the most important trends in modern Humanism is its reliance on the application of scientific enquiry and its evaluation of truth, reality and morals in purely human terms.

We may take each of these main elements and illustrate them in turn.

The autonomy of man.

Blackham:

Humanism proceeds from the assumption *that* man is on his own and this life is all and an assumption *of* responsibility for one's own life and for the life of mankind.

The simple theme of humanism is self-determination, for persons, for groups and societies, for mankind together.

Edmund Leach:

Men have become like gods. Isn't it about time that we understood our divinity? Science offers us total mastery over our environment and over our destiny, yet instead of rejoicing we feel deeply afraid . . . All of us need to understand that God, or Nature, or Chance, or Evolution, or the Course of History, or whatever you like to call it, can't be trusted any more. We simply must take charge of our own fate . . . It has ceased to be true that nature is governed by inevitable laws external to ourselves. We ourselves have become responsible.

Progress and improvement of man's condition.

Lord Willis:

Humanism is a faith, a faith by which it is possible to live. To sum it up very briefly, I believe that this life is the only one of which we have any knowledge, and it is our job to improve it.

Sir Julian Huxley, Professor of Zoology and humanist writer.

Reliance on reason.

Geoffrey Scott:

Humanism is the effort of men to think, to feel, and to act for themselves, and to abide by the logic of results . . . A new method is suddenly apprehended, tested, and carried firmly to its conclusion. Authority, habit, orthodoxy, are disregarded or defied. The argument is pragmatic, realistic, human. The question, 'Has this new thing a value?' is decided directly by the individual in the court of his experience; and there is no appeal. That is good which is seen to satisfy the human test, and to have brought an enlargement of human power.

A. J. Ayer:

I do not like to think of Humanism as a religion because one of its great merits, one of the things that has attracted me to it and caused me to become a Humanist, is its lack of dogma. One of the fundamental positions taken by Humanists is that men should have freedom to think out for themselves how they ought to live, to think out their own principles.

H. J. Blackham:

Each must think and decide for himself on important questions concerning the life he has and his conduct of it; and, most general, that nothing is exempt from human question. This means that there is no immemorial tradition, no revelation, no authority, no privileged knowledge (first principles, intuitions, axioms) which is beyond question because beyond experience and which can be used as a standard by which to interpret experience. There is only experience to be interpreted in the light of further experience, the sole source of all standards of reason and value, for ever open to question. This radical assumption is itself, of course, open to question, and stands only in so far as it is upheld by experience.

Reliance on science.

Julian Huxley:

This new idea-system, whose birth we of the mid twentieth-century are witnessing, I shall simply call *Humanism*, because it can only be based on our understanding of man and his relations with the rest of his environment . . .

Science has attained a new and very real unity and firmness of organization and is giving us a scientifically-based picture of human destiny and human possibilities. For the first time in history, science can become the ally of religion instead of its rival or its enemy, for it can provide a 'scientific' theology, a scientifically-ordered framework of belief, to whatever new religion emerges from the present idealogical disorder.

Existentialism

It is impossible to give a precise definition of Existentialism, because it is not a precise philosophy. One of its basic ideas is that there can be no complete philosophical system which answers all our questions. It insists that instead of talking about 'objective truth', which can never be obtained, we should begin with the actual individual and his experience as a human being—with his freedom, his despair and his anguish. The following extracts give some idea of what Existentialism stands for.

E. L. Allen defines it as:

the attempt to philosophize from the standpoint of the actor rather than from that of the detached spectator.

Karl Heim:

A proposition or truth is said to be *existential*

when I cannot apprehend or assent to it from the standpoint of a mere spectator but only on the ground of my total existence.

The Humanist Glossary, under Existentialism:

Kierkegaard and Heidegger, who are religious existentialist philosophers, and Sartre, who is an atheist, all share certain fundamental ideas. The starting point of their philosophy is the plight of the individual, thrust, as it were, into a world without authority, system of values, of law or human nature. Their basic tenet is that there is an inescapable tension between thought and existence; existence cannot be thought and thought departs from existence into abstraction. Man, being both thinker and in existence, has to live this tension, which he can never resolve once for all. Similarly, there are other oppositions which man has to live and cannot resolve because they make the human condition, e.g. faith and reason, the other and myself as persons. Human beings are always finding ways to escape from instead of living by, the conditions of the human situation.

Sartre:

Existentialism is nothing else but an attempt to draw the full conclusions from a consistently atheistic position.

Atheistic existentialism, of which I am a representative, declares with greater consistency that if God does not exist there is at least one being whose existence comes before its essence, a being which exists before it can be defined by any conception of it. That being is man or, as Heidegger has it, the human reality. What do we mean by saying that existence precedes essence? We mean that man first of all exists, encounters himself, surges up in the world—and defines himself afterwards. If man as the existentialist sees him is not definable, it is because to begin with he is nothing . . . Man is nothing else but that which he makes of himself. That is the first principle of existentialism.

The first effect of existentialism is that it puts every man in possession of himself as he is, and places the entire responsibility for his existence squarely upon his own shoulders. And, when we say that man is responsible for himself, we do not mean that he is responsible only for his own individuality, but that he is responsible for all men.

H. J. Blackham:

The peculiarity of existentialism . . . is that it deals with the separation of man from himself and from the world, which raises the questions of philosophy . . . The main business of this philosophy therefore is not to answer the questions which are raised but to drive home the questions themselves until they engage the whole man and are made personal, urgent, and anguished . . . Existentialism goes back to the beginning of philosophy and appeals to all men to awaken from their dogmatic slumbers and discover what it means to become a human being . . .

The second business of philosophy . . . is to cure the mind of looking for illusory objective universal answers, and to aid the person in making himself and getting his experience.

Communism

The particular aspects of Communism which concern us here are not its political and economic theory, but rather its basic humanism.

John Lewis, writing about Karl Marx:

We must not consider Marx as an economist . . . but as a sociologist, a philosopher . . . His thought remains that of a philosopher. Beyond the economic 'appearances' it plunges into the human reality that causes them. For the *factual* view of things, Marx substitutes a profound insight into human needs. His is a new humanism, new because it is incarnate.

Humanism, the *philosophy of humanism*, rather than economics, is the basic character and positive contribution of Marxian thought.

Marxism is humanism in its contemporary form . . . And the Marxist has this to convince the disinherited, whether in the great industrial cities of the West or the fields and mines of the colonial countries, that their very oppression could be the instrument of their emancipation, their entrance into an earthly paradise of material plenty and human justice.

It is not sufficiently understood that Marx's own thinking was basically humanist. He recognized the worth of the individual personality, he blazed with indignation at social injustice; there was prophetic fire in his passion for righteousness . . .

Behind the whole philosophy of Marxism there is a passionate opposition to all relations, all conditions in which man is a humiliated, enslaved,

Left: *Karl Marx, economist, philosopher and originator of Communism.*
Right: *Some freedom of religion is still allowed in Communist states. A city church in the USSR.*

despised creature. That is why Marxism is a humanism.

Guy Wint, writing about Communism in East Asia:

Communism, seen in one light, is an effort by a group of the intelligentsia, inspired by moral ideas borrowed from the West . . . to end or lessen the exploitation, to see that more justice is done to the mass of the people, and to open to them the opportunities of better life made possible by science.

Richard Crossman, in the introduction to his book *The God that Failed* (essays by six people who were all at one time members of the Communist Party or very sympathetic to it) writes:

The only link . . . between these six very different personalities is that all of them—after tortured struggles of conscience—chose Communism because they had lost faith in democracy and were willing to sacrifice 'bourgeois liberties' in order to defeat Fascism. Their conversion, in fact, was rooted in despair—a despair of western values.

Eastern religions

Hinduism. The clue to all eastern thinking about man is contained in one of the most significant sayings of Hinduism: 'Thou art That'—i.e. the individual soul is to be identi- fied with the Brahman, the all-pervading God.

K. M. Sen:

The *Upanishads* point out that the *Brahman* and the *Atman* are the same. The Supreme has mani- fested Himself in every soul, and the student of religion is dramatically told in the *Upanishads*, 'Thou art That' (*tat tvam asi*). This idea provides the core of most Hindu religious thought and is developed later by Samkara into his doctrine of *advaita* (lit. non-duality). This is a monistic doctrine, which denies the existence of the world as separate from God.

W. Cantwell Smith, writing about the sentence 'Thou art That':

The phrase . . . consists of three Sanskrit words, generally regarded in India as the most important sentence that that country has ever pronounced; the succinct formulation of a profound and ultimate truth about man and the universe. The phrase is: *tat tvam asi. Tat* means 'that'; *tvam* means 'thou'; and *asi* is the second person singular of the verb 'to be'. 'That thou art';

The Yin Yang sign symbolizes the equality of the active and passive principles in life.

tat tvam asi. It means, thou art that reality, thou art God. The same truth is expressed in other ways; for instance, in the famous equation 'atman equals *Brahman*'—or the soul of man is God, or the Ultimate Reality, with a very large capital U and capital R; the really real. The individual self is the world soul. The soul of man equals the ultimate of the universe. 'Thou', or to use our more colloquial term, 'you'—each one of you reading this book—are in some final, cosmic sense the total and transcendent truth that under- lies all being, *Brahman* who precedes and trans- cends God himself, the Infinite and Absolute Reality beyond all phenomena, beyond all apprehension and beyond all form.

Buddhism. Buddhism accepts the same starting-point as Hinduism, and looks for- ward to the state of Nirvana, in which man becomes one with the universe.

Christmas Humphreys:

At the heart of the Universe is the One Reality of which the universe as we know it is but a periodic manifestation. This is the only Supreme Deity known to Indian thought, for the Upanishadic philosophy, like Buddhism, 'revolts against the deistic conception of God' (Radhakrishnan) . . .

The quintessence of Indian thought may be summed up by saying that the Atman of man and the Atman of the universe are one.

Nirvana . . . is not the goal of escapism, a refuge from the turning Wheel; it *is* the Wheel, and he who realizes himself in this discovery makes his daily life divine. For him all things are Suchness, and he sees but the Suchness of things. His *Citta*, or inmost heart and mind, is one with the Universe; he *is* Mind Only.

In spite of the many differences between Humanism, Existentialism, Communism and the Eastern religions, they all share the same basic starting-point in their attitude to man. They therefore also share many of the same dilemmas.

THE ANSWER THIS APPROACH GIVES TO THE BASIC QUESTIONS ABOUT MAN

THE INDIVIDUAL

If I am not a creature created in the image of God and therefore having meaning and value as an individual, what reason do I have for holding on to the feeling that my personality is unique and individual? The following extracts are from writers who have felt the problem in different ways.

Pearl Buck sees no difficulty in asserting the freedom and uniqueness of the individual:

I believe we are born free—free of inheritance in that we can by our wills determine to be free of it, free of environment because no environment can shape one who will not be shaped. We are born free, in other words, of every sort of predestination. In each of us there is a little germ of individual being, compounded, it may be, of everything, inheritance, environment and all else, but the compound itself is new. It is forever unique. This *I* is never *You* or *He*. And this *I* is free, if I only know it and act upon that freedom.
   Does this make a philosophy? Such as it is, it is all I have.

E. M. Forster feels the problem more keenly, but has the optimistic hope that the individual can hold on to the feeling of his own individuality:

These are the reflections of an individualist and a liberal who has found liberalism crumbling beneath him and at first felt ashamed. Then, looking around, he decided there was no special reason for shame, since other people, whatever they felt, were equally insecure. And as for individualism—there seems no way out of this, even if one wants to find one . . .

Until psychologists and biologists have done much more tinkering than seems likely, the individual remains firm and each of us must consent to be one, and to make the best of the difficult job.

Colin Wilson describes the problem as it is felt by 'The Outsider', and is not as confident as Forster about the security of the individual:

Their problem is the unreality of their lives. They become acutely conscious of it when it begins to pain them, but they are not sure of the source of the pain. The ordinary world loses its values, as it does for a man who has been ill for a very long time. Life takes on the quality of a nightmare, or a cinema sheet when the screen goes blank. These men who had been projecting their hopes and desires into what was passing on the screen suddenly realise they are in a cinema. They ask: Who are we? What are we doing here? With the delusion of the screen identity gone, the causality of its events suddenly broken, they are confronted with a terrifying dream. In Sartre's phrase, they are 'condemned to be free'. Completely new bearings are demanded; a new analysis of this real world of the cinema has to be undertaken. In the shadow world on the screen, every problem had an answer; this may not be true of the world in the cinema. The fact that the screen world has proved to be a delusion arouses the disturbing possibility that the cinema world may be unreal too. 'When we dream that we dream, we are beginning to wake up!' Novalis says. Chuang Tzu had once said that he had dreamed he was a butterfly, and now wasn't sure if he was a man who dreamed he was a butterfly or a butterfly dreaming he was a man.

Eugene Ionesco writes of the problem of the individual as he expresses it in his plays:

Two fundamental states of consciousness are at the root of all my plays . . . These two basic feelings are those of evanescence on the one hand, and heaviness on the other; of emptiness and of an over-abundance of presence; of the unreal transparency of the world, and of its opaqueness . . . The sensation of evanescence results in a feeling of anguish, a sort of dizziness. But all of this can just as well become euphoric; anguish is suddenly transformed into liberty . . . This state of consciousness is very rare, to be sure . . . I am most often under the dominion of the opposite feeling: lightness changes to heaviness, transparence to thickness; the world weighs heavily; the universe crushes me. A curtain, an insuperable wall, comes between me and the world, between me and myself. Matter fills everything, takes up all space, annihilates all liberty under its weight . . . Speech crumbles.

Harold Pinter expresses the despair of one who does not know who he is himself, and is enraged at the complacency of others who think they do know:

Occasionally I believe I perceive a little of what you are, but that's pure accident. Pure accident on both our parts, the perceived and the perceiver. It's nothing like an accident, it's deliberate, it's a joint pretence. We depend on these contrived accidents, to continue . . . What you are, or appear to be to me, or appear to be to you, changes so quickly, so horrifyingly, I certainly can't keep up with it and I'm damn sure you can't either. But who you are I can't even begin to recognize, and sometimes I recognize it so wholly, so forcibly, I can't look, and how can I be certain of what I see? You have no number. Where am I to look, where am I to look, what is there to locate, so as to have some surety, to have some rest from this whole bloody racket? You're the sum of so many reflections. How many reflections? Is that what you consist of? What scum does the tide leave? What happened to the scum? When does it happen? I've seen what happens. But I can't speak when I see it. I can only point a finger. I can't even do that. The scum is broken and sucked back. I don't see where it goes, I don't see when, what do I see, what have I seen? What have I seen, the scum or the essence? What about it? Does all this give you the right to stand there and tell me you know who you are? It's a bloody impertinence.

Aldous Huxley, in *Brave New World Revisited* is aware of the problem of the freedom of the individual even in the so-called 'free world' of the west:

Meanwhile there is still some freedom left in the world. Many young people, it is true, do not seem to value freedom. But some of us still believe that, without freedom, human beings cannot become human and that freedom is therefore supremely valuable. Perhaps the forces that now menace freedom are too strong to be resisted for very long.

Virginia Woolf's novels reflect a kind of disintegration of personality. Her declared aim is to:

record the atoms as they fall upon the mind in the order in which they fall, tracing the pattern, however disconnected and incoherent in appearance, which each sight or incident scores upon the consciousness.

This attitude is interpreted by *C. E. M. Joad* as the effect of a particular kind of psychological theory:

Under the influence of psychology there is today a widespread belief that personality is a myth. A man is not a continuing entity; he is a series of separate psychological states. The ego, the thread upon which the states used to be strung like beads on a necklace, has disappeared. This disintegration of the *person* is bound up with the discrediting of reason, for it was reason that gave the background of cohesion and continuity to the essentially discontinuous series of moods and feelings. If reason is dismissed as unimportant, a human being becomes not a personality enduring through change, but a succession of changing moods. A man, on this view, is like a cinematographic man; that is to say, he is like a series of separate momentary men, succeeding one another with such rapidity as to create the illusion of continuity. The truth about a man so conceived will be the truth about the separate states; it will be a collection of accounts of successive little pieces of him, the tiny physical acts, the fleeting psychological moods, the semiconscious wishes, the memories half-evoked. And in order to get as close as possible to this succession of little pieces, one writes a succession of little pictures, matching the discontinuity of life with a discontinuity of style. By this means, it is thought, the essential reality of life will be captured, its essence distilled into one's pages.

Jean-Paul Sartre's novel *Nausea* expresses these feelings about the individual in the experience of the main character, Roquentin:

Now when I say 'I', it seems hollow to me. I can no longer manage to feel myself, I am so forgotten. The only real thing left in me is some existence which can feel itself existing. I give a long, voluptuous yawn. Nobody. Antoine Roquentin exists for Nobody. That amuses me. And exactly what is Antoine Roquentin? An abstraction. A pale little memory of myself wavers in my consciousness. Antoine Roquentin . . . And suddenly the I pales, pales, and finally goes out . . .

Many are aware of the possibility of losing the individual completely, and therefore see the individual as being absorbed in some greater entity such as 'the race' or 'the universe'.

H. G. Wells:

I think Man may be immortal, but not men.

Our individuality is, so to speak, an inborn obsession from which we shall escape as we become more intelligent.

Julian Huxley sees the individual as involved in the evolution of the whole human race:

In the light of the evolutionary vision the individual need not feel just a meaningless cog in the social machine, nor merely the helpless prey and sport of vast impersonal forces. He can do something to develop his own personality, to discover his own talents and possibilities, to interact personally and fruitfully with other individuals, to discover something of his own significance. If so, in his own person he is realizing an important quantum of evolutionary possibility: he is contributing his own personal quality to the fulfilment of human destiny; and he has assurance of his own significance in the vaster and more enduring whole of which he is a part.

Aldous Huxley describes the experience of the mystics who lose consciousness of their individuality and personality, and feel themselves part of 'an impersonal spiritual reality underlying all being':

They find that their visions disappear, that their awareness of a personality fades, that the emotional outpourings which were appropriate when they seemed to be in the presence of a person, become utterly inappropriate and finally give place to a state in which there is no emotion at all . . .

This new form of experience—the imageless and emotionless cognition of some great impersonal force—is superior to the old and represents a closer approach to ultimate reality.

Buddhism tries to be utterly consistent, and looks forward to the state of Nirvana, in which the individual no longer exists as a separate individual.

Christmas Humphreys:

Nirvana is the extinction of the not-Self in the completion of the Self. It is, therefore, to the limited extent that we can understand it, a concept of psychology, a state of consciousness. As such it is, as Professor Radhakrishnan points out, 'the goal of perfection and not the abyss of annihilation. Through the destruction of all that is individual in us, we enter into communion with the whole universe, and become an integral part of the great purpose. Perfection is then the sense of oneness with all that is, has ever been and can ever be. The horizon of being is extended to the limits of reality.' It is therefore not correct to say that the dewdrop slips into the Shining Sea; it is nearer to the truth to speak of the Shining Sea invading the dewdrop. There is here no sense of loss but of infinite expansion when, 'Foregoing self, the Universe grows I.'

D. T. Suzuki explains the doctrine of 'non-ego' in Buddhism:

The doctrine of non-ego not only repudiates the idea of an ego-substance but points out the illusiveness of the ego-idea itself. As long as we are in this world of particular existences we cannot avoid cherishing the idea of an individual ego. But this by no means warrants the substantiality of the ego. Modern psychology has in fact done away with an ego-entity.

Problems and questions arising out of this answer in relation to the individual are raised on p. 103.

MEANING

If there is no Creator-God who gives man meaning and value, one immediate reaction is to say that the question about meaning in life is itself meaningless.

Arthur Koestler, writing about the crucial change in the thinking of many in the west in the seventeenth century:

Before the shift, the various religions had provided man with explanations of a kind which gave everything that happened to him meaning in the wider sense of transcendental causality and transcendental justice. But the explanations of the new philosophy were devoid of meaning in this wider sense . . . In a word, the old explanations, with all their arbitrariness and patchiness, answered the question after 'the meaning of life' whereas the new explanations, with all their precision, made the question of meaning itself meaningless.

Another reaction is to say that we cannot hope to know the meaning of life.

Albert Camus:

I do not know whether this world has a meaning that is beyond me. But I know that I am unaware of this meaning and that, for the time being, it is impossible for me to know it. What can a meaning beyond my condition mean to me? I can understand only in human terms. I understand the things I touch, things that offer me resistance.

The vast majority of writers who are vocal on the subject have reached a pessimistic answer:

Somerset Maugham:

If one puts aside the existence of God and the possibility of survival as too doubtful to have any effect on one's behaviour, one has to make up one's mind what is the meaning and use of life. If death ends all, if I have neither to hope for good to come nor to fear evil, I must ask myself what I am here for, and how in these circumstances I must conduct myself. Now the answer to one of these questions is plain, but so unpalatable that most men will not face it. There is no reason for life, and life has no meaning.

Bertrand Russell:

That man is the product of causes which had no prevision of the end they were achieving; that his origin, his growth, his hopes and fears, his loves and his beliefs, are but the outcome of accidental collocations of atoms; that no fire, no heroism, no intensity of thought and feeling, can preserve an individual life beyond the grave; that all the labour of the ages, all the devotion, all the inspiration, all the noonday brightness of human genius, are destined to extinction in the vast death of the solar system, and that the whole temple of man's achievement must inevitably be buried beneath the debris of a universe in ruins—all these things, if not quite beyond dispute, are yet so nearly certain, that no philosophy which rejects them can hope to stand. Only within the scaffolding of these truths, only on the firm foundation of unyielding despair, can the soul's habitation henceforth be safely built.

H. J. Blackham, who is an optimistic humanist, starts from the position of 'recognizing the pointlessness of it all':

There is no end to hiding from the ultimate end of life, which is death. But it does not avail. On humanist assumptions, life leads to nothing, and every pretence that it does not is a deceit. If there is a bridge over a gorge which spans only half the distance and ends in mid-air, and if the bridge is crowded with human beings pressing on, one after another they fall into the abyss. The bridge leads to nowhere, and those who are pressing forward to cross it are going nowhere. It does not matter where they think they are going, what preparations for the journey they may have made, how much they may be enjoying it all . . . such a situation is a model of futility.

Francis Bacon:

Man now realises that he is an accident, that he is a completely futile being, that he has to play out the game without reason. I think that even when Velasquez was painting, even when Rembrandt was painting, they were still, whatever their attitude to life, slightly conditioned by certain types of religious possibilities, which man now, you could say, has had cancelled out for him. Man now can only attempt to beguile himself for a time, by prolonging his life—by buying a kind of immortality through the doctors. You see, painting has become—all art has become— a game by which man distracts himself. And you may say that it always has been like that, but now it's entirely a game.

Martin Esslin, writing about the Theatre of the Absurd:

The Theatre of the Absurd . . . can be seen as the reflection of what seems to be the attitude most genuinely representative of our own time.
The hallmark of this attitude is its sense that the certitudes and unshakable basic assumptions of former ages have been swept away, that they have been tested and found wanting, that they have been discredited as cheap and somewhat childish illusions.

Eugene Ionesco:

Absurd is that which is devoid of purpose . . . Cut off from his religious, metaphysical, and transcendental roots, man is lost; all his actions become senseless, absurd, useless.

Martin Esslin, writing about Samuel Beckett:

Language in Beckett's plays serves to express the breakdown, the disintegration of language. Where there is no certainty, there can be no definite meanings—and the impossibility of ever attaining certainty is one of the main themes of Beckett's plays. Godot's promises are vague and uncertain. In *Endgame*, an unspecified something is taking its course, and when Hamm anxiously asks, 'We're not beginning to . . . to . . . mean something?' Clov merely laughs. 'Mean something! You and I mean something!'

Sartre's novel *Nausea* conveys the feeling of meaninglessness in the experience of Roquentin:

His judgement pierced me like a sword and called in question my very right to exist. And it was true, I had always realized that: I hadn't any right to exist. I had appeared by chance, I existed like a stone, a plant, a microbe. My life grew in a haphazard way and in all directions. Sometimes it sent me vague signals; at other times I could feel nothing but an inconsequential buzzing.

I was just thinking . . . that here we are, all of us, eating and drinking, to preserve our precious existence, and that there's nothing, nothing, absolutely no reason for existing.

Allen Ginsberg:

I feel as if I am at a dead
end and so I am finished.
All spiritual facts I realize
are true but I never escape
the feeling of being closed in
and the sordidness of self,
the futility of all that I
have seen and done and said.

Many who reach the point of saying that human life is meaningless find it difficult, if not impossible, to *live* with this conclusion. They feel compelled to cast around for a way to create at least some measure of meaning somewhere.

Some attempts to create meaning

▷ **'Say a defiant "yes" to life in spite of its absurdity.'**

Allen Ginsberg, beat poet,
philosopher and mystic, in Haight Ashbury.

George Eliot:

The 'highest calling and election' is to *do without opium*, and live through all our pain with conscious, clear-eyed endurance.

Bertrand Russell:

Brief and powerless is man's life; on him and all his race the slow, sure doom falls pitiless and dark. Blind to good and evil, reckless of destruction, omnipotent matter rolls on its relentless way; for man, condemned today to lose his dearest, tomorrow himself to pass through the gate of darkness, it remains only to cherish, ere yet the blow fall, the lofty thoughts that ennoble his little day; disdaining the coward terrors of the slave of Fate, to worship at the shrine that his own hands have built; undismayed by the empire of chance, to preserve a mind free from the wanton tyranny that rules his outward life; proudly defiant of the irresistible forces that tolerate, for a moment, his knowledge and his condemnation, to sustain alone, a weary but unyielding Atlas, the world that his own ideals have fashioned despite the trampling march of unconscious power.

Nietzsche:

The kind of *experimental philosophy* which I am living, even anticipates the possibility of the most fundamental Nihilism, on principle: but by this I do not mean that it remains standing at a negation, at a *no*, or at a will to negation. It would rather attain to the very reverse—to a *Dionysian affirmation* of the world, as it is, without subtraction, exception, or choice . . .

To overcome pessimism effectively and, at last, to look with the eyes of a Goethe full of love and goodwill.

Nikos Kazantzakis, the Greek novelist, author of *Zorba the Greek*, writing to a friend in 1947·

To conquer illusion and hope, without being overcome by terror: this has been the whole endeavour of my life these past twenty years; to look straight into the abyss without bursting into tears, without begging or threatening, calmly, serenely preserving the dignity of man; to see the abyss and work as though I were immortal . . .

▷ **'Live with the absurd.'**

Maurice Friedman:

Today meaning can be found, if at all, only through the attitude of the man who is willing to *live* with the absurd, to remain open to the mystery which he can never pin down.

Jean-Paul Sartre in his autobiographical work *Words*:

I felt superfluous so I had to disappear. I was a sickly bloom under constant sentence of extinction. In other words, I was condemned, and the sentence could be carried out at any time. Yet I rejected it with all my strength: not that my life was dear to me—quite the contrary, for I did not cling to it: the more absurd life is, the less tolerable death.

For many, the only way to *live* with the absurd is to *write* about it. The very fact that one feels the meaninglessness of life and yet is able to give artistic expression to it is a kind of defiance.

André Malraux:

The greatest mystery is not that we have been flung at random among the profusion of the earth and the galaxy of the stars, but that in this prison we can fashion images of ourselves sufficiently powerful to deny our nothingness.

Arthur Adamov:

Everything happens as though I were only one of the particular existences of some great incomprehensible and central being . . . . Sometimes this great totality of life appears to me so dramatically beautiful that it plunges me into ecstasy. But more often it seems like a monstrous beast that penetrates and surpasses me and which is everywhere, within me and outside me . . . And terror grips me and envelopes me more powerfully from moment to moment . . My only way out is to write, to make others aware of it, so as not to have to feel all of it alone, to get rid of however small a portion of it.

Jean-Paul Sartre:

My retrospective illusions are in pieces. Martyrdom, salvation, immortality: all are crumbling; the building is falling in ruins. I have caught the Holy Ghost in the cellars and flung him out of them. Atheism is a cruel, long-term business: I believe I have gone through it to the end. I see clearly, I am free from illusions . . . I have renounced my vocation, but I have not unfrocked myself. I still write. What else can I do?

▷ **'Just live—life itself is the only value.'**

Colin Wilson, writing about Ernest Hemingway:

The key sentence, 'most men die like animals, not like men', is his answer to the humanist notion of the perfectibility of man . . . There is nothing that man cannot lose. This doesn't mean that life is of no value; on the contrary, life is the only value; it is ideas that are valueless.

Rebecca West:

The living philosophy which really sustains us, which is our basic nourishment, more than any finding of the mind, is simply the sensation of life, exquisite when it is not painful.

Santayana:

To live, to live just as we do, that is the purpose and the crown of living . . . The worth of life lies in pursuit, not in attainment; therefore everything is worth pursuing, and nothing brings satisfaction—save the endless destiny itself.

Lin Yutang:

Great wisdom consists in not demanding too much of human nature, and yet not altogether spoiling it by indulgence. One must try to do one's best, and at the same time, one must, when rewarded by partial success or confronted by partial failure, say to himself, 'I have done my best'. That is about all the philosophy of living that one needs.

Albert Camus:

It is plain that absurdist reasoning . . . recognizes human life as the single necessary good, because it makes possible that confrontation, and because without life the absurdist wager could not go on. To say that life is absurd, one must live. How can one, without indulging one's desire for comfort, keep for oneself the exclusive benefits of this argument? The moment life is recognized as a necessary good, it becomes so for all men.

. . . the living warmth that gives forgetfulness of all . . .

H. J. Blackham rejects the pessimism and despair which he sees in Francis Bacon and Jean-Paul Sartre, and believes that these are 'distorted and immature forms of humanist expression'. He then goes on to ask:

But can humanism really and justifiably maintain equanimity in the face not only of probable ultimate annihilation but also of actual human suffering and stupidity and brutality on the present scale? Is there any satisfaction at all to be found in the general behaviour of mankind or in the trends and tendencies that can be discerned? There is no answer to such a question, or no general answer, for there is no general behaviour of mankind. Everybody must balance his own account here. In any such reckoning, the ready money of daily cheerfulness and unalloyed pleasures is not too small to count. One dimension

Rebecca West, literary critic and political writer.

of finality is here and now. On the public fronts, defeatism may sometimes be the part of reason acting as prudence, but who will responsibly say that the time is not? So long as there are better or worse possibilities there is time for action. Today the better and the worse are better and worse than they have ever been. That is the summons to humanists and the summons of humanism.

▷ **'Evolution gives meaning to life.'** While there may be little or no meaning in the life of the individual by himself, there *is* some meaning to life when it is seen in the context of the evolution of the human race as a whole.

Julian Huxley believes that a philosophy based on evolution can meet man's need for a new religious system:

The evolutionary vision is enabling us to discern, however incompletely, the lineaments of the new religion that we can be sure will arise to serve the needs of the coming era. Just as stomachs are bodily organs concerned with digestion, and involving the biochemical activity of special juices, so are religions psychological organs concerned with the problems of human destiny, and involving the emotion of sacredness and the sense of right and wrong. Religion of some sort is probably necessary. But it is not necessarily a good thing.

Colin Wilson diagnoses the problem in this way:

He (man) is not yet a 'spiritual being', for spiritual, in its ultimate sense, means capable of exercising freedom, and freedom is meaningless without ultimate purpose . . . The one thing that is required to complete the transition from ape to man is the birth of a new kind of purpose *inside* man. Sir Julian Huxley is right in calling this sense of evolutionary purpose a 'new religion'.

He suggests as his answer what he calls 'evolutionary phenomenology':

What has been suggested is that the answer is to be sought in the idea of evolution, as described by Shaw, Wells, or Sir Julian Huxley . . . What if science *could* replace that sense of individual meaning, the feeling of having a direct telephone line to the universal purpose? For this is precisely the aim of evolutionary phenomenology: to change man's conception of himself and of the *interior forces* he has at his command, and ultimately to establish the new evolutionary type, foreshadowed by the 'outsiders'.

▷ **'Man has meaning only as he is absorbed into the universe.'** Life has meaning only as the individual sees himself as part of the universe and looks forward to a more complete absorption in it.

Henry Miller:

I see that behind the nobility of (man's) gestures there lurks the spectre of the ridiculousness of it all . . . he is not only sublime, but absurd. Once I thought that to be human was the highest aim man could have, but I see now that it was meant to destroy me. Today I am proud to say that I am inhuman, that I belong not to men and governments, that I have nothing to do with creeds and principles. I have nothing to do with the cracking machinery of humanity—I belong to the earth! . . . If I'm unhuman it is because my world has slopped over its human bounds, because to be human seems like a poor, sorry, miserable affair, limited by the senses, restricted by moralities and codes, defined by platitudes and isms . . . It may be that we are doomed, that there is no hope for us, any of us, but if that is so then let us set up a last agonizing, blood-curdling howl, a screech of defiance, a war-whoop! Away with lamentations! Away with elegies and dirges! Away with biographies and histories, and libraries and museums! Let the dead eat the dead. Let us living ones dance about the rim of the crater, a last expiring dance. But a dance! . . . The great incestuous wish is to flow on, one with time, to merge the great image of the beyond with the here and now. A fatuous, suicidal wish that is constipated by words and paralysed by thought.

Rabindranath Tagore, writing against a Hindu background:

Dark is the future to her, and the odour cries in
    despair,
  'Ah me, through whose fault is my life so
    unmeaning?
  Who can tell me, why I am at all?'
Do not lose heart, timid thing!
The perfect dawn is near when you will mingle
    your life with all life and know at last your
    purpose.

Problems and questions arising out of this answer in relation to meaning are raised on pp. 104f.

VALUES

If I am not a creature subject to the moral law of God, I cannot look beyond myself for values by which to live.

Pete Townshend:

I'm happy when life's good, and when it's bad I cry.

I've got values but I don't know how or why.

Jean-Paul Sartre:

If I have excluded God the Father, there must be somebody to invent values.

The 'death' of God thus creates a kind of moral vacuum.

Proust's character Oriane in the novel

Remembrance gives an example of the kind of situation in which this moral vacuum shows itself:

Placed for the first time in her life in the presence of two duties as different as whether to leave by car and dine in town, or to show pity to a man who was going to die, she saw nothing in her code which told her which choice to make, and not knowing where her preference should be directed, she decided to pretend that the second option had not been presented to her, which would allow her to follow the first course of action and demanded less effort, thinking that the best way of resolving the conflict was to deny it.

Arthur Koestler:

The logic of expediency leads to the atomic disintegration of morality; a kind of radioactive decay of all values.

Donald Kalish, writing about the present state of moral philosophy:

There is no system of philosophy to spin out. There are no ethical truths, there are just clarifications of particular ethical problems. Take advantage of these clarifications and work out your own existence. You are mistaken to think that anyone ever had the answers. There are no answers. Be brave and face up to it.

Gerald Emanuel Stern, writing about Marshall McLuhan:

McLuhan's ideas are not susceptible to the rigid formalism of genteel discussion; the question of right or wrong ('categories, categories') is, in many ways, irrelevant.

George Eliot, writing about McLuhan:

It is easy to see why McLuhan is listened to so eagerly: With the highest of intellectual credentials, he sounds like a Future-salesman assuring us that there are great days ahead and that what seems to be so terrible now arises only from resistance to change. What if admen do use TV as a way to spread lies and distortions and idiocy? It doesn't matter much anyway: The medium is the message, and a medium is neither moral nor immoral.

Edmund Leach points out the dangers involved in any so-called morality, and the impossibility of saying whether one code or another is right:

The question I am asking is: can scientists and politicians who have acquired god-like power to alter our way of life be restrained by the application of moral principles? If so, what moral principles? And the sort of answer that seems to be coming up is this: 'Beware of moral principles . . .'

When we elevate other people's behaviour we do so according to a code which we have been taught. The code is arbitrary. It changes as we move across the map from one place to another, or through time from one generation to another . . . The old start to denounce the young for their immorality because the code is changing, and they can no longer interpret the signals. But it is still all a question of interpretation; there is no way of saying what the facts really are. In their own estimation the psychedelic hippies with their marijuana and their LSD are primitive Christians proclaiming the brotherhood of man; in the eyes of many of their seniors their activities are a close approximation to witchcraft and the Black Masses. Either may be right.

Faced with this moral vacuum, then, what can we do about it? There are in principle only five possible answers.

Ways of dealing with the moral vacuum

▷ **'Live as if there are absolutes.'** We cannot be sure whether there are any moral standards. But we can at least act on the assumption that they do exist.

Sartre describes French Radicalism towards the end of the nineteenth century, holding on to traditional values long after their basis had dissolved:

Towards 1880, when the French professors endeavoured to formulate a secular morality, they said something like this: God is a useless and costly hypothesis, so we will do without it. However, if we are to have morality, a society and a law-abiding world, it is essential that certain values should be taken seriously; they must have an *a priori* existence ascribed to them. It must be considered obligatory *a priori* to be honest, not to lie, not to beat one's wife, to bring up children and so forth; so we are going to do a little work on this subject, which will enable us to show that these values exist all the same, inscribed in an intelligible heaven although, of course, there is no God. In other words—and this is, I believe, the purport of all that we in France call radicalism—nothing will be changed if God does not exist; we shall re-discover the same norms of honesty, progress and humanity and we shall have disposed of God as an out-of-date hypothesis which will die away quietly of itself.

Arthur Koestler, writing in the 1940s:

I am not sure whether what the philosophers call

the ethical absolutes exist, but I am sure that we have to act as if they existed.

J. B. Priestley:

We can try to feel and think and behave, to some extent, *as if* society were already beginning to be contained by religion, as if we were certain that Man cannot even remain Man unless he looks beyond himself, as if we were finding our way home again in the universe.

A problem arising from this way of dealing with the moral vacuum is raised on pp. 105f.

▷ **'Find a new absolute.'** Many attempts have been made to find some new absolute, some new principle which would provide a standard by which all moral values and judgements could be tested. For example, people have pointed to 'Nature' or 'Happiness' or 'Love' as the ultimate criterion by which to decide values.

1. NATURE. The Deists of the eighteenth century believed that 'Nature' and 'Reason' could combine to point to moral standards which would be evident and acceptable to all thinking people. This idea is still held by some.

Lin Yutang, developing Taoist ideas:

I believe that the only kind of religious belief left for the modern man is a kind of mysticism in the broadest sense of the word, such as preached by Lao-tse. Broadly speaking, it is a kind of reverence and respect for the moral order of the universe, philosophic resignation to the moral order, and the effort to live our life in harmony with this moral order. The *tao* in Taoism exactly means this thing. It is broad enough to cover the most advanced present and future theories of the universe. It is, for me, the only antidote against modern materialism.

Somerset Maugham:

What then is right action? For my part the best answer I know is that given by Fray Luis de Léon. To follow it does not look so difficult that human weakness quails before it as beyond its strength. With it I can end my book. The beauty of life, he says, is nothing but this, that each should act in conformity with his nature and his business.

BUT: 'Nature' is incapable of teaching us values.

T. H. Huxley:

The thief and the murderer follow nature just as much as the philanthropist. Cosmic evolution may teach us how the good and the evil tendencies of man may have come about; but, in itself, it is incompetent to furnish any better reason why what we call good is preferable to what we call evil than we had before.

2. HAPPINESS. The Utilitarian Principle of J. S. Mill says that an action is right if it promotes the greatest happiness of the greatest number. Many modern humanists hold a similar position, and claim that we can derive a system of values by the scientific study of life as it is actually lived.

H. J. Blackham:

The humanist's system of morality is a consecration of the actual facts of life as men live it. He proceeds in the reverse direction from that taken by the super-humanist; for, instead of passing from the arbitrary imperative to the corresponding fantastic indicative, he moves from the indicative of the observed and experienced facts to the imperative of a realistic morality and a rational legislation.

Adam Schaff asks the question 'What is the aim of life?' and gives the answer:

Marxist theory . . . leads to the general position that may be called 'social hedonism'—the view that the aim of human life is to secure the maximum happiness for the broadest mass of the people, and that only within the compass of this aim can personal happiness be reached.

BUT: happiness is generally a by-product of action pursued for other reasons than the attainment of happiness.

J. S. Mill himself recognized this later in life:

I never, indeed, wavered in the conviction that happiness is the test of all rules of conduct, and the end of life. But now I thought that this end was only to be attained by not making it the direct end. Those only are happy (I thought) who have their minds fixed on some subject other than their own happiness; on the happiness of others, on the improvement of mankind, even on some art or pursuit, followed not as a means, but as itself an ideal end. Aiming thus at something else, they find happiness by the way.

A second objection is that it is not possible, logically, to derive an 'ought' statement from an 'is' statement.

We cannot move from a simple statement about a state of affairs (how things actually are) to make a further statement about an obligation (how things ought to be). If we say 'people *do in fact act* like this . . .' we have no right to base a moral judgement on this and say 'therefore people *ought to act* as follows . . .' For example, not even the most exhaustive study of the sexual habits and customs of a particular society would enable us to say what customs people ought to accept or reject.

3. 'LOVE.' It is often suggested that the ultimate principle by which all moral values should be decided is the principle of 'Love'. It is usually assumed that in every situation it is self-evident what the principles of love would point to.

John Wren-Lewis speaks of love as:

. . . the concrete ultimate good.

John Robinson:

Assertions about God are in the last analysis assertions about Love . . .

Life in Christ Jesus . . . means having no absolutes but his love . . . And this utter openness in love to the 'other' for his own sake is equally the only absolute for the non-Christian . . .

Love alone, because, as it were, it has a built-in moral compass, enabling it to 'home' intuitively upon the deepest need of the other, can allow itself to be directed completely by the situation . . . It is the only ethic which offers a point of constancy in a world of flux and yet remains absolutely free for, and free over, the changing situation . . .

Nuclear power, a force for good or ill.
Left: *A materials testing reactor at Dounreay in Scotland.*
Right: *An atomic bomb test in the Nevada desert.*

BUT: It is not obvious and self-evident in *every* situation what the demands of love are. This argument assumes that the person who makes 'love' the absolute moral principle will know the right thing to do. But in practice people have widely differing views of what love demands in particular situations. 'Love' cannot help us to define moral standards any more than 'Reason' or 'Nature' or 'Happiness'.

Nor is it possible, logically, to move from statements of fact to statements of value (see p. 90). It is obvious that every person *does* show love to others to a greater or lesser extent. But why *should* we love? How can we move from the fact that men *do* love to build on this the moral command that men *ought* to love. This is a logical fallacy.

4. THE VALUES OF SCIENCE. *Bronowski* believes that science can actually 'create' values:

The values of science derive neither from the virtues of its members, nor from the finger-wagging codes of conduct by which every profession reminds itself to be good. They have grown out of the practice of science, because they are the inescapable conditions for its practice . . .

Like the other creative activities which grew from the Renaissance, science has humanized our values. Men have asked for freedom, justice, and respect precisely as the scientific spirit has spread among them . . .
The inspiration of science . . . has created the values of our intellectual life and, with the arts, has taught them to our civilization.

These are some of the values which he believes have been 'created' by science:

Independence and originality, dissent and freedom and tolerance: such are the first needs of science; and these are the values which, of itself, it demands and forms . . .
In societies where these values do not exist, science has had to create them.

From these basic conditions, which form the prime values, there follows step by step a range of values: dissent, freedom of thought and speech, justice, honour, human dignity and self-respect.
Our values since the Renaissance have evolved by just such steps.

This, therefore, is the principle which he puts forward as the scientific basis for values: *We OUGHT to act in such a way that what IS true can be verified to be so.*

Arthur Koestler:

Can science heal the neurotic flaw in us? If science cannot, then nothing can. Let us stop pretending. There is no cure in high moral precepts ... The insight of science is not different from that of the arts. Science will create values, I believe, and discover virtues, when it looks into man; when it explores what makes him man and not an animal, and makes his societies human and not animal packs.

BUT: making scientific values our 'absolute' creates some problems. In the first place, it is a confusion of language to say that science can 'create' values. Science is a human activity pursued by individual scientists. 'Science' cannot create values any more than other human activities like art or sport. Science may proceed more effectively if scientists recognize certain values; but the values which are said to have been created by science were recognized and practised long before the development of modern science.

Second, there are certain values which have little or nothing to do with science.

Bronowski admits in the Preface to the later edition of his book, that there are some values

which are not generated by the practice of science—the values of tenderness, of kindliness, of human intimacy and love.

Third, when it comes to particular moral problems, it will always be particular scientists or groups of scientists who will have to make the choices and point out the values. The tyranny of scientists could be just as frightening as the tyranny of soldiers or politicians.

Koestler, although he holds this view, shows elsewhere that he is well aware of the possible consequences:

Within the foreseeable future, man will either destroy himself or take off for the stars ...

Our hypnotic enslavement to the numerical aspects of reality has dulled our perception of non-quantitative moral values; the resultant end-justifies-the-means ethic may be a major factor in our undoing.

He describes science as

... the new Baal, lording it over the moral vacuum with his electronic brain.

5. 'DHARMA'. Values in Hinduism are based on the concept of '*dharma*'.

Radhakrishnan:

Dharma is right action. In the *Rg Veda*, *rta* is the right order of the universe. It stands for both the *satya* or the truth of things as well as the dharma or the law of evolution. Dharma formed from the root *dhr*, to hold, means that which holds a thing or maintains it in being. Every form of life, every group of men has its dharma, which is the law of its being. Dharma or virtue is conformity with the truth of things; adharma or vice is opposition to it. Moral evil is disharmony with the truth which encompasses and controls the world.

This concept of *dharma* comes close to the concept of 'Nature' (see p. 89). In practice, Hinduism teaches a strict code based on the traditions of society:

Radhakrishnan:

Hinduism is more a way of life than a form of thought. While it gives absolute liberty in the world of thought it enjoins a strict code of practice. The theist and the atheist, the sceptic and the agnostic may all be Hindus if they accept the Hindu system of culture and life.

In Buddhism there is the similar concept of *karuna*, love.

D. T. Suzuki:

Karuna corresponds to love. It is like the sands of the Ganges: they are trampled by all kinds of beings: by elephants, by lions, by asses, by human beings, but they do not make any complaints. They are again soiled by all kinds of filth scattered by all kinds of animals, but they just suffer them all and never utter a word of ill-will. Eckhart would declare the sands on the Ganges to be 'just', because 'the just have no will at all: whatever God wishes it is all one to them, however great the discomfort may be'.

Christmas Humphreys quotes some words of Radhakrishnan to the effect that good and evil are ultimately merely different aspects of one great reality:

The antitheses of cause and effect, substance and attribute, good and evil, truth and error, are due to the tendency of man to separate terms which are related. Fichte's puzzle of self and not-self, Kant's antinomies, Hume's opposition of facts and laws, can all be got over if we recognize that the opposing factors are mutually complementary elements based on one identity.

In practice the Buddhist code of morals is summed up in what is known as 'The Eightfold Path': Right Belief, Right Thought, Right Speech, Action, Means of Livelihood, Exertion, Remembrance, and Meditation. And the essence of Buddhism is summed up in the words:

'To cease from all sin,
To get virtue,
To purify the heart.'

BUT: If good and evil are both aspects of the One Great Reality, ultimately there is no sure way of deciding between what is good and what is evil.

Francis Schaeffer relates the following incident to illustrate this dilemma:

One day I was talking to a group of people in the digs of a young South African in Cambridge. Among others, there was present a young Indian who was of Sikh background but a Hindu by religion. He started to speak strongly against Christianity, but did not really understand the problems of his own beliefs. So I said, 'Am I not correct in saying that on the basis of your system, cruelty and non-cruelty are ultimately equal, that there is no intrinsic difference between them?'

He agreed. The people who listened and knew him as a delightful person, an 'English gentleman' of the very best kind, looked up in amazement. But the student in whose room we met, who had clearly understood the implications of what the Sikh had admitted, picked up his kettle of boiling water with which he was about to make tea, and stood with it steaming over the Indian's head. The man looked up and asked him what he was doing and he said, with a cold yet gentle finality, 'There is no difference between cruelty and non-cruelty.' Thereupon the Hindu walked out into the night.

▷ **'The individual must decide for himself.'** *Rousseau* rejects reason as a reliable guide for morals, and looks instead to conscience and feelings:

Whatever I feel to be right is right. Whatever I feel to be wrong is wrong. The conscience is the best of all casuists . . . Reason deceives us only too often and we have acquired the right to reject it only too well but conscience never deceives.

Charles Darwin:

A man who has no assured and ever present belief in the existence of a personal God or of a future existence with retribution and reward, can have for his rule of life, as far as I can see, only to follow those impulses and instincts which are the strongest or which seem to him the best ones.

Albert Camus believes that man's natural impulse to rebellion should be the source from which values can be derived:

The controversial aspect of contemporary history compels us to say that rebellion is one of man's

Wheel of the Law, from the Tibetan "Book of the Dead." The eight-spoked wheel circled by flowers of wisdom shows the symmetry and completeness of the sacred Law.

essential dimensions. It is our historical reality. Unless we ignore reality, we must find our values in it. Is it possible to find a rule of conduct outside the realm of religion and absolute values? That is the question raised by revolt . . .

Rebellion is the common ground on which every man bases his first values. I *rebel*—therefore we *exist*.

The excesses to which rebellion has led in the last few centuries, he argues, point to certain 'limits' or a new 'law of moderation'. It is up to the individual to perceive what these limits are, because they should be almost self-evident.

We know at the end of this long inquiry into rebellion and nihilism that rebellion with no other limits but historical expediency signifies unlimited slavery. To escape this fate, the revolutionary mind, if it wants to remain alive, must therefore return again to the sources of rebellion and draw its inspiration from the only system of thought which is faithful to its origins; thought which recognizes limits.

Sartre believes that freedom is the foundation of all values:

Dostoievsky once wrote 'If God did not exist, everything would be permitted'; and that, for existentialism, is the starting point. Everything is indeed permitted if God does not exist, and man is in consequence forlorn, for he cannot find anything to depend upon either within or outside himself. He discovers forthwith, that he is without excuse. For if indeed existence precedes essence, one will never be able to explain one's action by reference to a given and specific human nature; in other words, there is no determinism—man is free, man *is* freedom. Nor, on the other hand, if God does not exist, are we provided with any values or commands that could legitimise our behaviour. Thus we have neither behind us, nor before us in a luminous realm of values, any means of justification or excuse. We are left alone, without excuse. That is what I mean when I say that man is condemned to be free.

My freedom is the unique foundation of values. And since I am the being by virtue of whom values exist, nothing—absolutely nothing—can justify me in adopting this or that value or scale of values. As the unique basis of the existence of values, I am totally unjustifiable. And my freedom is in anguish at finding that it is the baseless basis of values.

This freedom does not mean that the individual can be irresponsible; on the contrary it places on man an even heavier burden of responsibility. 'In fashioning myself', says Sartre, 'I fashion man.'

This means, in practice, that the individual must 'create' his values. His freedom is similar to the free creativity of the artist:

Moral choice is comparable to the construction of a work of art.

We are in the same creative situation. We never speak of a work of art as irresponsible . . . There is this in common between art and morality, that in both we have to do with creation and invention. We cannot decide *a priori* what it is that should be done.

BUT: to follow this out consistently could lead to a position in which all morals are arbitrary. If we cannot point to any firm standard of values, we have no right to protest when each individual *does* decide what is right for himself. If we are completely free in this sense, we have no right to expect others to accept our values, no right to say 'You *ought* to do this . . .' or 'you *ought not* to do that.'

To the ordinary reader Sartre's position sounds like this summary by *Colin Wilson:*

His philosophy of 'commitment' . . . is only to say that since all roads lead nowhere, it's as well to choose any of them and throw all the energy into it . . .
. . . Any purpose will do provided it is altruistic.

John D. Wild, writing about the weaknesses of the existential understanding of man, speaks of:

the supposed arbitrariness of human choice, and the lack of any firm grounds. For Sartre, the whole effort to justify an act is a cowardly abandonment of freedom and responsibility, the turning of myself into a thing. Whether I decide to die for justice or drink at a bar, the matter is indifferent.

In practice this approach means that the individual has to rely on his own instincts. *Sartre* himself makes this admission:

If values are uncertain, if they are still too abstract to determine the particular, concrete case under consideration, nothing remains but to trust in our instincts.

One can never hope to *know* for certain whether one's values are good or bad. His extreme agnosticism becomes evident at this point:

Who, then, can prove that I am the proper person

to impose, by my own choice, my conception of man upon mankind? I shall never find any proof whatever; there will be no sign to convince me of it. If a voice speaks to me, it is still I myself who must decide whether the voice is or is not that of an angel. If I regard a certain course of action as good, it is only I who choose to say that it is good and not bad.

No state can function on a philosophy of complete freedom. Here Sartre himself is inconsistent. As *Adam Schaff* points out, Sartre the existentialist is committed to total freedom, while Sartre the Communist sympathiser pays tribute to a political system which restricts the freedom of the individual in the interests of the state:

Does the individual create society, by choosing the manner of his behaviour in complete spontaneity and freedom of choice? Or is it society that creates the individual and determines his mode of behaviour?—These questions lie at the heart of the antagonism between Existentialism and Marxism.

There is a contradiction between the Sartre who clings to traditional Existentialism and the Sartre who pays tribute to the philosophy of Marxism. The contradiction can be overcome only by abandoning one or other of the two antagonistic views he now holds.

▷ **'Find values based on agreement.'** The solution proposed by many humanists today is to find values by studying how people actually live and by agreeing on basic principles.

H. J. Blackham:

Only too obviously, there is precious little agreement in the world outside the province of the natural sciences—and perhaps less inside than is popularly supposed. Nevertheless, agreement is the ultimate criterion for values as well as for facts, some humanists would hold, and at any rate for rules which concern everybody in a society . . .

All humanists want to see a consensus on the secular *foundations* of society fully prevail.

Edmund Leach, summing up some basic ideas in his Reith Lectures of 1966, stakes his hopes on the value of tolerance:

I suppose the idea underlying them all was this problem of: How can we arrive at a moral consensus throughout society? . . . I do not feel that we could reach a moral consensus, but I did suggest that if we could only introduce the value of tolerance, that if we could only lead people to expect that other people within your own society might think differently from yourself, we might perhaps to some extent get over this problem—that in a changing society it's impossible for everybody to have an agreed moral consensus.

But in saying this, as *Alasdair MacIntyre* points out in reply, Leach—while insisting that *all* moral codes are relative—is himself insisting that there are some things which are right—absolutely right:

You are in effect saying that to be tolerant is clearly and absolutely right and to be intolerant and too hasty is wrong.

BUT: the problem is to decide what the 'agreed principles' are. Furthermore, quite apart from the inconsistency in declaring dogmatically what the agreed principles must be, there is the difficulty of seeing how agreement could ever be the ultimate criterion of values. One could hardly hope for 100 per cent agreement on a code of values. Failing such a consensus, what kind of majority vote would be acceptable—80 per cent or 51 per cent? In many situations, a society would be at the mercy of individual experts who would claim to *know* what is best for society. And in this case the concept of agreement cannot mean 'agreement of the majority' but rather 'agreement of the experts'.

▷ **'Let some powerful authority decide what is right.'** If we cannot allow each individual to work out his own values, then powerful individuals or groups are at liberty to impose their values on society. It hardly needs saying that this 'solution' is in itself a problem, which can lead to all the horrors of the totalitarian state.

Norman Hampson describes how this dilemma appeared to thoughtful minds at the time of the Enlightenment in the eighteenth century:

The escape from moral anarchy was already beginning to point towards a new totalitarian nightmare.

An attempt to base a code of ethics on purely human values was likely to lead, not to the emancipation of the individual, but to his immolation on the altar of society.

Dostoievsky:

Starting from unlimited liberty, I arrive at unlimited despotism.

C. S. Lewis, writing about the implications of the bold claims about the powers of modern man:

The power of Man to make himself what he pleases means . . . the power of some men to make other men what *they* please . . . the man-moulders of the new age will be armed with the powers of an omnicompetent state and an irresistible scientific technique: we shall get at last a race of conditionere who really can cut out all posterity in what shape they please.

C. E. M. Joad, writing in 1942:

Christianity preached the virtues of kindliness, gentleness, humanity, tolerance, justice, charity and respect for the personality of others. Its virtues, we doubt, were rarely practised; but they were at least professed. It will be a long time yet before the practice of mankind squares with its profession, but the first step is for its profession to condemn its practice. That step Christianity has taken.

In the philosophies of the Fascist people this step has been reversed; the Christian virtues are condemned as the weakness of cowards and half-wits, unable to meet, as good men should, the challenge of the hard world, and the contrary (Christian) vices of arrogance, ruthlessness and ferocity, combined with a professed determina-tion to treat one's neighbours as inferior, are held in honour. The result of this substitution of one code of values for another is all too visible before us.

Leslie Paul, writing about the practical morality of Communist revolutionaries:

If moral indignation is the motivator of Marxist parties in opposition, it disappears from their baggage once they attain power. There is a clear conflict between this morality in opposition and the immorality in power which has nothing to do with the ordinary process of corruption by office . . .

It was the moral passion of Marxism, and its principal child, Communism, which commended Marxism to so many social consciences in the interwar years and it was the disillusion with its moral consequences which has done so much to tarnish its image since. All over the world it has behaved with a moral indifference to human rights and sufferings. Its penal camps in Russia, which operated over at least a generation, probably succeeded in killing as many people as the Nazi

Nazi storm troopers salute Hitler in Vienna. They have become the symbol of the totalitarian regime, uniform, disciplined and military.

extermination camps for the Jews. In lying, terror, secrecy, judicial murder, there has been little to choose between Nazi and Communist dictatorships.

RELATIONSHIPS

Communication

Many modern writers express what they feel is an almost complete breakdown of communication.

Dramatist *Harold Pinter:*

I feel that instead of any inability to communicate there is a deliberate evasion of communication. Communication itself between people is so frightening that rather than do that there is continual cross-talk, a continual talking about other things, rather than what is at the root of their relationship.

Martin Esslin, writing about Samuel Beckett's plays:

The experience expressed in Beckett's plays is of a far more profound and fundamental nature than mere autobiography. They reveal his experience of temporality and evanescence; his sense of the tragic difficulty of becoming aware of one's own self in the merciless process of renovation and destruction that occurs with change in time; of the difficulty of communication between human beings; of the unending quest for reality in a world in which everything is uncertain and the borderline between dream and waking is ever shifting; of the tragic nature of all love relationships and the self-deception of friendship . . .

BUT: they have to use words to show the impossibility of conveying meaning in words.

Martin Esslin shows Beckett's awareness of this tension:

When Gessner asked him about the contradiction between his writing and his obvious conviction that language could not convey meaning, Beckett replied, '*Que voulez-vous, Monsieur? C'est les mots; on n'a rien d'autre.*'

John Wild points out a similar tension in much existentialist thinking. One of the weaknesses of the existentialist theory of man is

its failure to account for human communication. According to Heidegger, my ordinary mode of being with others is impersonal, debased, and unauthentic. He briefly refers to the possibility of authentic communication between persons, but nowhere explains how this is possible or even reconcilable with his picture of the genuine person who has broken from his fellows to live alone with himself in a world of his own choice. The more authentic we become, the more isolated we seem to be. Jaspers has struggled with this problem, but his rejection of universal concepts and judgements makes an intelligible solution impossible. In Sartre, this weakness emerges with brutal clarity. When two persons meet, each tries to absorb the other as an object into his world. Communication is thus restricted to conflict. Love, friendship, and devoted cooperation for common ends are excluded *a priori*.

Love

Many writers profoundly question the possibility of love; yet if it *is* possible, it may become the *only* thing that can make life worth living.

Cyril Connolly in conversation with *Jonathan Miller:*

Would it be a fair summary of your position to say that in this universe—which presumably you regard, as I do, as a deserted universe—friendship perhaps is the only solace, and that some sort of exercise of belief in the nature of friendship is perhaps the most important thing that one can spend one's time on?

I think friendship is one form of love; there is also sexual love; there is also marriage. Love is the prime source of communication between these lonely human organisms.

Camus speaks of friendship, and love between a man and a woman, as perhaps the only thing that can have meaning in an otherwise absurd universe:

If there is one thing one can always yearn for, and sometimes attain, it is human love.

Sartre's picture of love is much blacker. In *Nausea,* Roquentin speaks of his disgust at the way in which a man and a woman are behaving with each other—disgust simply because there is no such thing as love any more:

I stop listening to them: they annoy me. They are going to sleep together. They know it. Each of them knows that the other knows it. But as they are young, chaste, and decent, as each wants to keep his self-respect and that of the other, and as love is a great poetic thing which mustn't be shocked, they go several times a week to dances and restaurants, to present the spectacle of their ritualistic, mechanical dances . . .

After all, you have to kill time. They are young and well built, they have another thirty years in front of them. So they don't hurry, they take their time, and they are quite right. Once they have been to bed together, they will have to find something else to conceal the enormous absurdity of their existence. All the same . . . is it absolutely necessary to lie to each other? I look around the room. What a farce!

BUT: at this point it is in order to ask: If you don't *believe* in love, what happens when you find yourself falling in love?

Francis Schaeffer takes the example of lovers on the left bank of the Seine in Paris, who fall in love and then cry because they do not believe love exists:

If I met any of these I would put my hand gently on their shoulders and say, '. . . at this moment you understand something real about the universe. Though your system may say love does not exist, your own experience shows that it does.' They have not touched the personal God who exists, but, for a fleeting moment, they have touched the existence of true personality in their love. This is indeed an objective reality . . .

SUFFERING AND EVIL

The answer to this question usually amounts to one of four things: despair, resignation, optimism, or rebellion.

Despair

D. R. Davies, writing about his despair in the 30s as he came to understand the significance of what was happening in Europe:

As the significance of each group . . . of events became clear to my mind, my whole being underwent a most painful process of disintegration. I became oppressed with a dreadful sense of futility. As I came to realise the failure to establish peace; as the utter irrationality of the whole economic life of Europe gradually broke in upon me; and the meaning of Fascism gradually dawned upon me; and finally, as the illusion of Russia broke in upon me, I suffered a despair I had never previously known.

W. E. Hocking:

What we see is the moment-to-moment boundary of our being, the nothingness that completes itself in death, our own and that of the race: in such a world, riddled the while with horror-filled actualities, how can a being aspiring and infinite be other than condemned to frustration? And in this world we are nevertheless condemned to engage and to act as men: is it possible?

If this despair does not lead to resignation, it may lead to complete anarchy and destructiveness.

Aldous Huxley, writing in 1936, forsees what such an anarchic revolution might be like:

The time is not far off when the whole population and not merely a few exceptionally intelligent individuals will consciously realize the fundamental unlivableness of life under the present regime. And what then? . . . The revolution that will then break out will not be communistic— there will be no need for such a revolution . . . and besides, nobody will believe in the betterment of humanity or in anything else whatever. It will be a nihilist revolution. Destruction for destruction's sake. Hate, universal hate, and an aimless and therefore complete and thorough smashing up of everything.

Resignation

If the individual feels that life is full of suffering that he can do little to alleviate, he tends to resign himself to the thought that lasting happiness is hardly attainable, and see good and evil as purely relative terms. This has generally been the attitude of the Eastern religions.

Radhakrishnan, writing about Hinduism:

Evil, error and ugliness are not ultimate. Evil has reference to the distance which good has to traverse. Ugliness is half-way to beauty. Error is a stage on the road to truth. They have all to be outgrown. No view is so utterly erroneous, no man is so absolutely evil as to deserve complete castigation . . . In a continuously evolving universe evil and error are inevitable, though they are gradually diminishing.

Christmas Humphreys, writing about Buddhism:

Nothing can be manifested, in a finite world without its opposite. Light implies darkness, else it would not be known as light, and breathing could not be sustained unless we breathed both in and out. Like the double action of the human heart, the heartbeat of the universe implies duality, a cosmic pulse, an alternation of in-breathing and out-breathing, of manifestation and rest. To the Buddhist good and evil are relative and not absolute terms. The cause of evil is man's inordinate desires for self. All action directed to selfish separative ends is evil; all which tends to union is good.

John Robinson rejects the pantheism of the east, but his view of evil is not very different from that of the eastern religions. He does not regard evil as something distinct from God which he hates and fights. He writes of his sympathy with the outlook of Peter Dumitriu's book, *Incognito:*

It is the ability to take up *evil* into God and transform it that is the most striking—and shocking—feature of this theology . . .

God is everything and everything is in God—literally everything material and spiritual, evil as well as good.

God is not outside evil any more than he is outside anything else, and the promise is that he '*will be all in all*' *as love.*

BUT: this resigned attitude has far-reaching practical consequences.

G. T. Manley describes the results of Hinduism in India:

A man's life consists of actions, good and bad, each bearing fruit, and when he dies there is an accumulation of *karma*, merit and demerit, remaining to be worked off. This determines his status in the next life which may be that of a god, a Brahman, an outcaste, a woman, a dog, a plant, and so on. Once again he is caught up in the round of desire, action and consequences, as the water in the water-wheel is passed from one plate to the next, and finds no release.

This doctrine gives an easy explanation for all the differences in human life. Bad and good fortune, health or sickness, poverty or riches, are all ascribed to *karma*. Not only every calamity of the world, but the caste system itself is explained by this doctrine. It also accounts to a great extent for the pessimism found in Hindus today, and largely explains the apparent callousness towards suffering. A man's moral and spiritual state are not really under his control since it is the result of a former life.

Leslie Newbiggin:

It cannot be denied that the main thrust of the teaching of the ancient Asian religions has been away from a concern to change the world. Their dominant teaching has been that the wise man is he who seeks to be content with the world, to be released from attachment to it, but not to seek to change it. The idea of total welfare for all men as a goal to be pursued within history is foreign to the Asian religions, and modern Indian writers such as Sarma and Pannikar have no hesitation in acknowledging that, so far as India is concerned, it is part of the western invasion of the last few centuries.

Optimism

Those who refuse to despair or become resigned about the present suffering state of mankind, adopt a more optimistic outlook.

H. W. Van Loon:

I prefer to concentrate my powers upon that which is within my reach to do: to make this world with its tremendous, with its incredible potentialities for beauty and happiness—a place in which every man, woman, and child will be truly able to say, 'We are grateful that we are alive, for life is good!'

Today that sounds like mocking blasphemy. A hundred centuries hence, it will make sense. For by then man will have acquired the courage necessary to see himself as he really is—as a being equipped with a power of intellect which will eventually allow him to penetrate into every secret of nature until he will truly be the master of all he surveys, and endowed with such a complete freedom of will that he himself—and no one else—is the true master of his fate and therefore dependent for his ultimate happiness upon no one but *himself.*

This optimism about the future of man may be based on political action, on the sciences, or on philosophy.

▷ **Hope based on political action.**

Bertrand Russell:

I think we may hope that liberation from the load of fear, private economic fear and public fear of war, would cause the human spirit to soar to hitherto undreamt of heights. Men, hitherto, have always been cramped in their hopes and aspiration and imagination by the limitations of what has been possible . . . There is no need to wait for Heaven. There is no reason why life on earth should not be filled with happiness. There is no reason why imagination should have to take refuge in a myth. In such a world as men could now make, it could be freely creative within the framework of our terrestrial existence . . . If our present troubles can be conquered, Man can look forward to a future immeasurably longer than his past, inspired by a new breadth of vision, a continuing hope perpetually fed by a continuing achievement. Man has made a beginning creditable for an infant—for, in a biological sense, man, the latest of the species, is still an infant. No limit can be set to what he may achieve in the future. I see in my mind's eye, a world of glory and joy, a world where minds expand, where hopes remain undimmed, and what is noble is no longer condemned as treachery to this or that paltry aim. All this can happen if we let it happen. It rests with our generation to decide between this vision and the end decreed by folly.

Franz Fanon writes as an Algerian who is very conscious of the crimes of Europe as well as its profession of humanism. He looks to the 'Third World' to produce a new humanism:

Come, then, comrades . . . Leave this Europe where they are never done talking of Man, yet murder men everywhere they find them . . . Let us decide not to imitate Europe; let us combine our muscles and our brains in a new direction. Let us try to create the whole man, whom Europe has been incapable of bringing to triumphant birth . . . The Third World today faces Europe like a colossal mass whose aim should be to try to resolve the problems to which Europe has not been able to find the answers . . .

It is a question of the Third World starting a new history of Man, a history which will have regard to the sometimes prodigious theses which Europe has put forward, but which will also not forget Europe's crimes, of which the most horrible was committed in the heart of man, and consisted of the pathological tearing apart of his functions and the crumbling away of his unity. And in the framework of the collectivity there were the differentiations, the stratifications and the bloodthirsty tensions fed by classes; and finally, on the immense scale of humanity, there were racial hatreds, slavery, exploitation and above all the bloodless genocide which consisted in the setting aside of fifteen thousand millions of men . . .

For Europe, for ourselves and for humanity, comrades, we must turn over a new leaf, we must work out new concepts, and try to set afoot a new man.

▷ **Hope based on science.**

Arthur Koestler diagnoses the problem of

man in this way:

When one contemplates the streak of insanity running through human history, it appears highly probable that *homo sapiens* is a biological freak, the result of some remarkable mistake in the evolutionary process . . . somewhere along the line of his ascent something has gone wrong.

The cause underlying these pathological manifestations is the split between reason and belief—or more generally, insufficient co-ordination between the emotive and discriminating faculties of the mind . . . between instinct and intellect, emotions and reason.

He believes that science alone can provide a solution:

Biological evolution has let us down; we can only hope to survive if we develop techniques which supplant it by inducing the necessary changes in human nature.

He believes that a 'New Pill' could be developed which could change human nature by acting as a mental stabilizer:

The psycho-pharmacist cannot *add* to the faculties of the brain—but he can, at best, *eliminate* obstructions or blockages which impede their proper use. He cannot aggrandise us—but he can, within limits, normalise us; he cannot put additional circuits into the brain, but he can, again within limits, improve the coordination between existing ones, attenuate conflicts, prevent the blowing of fuses, and ensure a steady power supply. That is all the help we can ask for—but if we were able to obtain it, the benefits to mankind would be incalculable; it would be the 'Final Revolution' in a sense opposite to Huxley's—the break-through from maniac to man.

▷ **Hope based on evolution.**

Julian Huxley believes that the course of evolution itself will lead to a better future for mankind:

Evolution . . . is the most powerful and the most comprehensive idea that has ever risen on earth. It helps us to understand our origins, our own nature, and our relations with the rest of nature. It shows us the major trends of evolution in the past and indicates a direction for our evolutionary course in the future.

From the specifically religious point of view, the desirable direction of evolution might be defined as the divinization of existence—but for this to have operative significance, we must frame a new definition of 'the divine', free from all connotations of external supernatural beings.

This new point of view that we are reaching, the vision of evolutionary humanism, is essentially a religious one, and . . . we can and should devote ourselves with truly religious devotion to the cause of ensuring greater fulfilment for the human race in its future destiny.

▷ **Hope based on 'A New Humanism'.**

John Wren-Lewis:

The Renaissance failed precisely in so far as society failed to push the revolt against the traditional outlook right through, and here too it seems to me that we are today witnessing the gradual emergence of a new vision which fulfils the Renaissance promise because it *does* complete the revolution. We are witnessing, that is to say, the emergence of a deeper humanism based on a positive vision of human good in concrete experience, and it springs from the same discipline of psychological analysis that has exposed the neurotic character of mankind's traditional moral and social orientations.

Just what practical expression can be given to this faith is something which still remains to be worked out.

Thomas Mann looks forward to a 'new humanity':

I believe in the coming of a new, a third humanism, distinct, in complexion and fundamental temper, from its predecessors. It will not flatter mankind, looking at it through rose-coloured glasses, for it will have had experiences of which the others knew not. It will have a stout-hearted knowledge of man's dark, daemonic, radically 'natural' side; united with reverence for his superbiological, spiritual worth.

BUT: all these different kinds of optimism are based on a 'leap of faith'. There is not, in fact, a great deal to justify these utopian hopes. And it is hardly any encouragement to be told, 'If you look far enough ahead, all will be well.'

Some of the writers already quoted express their own fears as well as their hopes:

Michael Harrington speaks of the 'weary pessimism' which is found in *Thomas Mann* alongside his optimism:

Of all the great writers of the Devil's Party, Mann is the most relevant to a study of the contemporary decadence. He lived through the unnerving transitions of the period: the turn of the century, World War I, the stultification of the German middle class, the rise of fascism, World War II and the Cold War. Not only did he write of these incredible times; the times wrote his life as if it were one of his novels . . .

He died undecided, hesitating between a desperate optimism and a weary pessimism.

Bertrand Russell, in an interview with Ved Mehta, confesses:

I have to read at least one detective book a day to drug myself against the nuclear threat.

Arthur Koestler's novel *Darkness at Noon* was based on his knowledge of people involved in the Moscow Trials in the early 30s. The main character, Rubashov, has been condemned to death for crimes against the state and at any moment he expects the final summons. His feelings express the reaction of those who are not content to pin their hopes on a glorious future which they themselves will never see, and of which they see little evidence at the present time. The book ends with these words:

What happened to those masses, to this people? For forty years it had been driven through the desert, with threats and promises, with imaginary terrors and imaginary rewards. But where the Promised Land?

Did there really exist any such goal for this wandering mankind? That was a question to which he would have liked an answer before it was too late. Moses had not been allowed to enter the land of promise either. But he had been allowed to see it, from the top of the mountain, spread at his feet. Thus it was easy to die, with the visible certainty of one's goal before one's eyes. He, Nicolai Salmanowitch Rubashov, had not been taken to the top of a mountain; and wherever his eye looked, he saw nothing but desert and the darkness of night.

Rebellion

This attitude faces the absurdity of suffering and evil and a profound despair. In its determination to protest and rebel and fight suffering and evil it comes nearer than the rest to the Christian answer.

Albert Camus, addressing a Christian audience:

I share with you the same horror of evil. But I do not share your hope, and I continue to struggle against this universe where children suffer and die.

Jean-Paul Sartre, philosopher and author, leader of the existentialist movement in France.

Writing in *The Rebel:*

The words which reverberate for us at the confines of this long adventure of rebellion, are not formulae for optimism, for which we have no possible use in the extremities of our unhappiness, but words of courage and intelligence which, on the shores of the eternal seas, even have the qualities of virtue.

No possible form of wisdom today can claim to give more. Rebellion indefatigably confronts evil, from which it can only derive a new impetus. Man can master, in himself, everything that should be mastered. He should rectify in creation everything that can be rectified. And after he has done so, children will still die unjustly even in a perfect society. Even by his greatest effort, man can only propose to diminish, arithmetically, the sufferings of the world. But the injustice and the suffering of the world will remain and, no matter how limited they are, they will not cease to be an outrage. Dmitri Karamazov's cry of 'Why?' will continue to resound through history; art and rebellion will only die with the death of the last man on earth.

Camus' novel *The Plague* gives a vivid picture of what this rebellion in the face of suffering must mean. Rieux, the doctor, sees his work in the plague as 'fighting against creation as he found it'.

I have no idea what's awaiting me, or what will happen when all this ends. For the moment I know this; there are sick people and they need curing. Later on, perhaps, they'll think things over; and so shall I. But what's wanted now is to make them well. And I defend them as best I can, that's all . . .

Have you ever heard a woman scream 'Never!' with her last gasp? Well, I have. And then I saw that I could never get hardened to it. I was young then, and I was outraged by the whole scheme of things, or so I thought. Subsequently, I grew more modest. Only, I've never managed to get used to seeing people die. That's all I know . . .

At this moment he suffered with Grand's sorrow, and what filled his breast was the passionate indignation we feel when confronted by the anguish all men share.

BUT: this rebellion means fighting against the order of things without knowing why, and without hope.

Rieux, the doctor in Camus' *Plague*, expresses this dilemma:

For nothing in the world is it worth turning one's back on what one loves. Yet that is what I'm

Mère Ubu, a character from Jean-Louis Barrault's "Jarry Sur La Butte." Albert Jarry was a leading member of the Theatre of the Absurd movement in Paris in the 1920's.

doing—though *why* I do not know . . . That's how it is . . . and there's nothing to be done about it. So let's recognize the fact, and draw the conclusions . . . a man can't cure and *know* at the same time. So let's cure as quickly as we can. That's the more urgent job.

He knew that the tale he had to tell could not be one of a final victory. It could be only the record of what had had to be done, and what assuredly would have to be done again in the never-ending fight against terror and its relentless onslaughts, despite their personal afflictions, by all who, while unable to be saints but refusing to bow down to pestilences, strive their utmost to be healers.

And, indeed, as he listened to the cries of joy rising from the town, Rieux remembered that such joy is always imperilled.

PROBLEMS AND QUESTIONS

With regard to the individual; whatever we may think, we have to live here and now as if he is real

Dostoievsky writes:

Man's whole business is to prove that he is a man and not a cog-wheel . . .

Aldous Huxley is well aware of the dilemma of the person who says that the individual does not matter or is unreal. We can only deny the individual by going against all our normal experience of life.

Even if it were not so difficult to arrive at the vision of what philosophers and mystics assure us . . . to be the Truth; even if it were easy for us to pass in the spirit from the world of distinctions and relations to that of infinity and unity, we should be no nearer to being able to *live* in that higher world. For we live with our bodies; and our bodies grossly refuse to be anything but distinct and relative. Nothing can induce the body to admit its own illusoriness.

Our separateness is not wholly an illusion. The element of specifity in things is a brute fact of experience. Diversity cannot be reduced to complete identity even in scientific and philosophical theory, still less in life which is lived with bodies, that is to say, with particular patternings of the ultimately identical units of energy.

A consistent denial of the individual must lead to a philosophy of total negation and meaninglessness

C. E. M. Joad spells out the logical conclusion of the Eastern religions:

A condition in which I shall cease to think, to feel as an individual or, indeed to *be* an individual, is a condition in which *I* shall cease to be at all. Now why should I hope or seek to realise such a condition, unless I take my individual personality to be of no account?

Christmas Humphreys is convinced that Buddhism allows for the freedom of the will; but the rest of the Buddhist system hardly leaves room for this confident assertion:

The Buddhist fails to see any conflict between the hypotheses of freewill and predestination, for karma and freewill are two facets of the same spiritual truth. 'Buddhism', Ananda Coomaraswamy says, 'is fatalistic in the sense that the present is always determined by the past; but the future remains free. Every action we make depends on what we have come to be at the time, but what we are coming to be at any time depends on the direction of the will.

Is there a guarantee that the larger entity of which the individual is supposed to be a part, has meaning?

Aldous Huxley:

Individual salvation can have no real sense if existence in the cosmos is itself an illusion. In the monistic view the individual soul is one with the

Supreme, its sense of separateness an ignorance, escape from the sense of separateness and identity with the Supreme its salvation. But who then profits by this escape? Not the Supreme Self, for it is supposed to be always and inalienably free, still, silent, pure. Not the world, for that remains constantly in the bondage and is not freed by the escape of any individual soul from the universal illusion. It is the individual soul itself which effects its supreme good by escaping from the sorrow and the division into the peace and the bliss. There would seem then to be some kind of reality of the individual soul as distinct from the world and from the Supreme even in the event of freedom and illumination. But for the illusionist the individual soul is an illusion and non-existent except in the inexplicable mystery of maya. Therefore we arrive at the escape of an illusory soul from an illusory non-existent bondage in an illusory non-existent world as the supreme good which that non-existent soul has to pursue! . . .

The principle of negation prevails over the principle of affirmation and becomes universal and absolute. Thence arise the great world-negating religions and philosophies.

⚠ On the question of meaning: can anyone live with a philosophy of total meaninglessness?

Nietzsche tried perhaps harder than any person to *live* his philosophy of meaninglessness to the end. This is how H. J. Blackham describes his attempt:

In his own case, he provided himself with no means of getting out of the nihilism into which he plunged himself, precisely because it was a deliberate plunge over the edge. He tried to say at the same time: nihilism must be surmounted; nihilism cannot be surmounted; nihilism is good, nihilism is best. He imprisoned himself within the chalked circle of his own metaphysical assumptions.

Colin Wilson describes what the philosophy of meaninglessness meant for some in the nineteenth century:

Most of these poets of the late nineteenth century were only 'half in love with easeful death'; the other half clung very firmly to life and complained about its futility. None of them, not even Thomson, goes as far as Wells in *Mind at the End of Its Tether*. But follow their pessimism further, press it to the limits of complete sincerity, and the result is a completely life-denying nihilism that is actually a danger to life. When Van Gogh's 'Misery will never end', is combined with Evan Strowde's 'Nothing is worth doing', the result is a kind of spiritual syphilis that can hardly stop short of death or insanity. Conrad's story *Heart of Darkness* deals with a man who has brought himself to this point; he dies murmuring: 'The horror, the horror.' Conrad's narrator comments: '. . . I wasn't arguing with a lunatic either . . . His intelligence was perfectly clear; concentrated . . . upon himself with a horrible intensity, yet clear . . . But his soul was mad. Being alone in the Wilderness, it had looked within itself, and . . . it had gone mad: he had summed up; he had judged: the Horror.'

Albert Camus points out the contradiction in the absurdist position:

I proclaim that I believe in nothing and that everything is absurd, but I cannot doubt the validity of my own proclamation and I am compelled to believe, at least, in my own protest.

Writer Colin Wilson.

⚠ If life as a WHOLE has no meaning, why should we think that PARTS of life may have some meaning?

Aldous Huxley, writing in the 30s speaks of how some of his contemporaries accepted a philosophy of meaninglessness, but then went on to reintroduce meaning in different ways. It was the results of this thinking in practice and in history which forced Huxley to reconsider the truth of the philosophy:

Meaning was reintroduced into the world, but only in patches. The universe as a whole still remained meaningless, but certain of its parts, such as the nation, the state, the class, the party, were endowed with significance and the highest value. The general acceptance of a doctrine that denies meaning and value to the world as a whole, while assigning them in a supreme degree to certain arbitrarily selected parts of the totality, can only have evil and disastrous results . . .

It was the manifestly poisonous nature of the fruits that forced me to reconsider the philosophical tree on which they had grown.

⚠ How can one create meaning out of meaninglessness?

Many of these attempts to create meaning, in spite of their seriousness and intensity of feeling, sound very much like the attempt of the King in *Alice in Wonderland* to make sense of some nonsensical verses of poetry:

'That's the most important piece of evidence we've heard yet,' said the King, rubbing his hands; 'so now let the jury——'

'If any one of them can explain it,' said Alice (she had grown so large in the last few minutes that she wasn't a bit afraid of interrupting him), 'I'll give him sixpence. *I* don't believe there's an atom of meaning in it.'

The jury all wrote down on their slates, '*She* doesn't believe there's an atom of meaning in it,' but none of them attempted to explain the paper.

'If there's no meaning in it,' said the King, 'that saves a world of trouble, you know, as we needn't try to find any. And yet I don't know,' he went on, spreading out the verses on his knee, and looking at them with one eye; I seem to see some meaning in them, after all . . '

⚠ With regard to values: how can one hold on to Christian values when the beliefs on which they are based are no longer accepted?

Nietzsche pours scorn on those who reject Christian beliefs about God but at the same time want to hold on to Christian values:

They have got rid of the Christian God, and now feel obliged to cling all the more firmly to Christian morality: that is *English* consistency, let us not blame it on little blue-stockings *à la* Eliot. In England, in response to every little emancipation from theology one has to reassert one's position in a fear-inspiring manner as a moral fanatic. That is the *penance* one pays there.—With us it is different. When one gives up Christian belief one thereby deprives oneself of the *right* to Christian morality. For the latter is absolutely *not* self-evident: one must make this point clear again and again, in spite of English shallowpates. Christianity is a system, a consistently thought out and *complete* view of things. If one breaks out of it a fundamental idea, the belief in God, one thereby breaks the whole thing to pieces: one has nothing of any consequence left in one's hands. Christianity presupposes that man does not know, *cannot* know what is good for him and what is evil: he believes in God, who alone knows. Christian morality is a command: its origin is transcendental; it is beyond all criticism, all right to criticize; it possesses truth only if God is truth—it stands or falls with the belief in God.—If the English really do believe they know, of their own accord, 'intuitively', what is good and evil; if they consequently think they no longer have need of Christianity as a guarantee of morality; that is merely the *consequence* of the ascendancy of the Christian evaluation and an expression of the *strength* and *depth* of this ascendancy: so that the origin of English morality has been forgotten, so that the highly conditional nature of its right to exist is no longer felt. For the Englishman morality is not yet a problem.

But morality is very much of a problem—even for the English!

C. E. M. Joad, writing in 1942, when he was still an agnostic, was well aware of the difficulty, even the dishonesty, of the position Nietzsche scorned:

I have been led to place a new value upon the Christian code of ethics and the way of life that is based on their acceptance, and to see that this value remains, even if the metaphysical foundations upon which Christianity bases the codes are thought to be dubious or dismissed as untenable. But then comes the question: 'Can the code endure without the supernatural foundation, any more than a flower can endure that is cut from its roots?' That the Christian code and the Christian way of life may so endure *for a time* is clear. Plato has an interesting passage about the substitution of habit for principle in a society. He gives a vivid description of the power of habit, describing how men and women will continue to cultivate certain virtues and practise restraints, when the principles which would alone have justified the cultivating and the practising have ceased to be held. They may do this, he points out, for a time, even, if the times are quiet, for a long time, in ignorance that the basis of principle is no longer there; but the structure of habit lacking foundation collapses at the first impact of adversity.

Is it not doing so now? Is it well that it should do so? And if it is not well, is it wise to continue to erode the foundations in history and metaphysics upon which the Christian faith is based? If we can't accept them ourselves, may it not, nevertheless, be well that we should at least pretend, remembering in our emergency Plato's hint about the social beneficence of the useful lie?

Sartre:

When we speak of 'abandonment'—a favourite word of Heidegger—we only mean to say that God does not exist, and that it is necessary to draw the consequences of his absence right to the end. The existentialist is strongly opposed to a certain type of secular moralism which seeks to suppress God at the least possible expense. The existentialist, on the contrary, finds it ... embarrassing that God does not exist, for there disappears with Him all possibility of finding values in an intelligible heaven. There can no longer be any good *a priori*, since there is no infinite and perfect consciousness to think it. It is nowhere written that 'the good' exist, that one must be honest or must not lie, since we are now upon the plane where there are only men.

A magistrates' court in session. The motto 'God and my right' is still emblazoned on the royal coat of arms over the magistrates' bench.

BACK TO ANSWER ONE

"Man is a creature created in the image of God— the God of the Bible"

PROBLEMS AND QUESTIONS

Having examined other possible answers to the basic question, 'What is man?' we return to option one, the Biblical Christian answer, for a closer look at some of the questions and objections raised.

⚠ Doesn't calling man a 'creature' rob him of his dignity?

Colin Wilson associates belief in creation with a submissive passivity. He believes that religion gives

the sense of being a mere creature whose only business is passive obedience to a master.

Lord Willis, speaking as a humanist, sees belief in God and the divinity of Jesus as signs of weakness:

I disbelieve in them actively, I am afraid. In fact I would regard it as a weakness to believe in them. I do not believe they are necessary. I respect very much indeed the need that some people have for this particular belief and would not dream of attacking them in any way, but for myself I do not need this belief and I would regard it as an affront to my dignity as a human being to put my faith in something supernatural.

▷ It has to be admitted that Christians have at times held a view of man which makes him much less than the Bible's picture of him.

The Psalmist's words 'I am a worm and no man' (Psalm 22:6) have been used to give the impression that man is little more than an insignificant worm. But these words in their context express the feelings of a man in the depths of his suffering and humiliation, and cannot be taken as a summary of the whole biblical view of man.

▷ The Bible regards man's status as a created being, far from *degrading* man, as being the very thing that gives him his *dignity and greatness*. What kind of a creature is this who is created, not like the plants and the trees 'after their kind', but in the image and likeness of God himself? In the two passages where the Old Testament writers ask the question 'what is man . . .?' (Psalm 8:3-8 and Job 7:17-21, quoted on pp. 54 and 56) the basic thought is: 'O God, what is man that you *make so much of him?*'

▷ What happens if man is *not* regarded as a creature created in God's likeness? It may seem that the idea of the dignity and worth of every human being is so obvious and self-evident, that no one in his senses would ever deny it. But the history of the last three centuries shows that it is far from self-evident, and we cannot guarantee that this belief will continue indefinitely if it has no firm foundation. (See pp. 75ff.)

⚠ How can man be created and free at the same time?

I.e., doesn't the very idea of creation rule out the possibility that the created thing can be free and responsible? If God creates man in a certain way, how can he hold him responsible for his choices?

▷ We *all* behave in practice *as if* we have a certain measure of freedom and responsibility. However much a person doubts or denies the possibility of man's freedom in making choices, he cannot in fact live as if he has no freedom. Any discussion of determinism and freewill must start with this fact of our experience, not simply with our philosophy.

Jacob Bronowski describes the kind of freedom which is an essential part of being human:

When I say that I want to be myself, I mean as the existentialist does that I want to be *free* to be myself. This implies that I too want to be rid of constraints (inner as well as outward constraints) in order to act in unexpected ways. Yet I do not mean that I want to act either at random or unpredictably. It is not in these senses that I want to be free but in the sense that I want to be allowed to be different from others. I want to follow my own way—but I want it to be a way, recognizably my own, and not a zig-zag. And I want people to recognize it: I want them to say, 'How characteristic!'

He believes that the analogy of the machine—even the most sophisticated machine—is inadequate for describing human experience:

Until we find a concept of what a machine is which follows fundamentally different laws from any that we know now, my self contains a part that is certainly not a machine in any known sense.

▷ If we agree that a measure of freedom is an essential part of the human condition, what actually happens when a choice or decision is made?

Professor Donald Mackay, a brain scientist, approaches the problem by saying: 'Just suppose for the sake of argument that we could predict a person's actions with 100 per cent accuracy—what would it prove?' He argues that it doesn't prove the case of the determinist, because there would still be an unknown element: will the person concerned believe what is predicted about himself or will he not?

It follows that even if the brain were as mechanical as clockwork, no completely detailed present or future description of a man's brain can be equally accurate whether the man believes it or not. (a) It may be accurate *before* he believes it, and then it would automatically be rendered out of date by the brain-changes produced by his believing it; or (b) it might be possible to arrange that the brain-changes produced by his believing it would bring his brain into the state it describes, in which case it must be inaccurate *unless* he

Brain-waves being recorded on a graph for research purposes.

believes it, so he would not be in error to *disbelieve* it.

In either case, then, the brain-description lacks the 'take it or leave it' character of scientific descriptions of the rest of the physical world, since its validity depends precisely upon whether the subject takes it or leaves it! True, any number of detached observers could predict whether the subject will 'take it' or 'leave it'; but this prediction in turn, though valid for the observers in detachment, would lack any 'take it or leave it' validity for the subject. It would still be true that for such brain-states, and future events causally dependent upon them, no *universally valid (pre) determination exists*: no complete and certain prediction waits undiscovered upon which the subject and his observers would be correct to agree . . .

I suggest . . . that the question whether all human brain activity has a mechanistic explanation is one we can peacefully leave open for future investigation, no matter how high a view we take of man's power of decision and its moral and religious significance. A complete mechanistic explanation of the brain would not eliminate our freedom, and those who urge mechanistic behaviourism so as to abolish moral and spiritual categories seem to be pursuing an illusion.

▷ Mackay also suggests that there is a similarity between the problem of determinism and responsibility on the human level and the relation between *God*'s sovereignty and man's responsibility. He claims that just as there need be no antithesis between (possibly) mechanistic explanations and human responsibility, so in the same way there is no logical antithesis between divine sovereignty and human responsibility. It is possible for man to be created and at the same time to make choices for which he is responsible. Professor Mackay uses the analogy of the author and the story he creates.

It may help our thinking if we look first at the logical relation between the 'predestined course' of a human novel, and what the people in the story would have been correct to believe. The human author is sovereign over the whole of their created history, which for him is one coherent spatio-temporal fact. No event appears in it that he has not ordained, and we can share his complete knowledge of every decision made by his creatures. This does not mean that we know *in advance* an event still in the future for us, nor are the events over which the author is sovereign ahead of *him* in (his) time; so for us and him the prefix 'fore-' in such terms as 'fore-known' and 'fore-ordained' would be inappropriate. All events

in the synthetic history, from beginning to end, are for us not prospects but data.

Suppose now that we ask what the people in the story would be correct to believe about the events in their future. John, let us suppose, makes up his mind to ask Mary rather than Jane to marry him. Mary eventually decides to turn him down. Can we say that before either of these decisions was taken, the outcomes were already foreordained and therefore inevitable for John and Mary? Can we say that Mary was not really free to make up her mind, and that she was forced by her author to reject John?

Fortified by our earlier discussions, we can easily see that no such conclusion need follow. No doubt the author *could* write a story in which the characters were mindless puppets, but this is not our story. If John and Mary have been conceived by their author as normal human people, then their decisions will depend upon their cognitive processes in just the way we have already analysed, with the same logical consequences. Not even the author himself can produce a prediction of the outcome which John and Mary would be correct to accept as inevitable before they make up their minds; for no such prediction exists. On such matters our 'predestinarian' knowledge generates nothing definitive for them to know until they make up their minds—and then of course they know the outcome without our help! . . .

So their author's creative sovereignty and 'fore-knowledge', complete though it is, does not imply that while they are making up their minds, there exists a secret prediction of their decision, already known to their author, which they would be correct to believe as certain whether they liked it or not, and which thus proves the outcome to be inevitable for them; nor are they *forced* by their author to make the decisions they do, nor is their responsibility for them in any way reduced. But it does imply that although their author may be unknowable by them, they owe their whole existence and that of their world to him, since he decrees every fact of their history—including the fact that they themselves are free agents.

If there is this element of freedom in the relationship between God and man, God can address man and hold him responsible for his response.

Dialogue . . . is a relationship in which the parties necessarily know one another as undetermined agents. If then our Creator has chosen to offer Himself to us in that relationship, *even He must know us as free and responsible beings.* So in any discussion of the relationship between ourselves and God, we must sharply distinguish between what may be logically applicable to 'God-in-dialogue' and to 'God-in-eternity' respectively, just as we would have to do if we were speaking of a human author who had created a history in which he himself was one of the characters . . . Logically, we can depend for our existence upon the 'creative' will of God-in-eternity, and still be answerable for our response as free beings to the 'normative' will of God-in-dialogue. Whatever our attitude to the twin doctrines of divine sovereignty and human responsibility, no logical antithesis can be sustained between them in their biblical form.

▷ If we reject the Christian answer (or any kind of theistic answer), we still have the problem of *accounting for* our freedom. We are faced with a dilemma:

either we must say 'we know *that* we have some freedom, but we cannot hope to be able to explain *how* we have evolved in this way';

or we must deny that we have any freedom, and say that our feeling of being free is an illusion.

Thus, if there is a problem in understanding how divine creation can be reconciled with human freedom and responsibility, the problem is very much *more acute* for the agnostic or the atheist. (See pp. 80ff. for some illustrations of this dilemma.)

⚠ Is belief in a historic Adam an essential part of Christian beliefs about man?

The following are the main reasons why the biblical Christian generally holds that belief in a historic Adam *is* an essential part of Christian beliefs:

▷ It is a basic principle in interpreting the Bible that we must always ask: 'what did the original writer intend?' When we ask this question about the early chapters of Genesis, we find an important clue in the phrase 'these are the generations of . . .' This phrase is repeated in different forms 11 times in the course of the book, and its meaning is: 'this is the genealogy, or genealogical history, of . . .' For example,

These are the generations of the heavens and the earth	2 : 4
This is the book of the generations of Adam	5 : 1
These are the generations of Noah . .	6 : 9
These are the generations of the sons of Noah, Shem, Ham and Japheth . .	10 : 1

The writer thinks of Adam in the same way as all the other characters who come after him—i.e. as real historical characters. If the writer had wanted to convey the idea that Adam stands for 'Everyman' and that the story represents an existential myth about universal human experience, he would hardly have included Adam in this framework of genealogies and spoken of the 'descendants of Adam'.

▷ The Jews always understood that the creation account referred to a single pair, and *Jesus* clearly accepted this view without question.

Pharisees came up to him and tested him by asking, 'Is it lawful to divorce one's wife for any cause?' He answered, 'Have you not read that he who made them from the beginning made them male and female, and said, "For this reason a man shall leave his father and mother and be joined to his wife, and the two shall become one"?'

Luke traces the genealogy of Jesus back to Adam, the first man:

Jesus, when he began his ministry, was about thirty years of age, being the son (as was supposed) of Joseph, the son of Heli . . . the son of Enos, the son of Seth, the son of Adam, the son of God.

Paul assumes that Adam was the first man, the one through whom sin entered the world. His whole argument in the following passage about the effects of the death and resurrection of Jesus depends on the assumption that the fall of Adam was just as much a historical event as the death and resurrection of Jesus:

. . . sin came into the world through one man and death through sin, and so death spread to all men because all men sinned . . . If many died through one man's trespass, much more have the grace of God and the free gift in the grace of that one man Jesus Christ abounded for many. And the free gift is not like the effect of that one man's sin. For the judgement following one trespass brought condemnation, but the free gift following many trespasses brings justification. If, because of one man's trespass, death reigned through that one man, much more will those who receive the abundance of grace and the free gift of righteousness reign in life through the one man Jesus Christ.

Then as one man's trespass led to condemnation for all men, so one man's act of righteousness leads to acquittal and life for all men. For as by one man's disobedience many were made sinners, so by one man's obedience many will be made righteous.

▷ Rejection of the belief in a historic Adam creates far more problems than it solves. If the early chapters of Genesis have nothing to do with *origins*—the origin of the universe, of man and sin and suffering—then a host of very vital questions are left completely unanswered: e.g. what does it mean to say that man was 'created in the image of God'?

Did man grow into the image of God, and did the divine likeness in man evolve gradually? Was man created perfect, or was he created in the same condition as he is now? Was man always a sinner and a rebel by nature?

John Habgood;

Even if we believe, as most theologians now do, that the stories of Adam and Eve are profound myths and not literal history, some difficulties remain. The doctrines of the Fall and of the uniqueness of man are not just forced upon Christians because they happen to be there in Genesis 1:3. They are essential pieces of Christian theology, interlocking with the whole of the rest of theology, which cannot be removed without putting the whole structure in jeopardy.

⚠ Is creation compatible with evolution?

Our answer to this question must depend on the answers we give to the following questions:

How do we define 'creation' and 'evolution'? How do we understand the relation between science and revelation? How do we interpret the scientific evidence? How far are we influenced by other assumptions which have nothing to do with science?

How do we define 'creation' and 'evolution'? One of the opening scenes of de Laurentii's film *The Bible* shows Adam literally being formed out of dust—a heap of dust is transformed into a living man before our eyes in a few seconds. The text of Genesis, however, does *not* demand an interpretation of this kind. Nor does it demand the interpretation that man was created in an instant 'out of nothing'.

The writer of Genesis reserves the word 'create' for three decisive stages in the creation of the universe:

In the beginning God created the heavens and the earth . . .
(the initial creation of the 'raw material' of the universe, 1 : 1)

God created the great sea monsters and every living creature that moves, with which the waters swarm . . . and every winged bird . . .
(the creation of animal life, 1 : 21)

God created man in his own image . . .
(the creation of man, 1 : 27)

In the first of these stages the word 'create' must imply 'created out of nothing'. But in the other two stages, it is not a creation out of nothing, but rather a creation through working on matter that is already there:

And God said, 'Let the waters bring forth swarms of living creatures . . .' (1 : 20)

The Lord God formed man of dust from the ground, and breathed into his nostrils the breath of life; and man became a living being . . . (2 : 7)

Thus, when the writer speaks of God creating man, he speaks of it as a decisively new stage in the unfolding process of creation. But he does not define precisely *how* God created man; and we must be careful not to read into the text ideas which are not there. If we are careful to distinguish between what the Bible *does say* and what it *does not say*, we can afford to have a more open mind over the process by which God created man.

The difficulty in defining 'evolution' arises from the fact that the word is used in at least three different senses:

▷ Used in a very *general sense*, it means little more than 'development', and describes the process whereby animals and plants change in such a way that new varieties are formed. In this case it normally refers to development within limited areas, and nothing is implied about 'natural selection'.

Charles Darwin, zoologist, botanist and naturalist. He published "The Origin of Species" in 1859.

▷ Used in the *technical sense*, it refers to the biological theory formulated by Charles Darwin, and is applied to all living things from the amoeba to man.

Professor W. R. Thompson, in the Introduction to the latest Everyman edition of *The Origin of Species*, summarizes Darwin's theory of evolution and the view of most representative modern Darwinians in this way:

. . . natural selection, leading to the survival of the fittest, in populations of individuals of varying characteristics and competing among themselves, has produced in the course of geological time gradual transformations leading from the simple primitive organism to the highest form of life, without the intervention of any directive agency or force . . .Purposeless and undirected evolution, says J. S. Huxley, eventually produced, in man, a being capable of purpose and of directing evolutionary change.

Those who believe that creation is compatible with evolution in this sense are forced to make a drastic reinterpretation of Genesis; for if the human race has evolved gradually without any special 'break', there cannot have been a single 'Adam'. They are also faced with the problem of how God is able to work purposefully through a process which, by definition, works by chance. Darwin himself spoke of 'a Creator', and may have thought that the idea of creation was not incompatible with his theory of evolution. But it was not long before he rejected the Christian belief in creation, and most of his modern followers find the theory a convincing reason for rejecting Christian beliefs:

Professor W. R. Thompson:

The doctrine of evolution by natural selection as Darwin formulated, and as his followers still explain it, has a strong anti-religious flavour. This is due to the fact that the intricate adaptations and co-ordinations we see in living things, naturally evoking the idea of finality and design and, therefore, of an intelligent providence, are explained, with what seems to be a rigorous argument, as the result of chance . . . It is clear that in the *Origin* evolution is presented as an essentially undirected process. For the majority of its readers, therefore, the *Origin* effectively dissipated the evidence of providential control.

▷ In many cases 'evolution' is understood to be *not only a biological theory but also a philosophical theory* which can be applied in many other fields and rules out the existence of God.

Julian Huxley writes of evolution as an all-embracing philosophy:

All reality is evolution . . . it is a one-way process in time; unitary, continuous; irreversible; self-transforming, and generating variety and novelty during its transformations.

How do we understand the relation between science and revelation? When this general question is related to the particular question of evolution, there are basically four different answers that can be given.

1. 'Accept the principle of evolution without question and revise our interpretation of Genesis accordingly.'

This means that we accept the probability that man has evolved gradually from ape-like ancestors. There cannot have been one Adam, as Genesis describes him, and the early chapters of Genesis cannot be understood as speaking about the origin of the human race.

The difficulty with this view is that it demands such a drastic reinterpretation of the book of Genesis and of the Bible as a whole. For the biblical Christian, belief in a single Adam is a vital part of his Christian beliefs, and rejection of this belief creates more problems than it solves (see 'Man', pp. 110f.).

2. 'Reject the principle of evolution completely and refuse to allow any scientific evidence to affect our understanding of the Bible.'

In this case we keep science completely separate from revelation, and are unwilling even to consider modifying our interpretation of what the Bible says in the light of the findings of the sciences.

The weakness of this view is that it creates a dichotomy of truth by making a total separation between the truth of revelation and the truth of science. If God is the author of *all* truth, truth must be *one*, and it must be possible to relate the truth of revelation to the truth of science. Another weakness of this view is that it refuses to make any distinction between the *authority* of the Bible itself and the authority of a particular *interpretation*. It allows only one way of interpreting the book of Genesis and gives to this particular interpretation the same authority as to the text of the Bible itself.

3. 'Be discriminating in interpreting the scientific evidence, but keep science and revelation completely separate'.

If we adopt this approach, we refuse to accept evolution as a dogma which cannot be challenged, and we may be critical of some aspects of evolutionary theory. But we also say that, whatever our views about evolution, we must realize that the scientist and the writer of Genesis are approaching the question of the origin of man from completely different standpoints. They are presenting two different views of man which are not necessarily incompatible, but rather complementary. Science is concerned with the 'how?' of creation, whereas the Bible is concerned with the 'why?' Both viewpoints are valid within their own sphere, and must be examined separately in the way that is most appropriate to each.

There is of course a great deal of truth in this, but the problem with this view is that it tends to put science and revelation in two apparently separate, water-tight compartments, and therefore makes it very difficult for the scientist or the non-Christian to examine the truth of Christian beliefs about the origin of man. If there are no points of contact between science and revelation, Christian beliefs have to be accepted 'by faith', and the questioner inevitably wonders how he is to find his 'way in' to the Christian faith.

4. 'Be discriminating in interpreting the scientific evidence, but try as far as possible to reconcile or harmonize science and revelation.'

This is the approach which is most consistent with the biblical understanding of truth which has been outlined in BOOK ONE (pp. 12ff.). It means that we are willing to accept the vulnerability of the Christian faith at this point: if Christian beliefs about man are open to verification, they are also open to falsification. Thus, if we find that there is no possible way of reconciling science and revelation, we must have grave doubts about the truth of these Christian beliefs.

How does this work out in practice?

We have to be *aware of the tentative nature of most scientific theories*. It is only too easy for the scientist to dogmatize about his theories, but then to find that they have to be revised radically in a few years time in the light of new knowledge. If we remember how confidently certain scientific theories were advanced, say 50 years ago, and how much they have had to be revised since then, we shall be less inclined to have an unjustifiable confidence in the theories which are propounded as certain today.

We have to be *willing to revise our interpretation of what the Bible means*. We must acknowledge that we may not always have understood the meaning which the author intended to convey. Revising our *interpretation* of the Bible, however, does not demand a change in our estimate of its *authority*.

We have to be *prepared to suspend judgement* when we find that we cannot make sense of all the different pieces of evidence. This means that we may have to say, 'Yes, there *is* a problem here, and we cannot *at present* see a solution to it. We are not running away from the evidence, and it *is* conceivable that compelling evidence would tell against Christian beliefs at this point and make us reject them. But the evidence is not so decisive as to make us abandon our understanding of the Bible's teaching. We must therefore simply suspend judgement now, and hope to be able to see a solution at some future date.' Far from being an escape or an excuse for lazy minds, this attitude can be a genuine expression of Christian and scientific humility.

Derek Kidner, writing in his Commentary on Genesis about his understanding of the relation between the story of Adam and science:

The exploratory suggestion is only tentative, as it must be, and it is a personal view. It invites correction and a better synthesis; meanwhile it may serve as a reminder that when the revealed and the observed seem hard to combine, it is because we know too little, not too much ...

How are we to interpret the scientific evidence about the origin of man? The problem here is that while one does not need to be a trained historian in order to study the documents concerning the life of Jesus, the vast majority of us find ourselves out of our depth when faced with the intricacies of biological and anthropological studies. The layman also finds that while there may be widespread acceptance of the *theory* of evolution, there are significant gaps in the *data* which ought to support the theory.

Julian Huxley speaks as if we can be reasonably certain about the stages by which man has evolved:

We can distinguish ... three stages in the physical evolution of man. First ... pre-men ... Next came the proto-men ... The broad picture of their prehistory which emerges from modern discoveries is something like this ... And then we reach the fully human phase—man in the proper sense of the word.

Romer, in his book *Man and the Vertebrates* is more cautious about the origins of man:

When he (Homo Sapiens) came is a question to which we have as yet no satisfactory answer ... Nor can we be dogmatic as to his pedigree.

David Lack, an ornithologist:

New species of animals normally arise from isolated populations, not individuals. But it is theoretically possible for one pair to give rise to a new species, and this may well have happened in various land animals that have found their way to remote islands. Hence on biological grounds it is not at all impossible, though it would be unusual, if the population ancestral to man were at one time reduced to a single pair through mortality, or more probably, emigration ...

The available biological and fossil evidence would allow the unity of the human race ... At the same time, the evidence is so scanty that nearly all biologists ... would prefer to leave the question open.

Professor W. R. Thompson:

Darwin himself considered that the idea of evolution is unsatisfactory unless its mechanism can be explained. I agree, but since no one has explained to my satisfaction how evolution could happen I do not feel impelled to say that it has happened. I prefer to say that on this matter our information is inadequate.

There is a great divergence of opinion among biologists, not only about the causes of evolution but even about the actual process. This divergence exists because the evidence is unsatisfactory and does not permit any certain conclusion. It is therefore right and proper to draw the attention of the non-scientific public to the disagreement about evolution. But some recent remarks of evolutionists show that they think this unreasonable. This situation, where scientific men rally to the defence of a doctrine they are unable to define scientifically, much less demonstrate with scientific rigour, attempting to maintain its credit with the public by the suppression of criticism and the elimination of difficulties, is abnormal and undesirable in science.

How far are we influenced by other assumptions which have nothing at all to do with science? If the purely scientific evidence is not decisive one way or the other, it may well be that our general assumptions about God and man enter far more fully than we realize into our thinking about creation and evolution— and this is probably true for the non-Christian as much as for the Christian.

Julian Huxley, for example, confuses purely scientific knowledge and his own philosophical assumptions when he makes the following claim:

Supernatural creation runs counter to the whole of our scientific knowledge . . . To postulate a divine interference with these exchanges of matter and energy at a particular moment in the earth's history is both unnecessary and illogical.

Professor D. S. M. Watson, who was himself a biologist, suggested that the consensus which accepts the theory of evolution (in the third sense noted above) may not be based on purely scientific evidence:

Evolution has been accepted by scientists, not because it has been observed to occur or proved by logical coherent evidence to be true, but because the only alternative, special creation, is clearly unacceptable.

If our general assumptions play such an important part in this question of evolution and creation, we must emphasize again that what is at stake is not simply the question of whether or not man is descended from the apes, but our total view of man. The person who uses evolutionary theory to reject divine creation has not solved all his problems: in fact they are only just beginning, because he is faced with other more personal questions— about the individual and the meaning of life,

about values, relationships, and suffering and evil. (See further BOOK ONE, pp. 21–23; and 'Man', pp. 75ff.).

Can we therefore say if creation is compatible with evolution in any sense?

John Stott gives a personal view:

It seems perfectly possible to reconcile the historicity of Adam with at least some (theistic) evolutionary theory. Many biblical Christians in fact do so, believing them to be not entirely incompatible. To assert the historicity of an original pair who sinned through disobedience is one thing; it is quite another to deny all evolution and to assert the separate and special creation of everything, including both subhuman creatures and Adam's body. The suggestion (for it is no more than this) does not seem to me to be against Scripture and therefore impossible that when God made man in His own image, what He did was to stamp His own likeness on one of the many 'hominids' which appear to have been living at the time.

Speaking hesitatingly as a non-scientist, the extraordinary homogeneity of the human race (physiological and psychological) has always appealed to me as the best available scientific evidence of our common ancestry.

The chief problem in the reconciliation of Scripture and science regarding the origins of mankind concerns the antiquity of Adam. If Adam and Eve were a historical pair, when do you date them? There are two main alternatives.

The first is that they were very early indeed, many thousands of years BC, so that all the cave-drawing, tool-making hominids were descended from them. The difficulty here is that we would then have to postulate immense gaps in the Genesis story and genealogies.

The second alternative is that they were comparatively recent, even as late as 5 or 10,000 BC. This reconstruction begins with the biblical witness that the dawn of civilization, adumbrated in Genesis 4 : 17–22, almost immediately follows the Fall. If this is correct, then even the fairly advanced (although prehistoric) cave-drawing hominids were pre-Adamic. The difficulty here is the claimed scientific evidence that true humans were living in some parts of the world long before this period. But were they Adamic? Anatomically they may have been virtually indistinguishable from modern man; but by what criteria can we judge if they bore the image of God in a biblical sense?

It may be that we shall not be able to solve this problem until we know more precisely what 'the image of God' means, and how much cultural (and even primitive religious!) development may have been possible to pre-Adamic hominids who nevertheless did not possess the divine likeness.

QUESTION FOUR

"What kind of universe do we live in?"

The basic question here is this:

☐ **Has the universe been created by some supernatural Being, or is it an 'uncreated' universe?**

Fred Hoyle:

The universe being what it is the creation issue simply cannot be dodged.

Julian Huxley:

Science has removed the obscuring veil of mystery from many phenomena, much to the benefit of the human race; but it confronts us with a basic and universal mystery—the mystery of existence in general, and of the existence of mind in particular. Why does the world exist?

Following on from the basic question are three further important questions which we should ask:

CAN WE BE SURE THE UNIVERSE IS REALLY THERE?

Bertrand Russell, in his book the *Problems of Philosophy* explains the problem in this way:

Is there a table which has a certain intrinsic nature, and continues to exist when I am not looking, or is the table merely a product of my imagination, a dream-table in a very prolonged dream? This question is of the greatest importance ... If we cannot be sure of the independent existence of objects, we shall be left alone in a desert—it may be that the whole outer world is nothing but a dream, and that we alone exist.

COSMOS OR CHAOS? DESIGN OR CHANCE?

C. E. M. Joad voices a question vital in the development of modern science.

Has the universe ... any design, or is it merely a fortuitous concourse of atoms?

IS THERE SUCH A THING AS BEAUTY?

Is beauty something which is 'there' in the universe? Or is it merely the name which we give to things that please us? Our answer to this question will affect our whole approach to art.

Art historian *H. R. Rookmaaker* writes about aesthetics, the theory of beauty and art:

It was first developed in the same Greece that conceived classical art ... the purpose of art was to reveal the ideal, beauty in the highest form. Where this beauty was to be found and how the artist was to realize it were the great questions in aesthetics.

Before the eighteenth century ... both the artist and the public judged with the same criteria. Since the Enlightenment, this has changed.

In the pages that follow, we take the three basic answers to the question 'What kind of universe do we live in?' and then see where each leads in relation to the three supplementary questions.

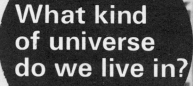

What kind of universe do we live in?

"A universe created by God — but not the God of the Bible"

PAGE 123

"A universe which is not the work of any Creator God"

PAGE 127

"A universe created and sustained by God — the God of the Bible"

PAGE 118

1. THE ANSWER OF BIBLICAL CHRISTIANITY

"The universe was created and is sustained by God—the God of the Bible"

THE UNIVERSE WAS CREATED BY GOD

The universe has been brought into existence by God. It is not eternal.

God created the universe of his own free choice. He was not under any compulsion to create the universe. He was not incomplete without it.

The universe is completely distinct from God; God is transcendent. The universe is not a part of God or an emanation from God, nor is God a part of the universe.

God created the universe 'out of nothing'; there was no raw material already there which he simply brought into order.

All these propositions can be derived from the first chapter of the Bible:

In the beginning God created the heavens and the earth. The earth was without form and void, and darkness was upon the face of the deep; and the Spirit of God was moving over the face of the waters.

And God said, 'Let there be light'; and there was light. And God saw that the light was good; and God separated the light from the darkness . . .

'God created' implies that he created 'out of nothing'.

'God said . . .' implies that the creation of the universe was a free act, a free choice of God.

'God saw . . .' implies that the universe is distinct from God.

The writer of the letter to the Hebrews:

Now faith is the assurance of things hoped for, the conviction of things not seen . . . By faith we understand that the world was created by the word of God, so that what is seen was made out of things which do not appear.

THE UNIVERSE IS SUSTAINED BY GOD

The universe was not only created by God; it is also sustained by him all the time. The universe could not exist without God.

God sustains the universe according to certain 'laws'; but these laws do not work independently of him. Both the normal and the abnormal ordering of natural phenomena are the work of God. God is able to work miracles at any time in his own universe for a particular purpose.

God is responsible for what we *do* know about the universe as well as for what we *do not* know. He is not simply the 'God of the gaps', brought in to account for the areas of life we do not yet understand.

▷ The Psalmist speaks of the activity of God in the regular and 'natural' processes of nature:

Thou makest springs gush forth in the valleys;
   they flow between the hills,
they give drink to every beast of the field;
   the wild asses quench their thirst.
By them the birds of the air have their habitation;
   they sing among the branches.
From thy lofty abode thou waterest the
     mountains;
   the earth is satisfied with the fruit of thy work.

Thou dost cause the grass to grow for the cattle,
 and plants for man to cultivate,
that he may bring forth food from the earth,
 and wine to gladden the heart of man,
oil to make his face shine,
 and bread to strengthen man's heart.

▷ Many writers do not draw any sharp line between God's work in creation and sustaining; they are aspects of the same activity.

It is he who made the earth by his power,
 who established the world by his wisdom,
and by his understanding stretched out the
 heavens.
When he utters his voice there is a tumult of
 waters in the heavens,
 and he makes the mist rise from the ends of
 the earth.
He makes lightenings for the rain,
 and he brings forth the wind from his storehouses.

▷ Several passages in the New Testament speak of the work of the eternal Son in the creation and sustaining of the universe.

He is the image of the invisible God, the first-born of all creation; for in him all things were created, in heaven and on earth, visible and invisible, whether thrones or dominions or principalities or authorities—all things were created through him and for him. He is before all things, and in him all things hold together.

. . . for us there is one God, the Father, from whom are all things and for whom we exist, and one Lord, Jesus Christ, through whom are all things and through whom we exist.

In the beginning was the Word, and the Word was with God, and the Word was God. He was in the beginning with God; all things were made through him, and without him was not anything made that was made.

▷ As originally created, the universe was 'very good':

And God saw everything that he had made, and behold, it was very good.

▷ The fall of Adam in some ways affected even the physical universe:

And to Adam he (God) said,
'Because you have listened to the voice of your
 wife.

and have eaten of the tree
of which I commanded you,
 "You shall not eat of it,"
cursed is the ground because of you;
 in toil you shall eat of it all the days of your life;
thorns and thistles it shall bring forth to you . . .

Paul speaks of the whole creation being 'subjected to futility'.

▷ The person who believes the universe to be created and sustained in this way can respond with amazement, worship and joy:

Bless the Lord, O my soul!
O Lord my God, thou art very great!
Thou art clothed with honour and majesty,
 who coverest thyself with light as with a
 garment,
who hast stretched out the heavens like a tent . . .

▷ This way of thinking about the universe is not inconsistent with the outlook of the modern scientist.

Professor D. M. Mackay, himself a scientist, explains what is meant by the biblical concept of creation and 'upholding':

What sense can we make of this unfamiliar idea of 'holding in being'? . . .
 An imaginative artist brings into being a world of his own invention. He does it normally by laying down patches of paint on canvas, in a certain special order (or disorder!). The *order* in which he lays it down determines the *form* of the world he invents. Imagine now an artist able to bring his world into being, not by laying down paint on canvas, but by producing an extremely rapid succession of sparks of light on the screen of a television tube. (This is in fact the way in which a normal television picture is held in being.) The world he invents is now not static but dynamic, able to change and evolve at will. Both its form and its laws of change (if any) depend on the way in which he orders the sparks of light in space and time. With one sequence he produces a calm landscape with quietly rolling clouds; with another, we are looking at a vigorous cricket match on a village green. The scene is steady and unchanging just for as long as he wills it so; but if he were to cease his activity, his invented world would not become chaotic; it would simply cease to be . . .

Creation in the biblical sense is the 'willing into reality' of the *whole* of our space-time: future, present and past.

THE ANSWER THIS APPROACH GIVES TO OTHER QUESTIONS ABOUT THE UNIVERSE

CAN WE BE SURE THE UNIVERSE IS REALLY THERE?

We can be sure that it is really there because God has created the universe 'outside of' himself. It exists outside of God, and is not part of his mind or of his 'dreaming'.

Praise him, sun and moon,
  praise him, all you shining stars!
Praise him, you highest heavens,
  and you waters above the heavens!
Let them praise the name of the Lord!
  for he commanded and they were created.
And he established them for ever and ever;
  he fixed their bounds which cannot be passed.

COSMOS OR CHAOS? DESIGN OR CHANCE?

The universe is not the product of chance, but of the purpose and design of God. It is God who is responsible for the 'natural' laws of the universe.

After the Flood, God says to Noah,

'While the earth remains, seedtime and harvest, cold and heat, summer and winter, day and night, shall not cease.'

The Psalmist speaks of the stability and reliability of the universe as the work of God:

Thou didst set the earth on its foundations,
  so that it should never be shaken.
Thou didst cover it with the deep as with a
    garment;
  the waters stood above the mountains.
At thy rebuke they fled;
  at the sound of thy thunder they took to flight.
The mountains rose, the valleys sank down
  to the place which thou didst appoint for them.
Thou didst set a bound which they should not
    pass,
  so that they might not again cover the earth.

Belief in the fundamental stability of the universe contributed significantly to the rise of modern science. We may say that the birth of modern science depended on:

  the geometry developed by the Greeks;

  the accumulation of astronomical knowledge from the classical period onwards;

the development of arithmetic and algebra among the Arabs;

the rejection of the Greek approach to science which relied on deduction from first principles rather than observation and experiment;

belief in the regularity of nature, the rationality of God, and the certainty that the universe is there;

the linking of the rational and the empirical, the combination of thought and fact.

Professor Hooykaas in his book *Religion and the Rise of Science*:

The confrontation of Graeco-Roman culture with biblical religion engendered, after centuries of tension, a new science. This science preserved the indispensable parts of the ancient heritage (mathematics, logic, methods of observation and experimentation), but it was directed by different social and methodological conceptions, largely stemming from a biblical world view. Metaphorically speaking, whereas the bodily ingredients of science may have been Greek, its vitamins and hormones were biblical.

C. F. Von Weizacker, a German physicist, summarizes his argument about the connection between modern science and Christian beliefs:

The concept of strict and generally valid laws of nature could hardly have arisen without the Christian concept of creation. Matter in the Platonic sense, which must be 'prevailed upon' by reason, will not obey mathematical laws exactly: matter which God has created from

nothing may well strictly follow the rules which its Creator had laid down for it. In this sense I called modern science a legacy, I might even have said a child, of Christianity.

Professor Donald Mackay writes of how the biblical outlook provides a solid basis for the activity of the scientist today:

The biblical doctrine . . . provides a more stable, rather than a less stable, foundation for our normal scientific expectations, in the stability of the will of a God who is always faithful.

We are emerging from a period of confused conflict during which the biblical doctrine of divine activity seems to have become largely distorted or forgotten. It is in this doctrine, untrimmed by any concessions to the spirit of our age, that I see the basis of the deepest harmony between Christian faith and the scientific attitude. There could be no higher guarantee of our scientific expectations than the rationality and faithfulness of the One who holds in being the stuff and pattern of our world.

IS THERE SUCH A THING AS BEAUTY?

The natural starting-point for the biblical answer to this question is contained in the words of Genesis:

And God saw everything that he had made, and behold it was very good.

Design under the microscope.
Left: *Egg of a Noctuid moth magnified 740 times. Marine diatom, magnified 1,130 times.*
Right: *Detail from the eye of a moth 9,620 magnification.*
Sea sponges.

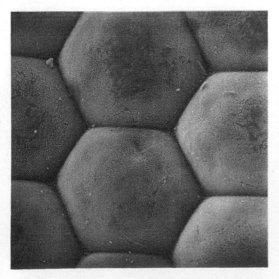

The word 'saw' implies that the universe is distinct from God; and the words that follow give God's description of the universe as he created it: 'it was very good'. Thus the 'goodness' is something inherent in the universe: it is not merely a feeling in the mind of God or of man. The word 'good' cannot refer to moral goodness and must imply at least that there was order and beauty in the universe.

The Christian believes, therefore, that beauty is not simply an idea in his own mind. Beauty is a quality of things as they are; *it is there*—even if we find it hard to define what beauty is or have different opinions about what is beautiful.

H. R. Rookmaaker discusses how the Christian's starting-point affects his understanding of art:

We may now ask: what is Christian art? It is clear that this term cannot mean only art with Biblical or ecclesiastical subject matter. It is quite possible for a painting of a crucifixion, for example, to have an unbiblical content or even be anti-Christian. And it must be clear that the inherent Christian qualities are not bound to one specific style—just as a sermon can be preached in different languages without losing its integrity. Yet it may be true that one style is better suited to 'do the truth' than another—just as Christianity when it enters into the cultural life of people, alters their language and adds new elements to it, and may eliminate certain peculiarities. In a way, the real Christian quality cannot be found by looking for specific elements. In a way, just the opposite is the case. When things are in accordance with God's created possibilities and His will for His world, they are just 'normal'. When love reigns in a community, that community is not strange but healthy. Problems, strangeness, conflicts, tensions, etc. always arise only from sin and its results. In a way, it is, therefore, perhaps even better to speak, not of Christian art, but of truthful art, art that is art in the fulness of the meaning as God intended it to be. Perhaps a still-life of a man like Heda (who worked in the Netherlands in the early seventeenth century) is more intrinsically 'Christian' than a crucifixion by El Greco.

Christian art is not to be defined as art made by a Christian. Christians can sin; they can make (even with the best of intentions) ugly, silly or shallow works of art. And a non-Christian can make beautiful and truthful ones. The criterion is the inherent truth of the work. This fact gives rise to another question: how can such truthful works of art come into being? The answer is that they can be made by man where the artist is fully human and true to his calling. This may happen anywhere and at any time, when man acts out of his created humanness. As soon as sinful elements, or tendencies not in accord with God's will as laid down in His creation, enter into the production of the work of art, its integrity is challenged and . . . ugliness, and mannerisms enter in.

Our being cannot be satisfied unless the thirst for Beauty is quenched. This is why the child of God fights for Beauty and Holiness, because at the Creation man was absolutely beautiful. The beautiful and the good for which Plato was searching will come when the Lord returns.

We must be fully aware that the truth is at stake, the question of whether God's creation is good, whether life is beautiful and worth the living of it, or whether evil is sin and a result of sin. It is the question of whether human life has value, whether our work has meaning, and the question of whether there is meaning outside God and Jesus Christ. It is not an academic question to ask what are the results of over-stepping the first and second commandments, refusing to acknowledge God, refusing to love our neighbour and dragging him through the mire because we do not recognize him in his humanness.

Professor H. R. Rookmaaker, Professor of History of Art at the Free University, Amsterdam.

2. THE ANSWER OF PRIMAL RELIGION AND JUDAISM, ISLAM AND DEISM

"The universe is created by God—but not the God of the Bible"

It is not enough to say that the universe is created by God. We must also define what we mean by the word 'God'. Different concepts of God are bound to lead to different ways of thinking about the universe.

The following are some of the main points in which these different religions differ from the biblical understanding:

☐ some deny that the creation is good;

☐ others see God's relationship with the universe in terms of that between a mechanic and his machine;

☐ some set the 'natural' over against the 'supernatural', seeing them as two distinct spheres.

Primal religion

John Mbiti describes how the African sees the universe:

It emerges clearly that for African peoples, this is a religious universe. Nature in the broadest sense of the word is not an empty impersonal object or phenomenon: it is filled with religious significance. Man gives life even where natural objects and phenomena have no biological life. God is seen in and behind these objects and phenomena: they are His creation, they manifest Him, they symbolize His being and presence. The invisible world is symbolized or manifested by these visible and concrete phenomena and objects of nature. The invisible world presses hard upon the visible: one speaks of the other, and African peoples 'see' that invisible universe when they look at, hear or feel the visible and tangible world.

Judaism

Because they are based on the Old Testament, Jewish beliefs can come close to the Christian understanding. (See pp. 118ff.)

Islam

Some of the most beautiful verses of the Qur'an are about the creative work of God in the universe.

We spread out the earth and set upon it immovable mountains. We brought forth in it all kinds of delectable plants. A lesson and an admonition to penitent men.
We send down blessed water from the sky with which We bring forth gardens and the harvest grain, and tall palm-trees laden with clusters of dates, a sustenance for men; thereby giving new life to some dead land.
We have decked the heavens with constellations and guarded them from all accursed devils. Eavesdroppers are pursued by fiery comets.
We have spread out the earth and set upon it immovable mountains. We have planted it with every seasonable fruit, thus providing sustenance for man and beast. We hold the store of every blessing and send it down in appropriate measure. We let loose the fertilizing winds and bring down water from the sky for you to drink; its stores are beyond your reach.

Deism

In order to understand how Deism developed it is important to see how Christian ideas about the universe were gradually contaminated by Greek ideas.

Hooykaas describes the difference between the biblical view of the universe and that of the ancient Greeks:

There is a radical contrast between the deification of nature in pagan religion and, in a rationalized form, in Greek philosophy, and de-deification of nature in the Bible. By contrast with the nature-worship of its neighbours, the religion of Israel was a unique phenomenon. The God of Israel, by his word, brings forth all things out of nothingness. He is truly all-powerful: He was not opposed by any matter that had to be forced into order, and He did not have to reckon with eternal Forms; His sovereign will alone created and sustains the world. In the first chapter of Genesis it is made evident that absolutely nothing, except God, has any claim to divinity; even the sun and the moon, supreme gods of the neighbouring peoples, are set in their places between the herbs and the animals and are brought into the service of mankind. The personal gods of the Greeks had an origin, in spite of their immortality. The God of the Bible is the only god who is immutable and eternal, unlike all created things which are liable to change and final destruction. Nothing else has divine power, not even by delegation: 'The Lord is one; there is no one but He.'

The New Testament proclaims again the message that there is no eternal cycle of nature or cycle of history. The history of the world moves towards its final destination and heaven and earth are destined to fall back into the nothingness from which they once emerged. Not only the creating, but also the upholding of the world belongs to God alone; that is to say, Jahveh is not a deistic supreme being who, after the creative act, leaves everything to the innate laws of nature, and He does not withdraw, like a platonic demiurge, into 'the way of being that belongs solely to Him.' He remains for ever the will and power behind all events . . . In total contradiction to pagan religion, nature is not a deity to be feared and worshipped, but a work of God to be admired, studied and managed. When we compare pagan and biblical religions, we find a fundamental contrast between the ideas concerning God and man which have emerged. In the Bible God and nature are no longer both opposed to man, but God and man together confront nature. The denial that God coincides with nature implies the denial that nature is god-like.

Some of these ideas from pagan religions

were carried over into the thinking of many Christians in the Middle Ages.

Nature was considered as a semi-independent power, and when things happened according to nature, this meant that they followed a pattern that seemed rational to the human mind, one which had been discovered by Aristotle . . . In the Middle Ages . . . the biblical view was only superimposed on, and did not overcome, the Aristotelian conception. The regular order of nature was considered to be something instituted by God, but liable to be over-ruled by Him in a *super*-natural way (the term is significant) when performing a miracle. Thomas Aquinas considered one of the useful functions of natural philosophy to be to enable us to distinguish that which belongs only to God (for example miracles, or the origin of things) from that which belongs to nature.

The lengths to which the devaluation of the natural universe could go is illustrated in these words from a medieval churchman, *Lallemant:*

We should marvel at nothing in Nature except the redeeming death of Christ.

This is a thoroughly *un*-Christian sentiment, and we are not surprised to learn that these words contain the essence of what Nietzsche detested about Christian sainthood.

Combined with this was the belief that the material universe is somehow part of the Satanic order.

Basil Willey, speaking of the medieval idea of science as 'the forbidden knowledge':

The Faustus legend testifies to the strength of the fascinated dread with which the Middle Ages had thought of natural science . . . 'Nature' had, in quite a special sense, been consigned to the Satanic order.

For practical purposes . . . we may perhaps take the later fifteenth and the sixteenth centuries as the epoch of the rebirth of confidence in 'Nature' . . .

This recrudescence of confidence in Nature was immensely strengthened by the scientific movement of the Renaissance, which reclaimed the physical world from its traditional association with Satan.

When we come to the seventeenth century, we find that as the Creator recedes more and more into the background, 'Nature' itself becomes almost like a god.

Basil Willey, writing about John Locke:

Locke's deity, in a word, is that of the contemporary reconcilers of science and religion, such as Glanvill or Boyle, and that of the eighteenth century as a whole—a Deity to be approached by demonstration, and whose existence, proclaimed by the spacious firmament on high, is as well attested as any proof in Euclid. This phase of religious thought, with which the term 'Deism' is often associated, was rendered possible largely by the completeness with which the findings of seventeenth-century science, up to that date, could be made to fuse with the inherited religious certainties. Newton's Great Machine needed a Mechanic, and religion was prepared ahead with that which could serve this purpose. Everywhere that science had so far disclosed was nothing but 'order, harmony, and beauty'; and finally the incomparable Newton had linked the infinitely great and the infinitely little in one inspired synthesis. The mighty maze was not without a plan, and Locke could declare with perfect candour that 'the words of Nature in every part of them sufficiently evidence a Deity'.

Shaftesbury in the seventeenth century addressed 'Nature' in this way:

O Glorious *Nature*! supremely Fair, and sovereignly Good! All-loving and All-lovely, All-divine! . . . Whose every single Work affords an ampler scene, and is a nobler Spectacle than all which ever Art presented! O mighty *Nature*! Wise Substitute of Providence! impower'd *Creatress*! Or Thou impowering Deity, supreme Creator! Thee I invoke, and Thee alone adore. To Thee this solitude, this place, these Rural Meditations are sacred . . .

Basil Willey comments on the significance of Shaftesbury:

Thus far . . . had the divinization of Nature proceeded a hundred years before Wordsworth. Already the injunction 'First follow Nature' had passed beyond the region of ethics and poetics,

and the Wordsworthian nature-religion can be regarded, less as something wholly new, than as the culmination of a process which had been implicit in the 'humanist' tradition ever since the Renaissance.
Ever since the Renaissance the Creation had been steadily gaining in prestige as the 'art of God', the universal divine Scripture which 'lies expans'd unto the eyes of all'. The emotion of the numinous formerly associated with super-nature, had become attached to Nature itself; and by the end of the eighteenth century the divinity, the sacredness of nature was, to those affected by this tradition, almost a first datum of consciousness.

Wordsworth's understanding of God and his relation to the universe is summed up in this passage from *Mark Rutherford*, writing about the effect which Wordsworth's Lyrical Ballads had on him:

God is nowhere formally deposed, and Wordsworth would have been the last man to say that he had lost his faith in the God of his fathers. But his real God is not the God of the Church, but the God of the hills, the abstraction Nature, and to this my reverence was transferred.

Charles Darwin at the time when he wrote *The Origin of Species* (published in 1859) described himself as a theist:

When thus reflecting, I feel compelled to look to a First Cause having an intelligent mind in some degree analogous to that of man; and I deserve to be called a Theist.

But disbelief gradually crept over him, and in his *Autobiography* (written in 1876) he wrote:

The mystery of the beginning of all things is insoluble to us; and I for one must be content to remain an Agnostic.

THE ANSWER THIS APPROACH GIVES TO OTHER QUESTIONS ABOUT THE UNIVERSE

Other questions on the universe are not too difficult for those who believe in a personal Creator. But for the Deist they may become real problems as God recedes into the background.

HOW CAN WE BE SURE THE UNIVERSE IS REALLY THERE

The existence of a personal Creator is

generally held to guarantee that the tangible world is real.

Descartes, however, with his principle of systematic doubt was forced to question the existence of the external universe. The only way in which he could solve the problem for himself was to say that we all feel that the material world really exists outside of ourselves. And it is inconceivable that God should give us this feeling if it is not in accordance with the truth, since God would not deceive us. Therefore, the external world must exist. So Descartes uses God as a guarantee that our convictions about the universe are true.

COSMOS OR CHAOS? DESIGN OR CHANCE?

Those who believe in the existence of a Creator usually believe there is design and order in the universe.

But the vaguer the belief in the existence of God, the more doubtful the concept of design and order, as *Charles Darwin* shows:

My theology is a simple muddle; I cannot look at the universe as the result of blind chance, yet I can see no evidence of beneficent design, or indeed of design of any kind, in details.

IS THERE SUCH A THING AS BEAUTY

The Deist believes that the creation is the handiwork of God, and therefore that its beauty is something given to it by God. But as the relationship between 'Nature' and God becomes more and more tenuous, beauty becomes less and less dependent on God.

Wordsworth found that his experience of ecstasy over Nature did not last. He could not find lasting peace and satisfaction through his attitude to Nature, and finally he was forced to turn to other things for inspiration.

Basil Willey writes:

In the later life of our greatest 'Nature' poet . . . there is a steady retreat towards the religious sources of his mysticism, and grace supplants the visionary gleam.

It is significant that Wordsworth to some extent abandoned Nature himself, as if he had discovered its inadequacy; abandoned it first for 'Duty' and then for Faith.

It would seem that beauty divorced from the God who has created beautiful things cannot long remain real and satisfying.

Charles Darwin, in his *Autobiography*, speaks

of how in later years he began to lose some of his appreciation of beauty. This may have been partly the effect of old age and sickness; but there is probably also some connection with his general understanding of the universe.

My mind seems to have become a kind of machine for grinding general laws out of large collections of facts, but why this should have caused the atrophy of that part of the brain alone, on which the higher tastes depend, I cannot conceive.

In my Journal I wrote that whilst standing in the midst of the grandeur of a Brazilian forest, 'it is not possible to give an adequate idea of the higher feelings of wonder, admiration, and devotion which fill and elevate the mind'. I well remember my conviction that there is more in man than the mere breath of his body; but now the grandest scenes would not cause any such conviction and feelings to arise in my mind. It may be truly said that I am like a man who has become colour-blind.

Nature can be beautiful and horrific at the same time.

3. THE ANSWER OF HINDUISM, EUROPEAN THINKERS, AND SOME MODERN THEOLOGIANS

"The universe is not the work of any Creator God"

Hinduism

Radhakrishnan, writing in *the Hindu View of Life* is content to remain agnostic about the origin of the universe:

The hypothesis of creation is a weak one, and it assumes that God lived alone for some time and then suddenly it occurred to him to have company, when he put forth the world. The theory of manifestation is not more satisfying, for it is difficult to know how the finite can manifest the infinite. If we say that God is transformed into the world, the question arises whether it is the whole of God that is transformed or only a part. If it is the whole, then there is no God beyond the universe and we lapse into the lower pantheism. If it is only a part, then it means that God is capable of being partitioned. We cannot keep one part of God above and another part below. It would be like taking half the fowl for cooking, leaving the other half for laying eggs. Samkara believes that it is not possible to determine logically the relation between God and the world. He asks us to hold fast both ends. It does not matter if we are not able to find out where they meet.

The history of philosophy in India as well as Europe has been one long illustration of the inability of the human mind to solve the mystery of the relation of God to the world. The greatest thinkers are those who admit the mystery and comfort themselves by the idea that the human mind is not omniscient. Samkara in the East and Bradley in the West adopt this wise attitude of agnosticism. We have the universe with its distinctions. It is not self-sufficient. It rests on something else, and that is the Absolute. The relation between the two is a mystery.

He rejects an extreme form of pantheism, but there is still no possibility of the existence of a personal Creator God.

The Hindu view rebels against the cold and formal conception of God who is external to the world, and altogether remote and transcendent. The natural law of the world is but a working of God's sovereign purpose. The uniformity of nature, the orderliness of the cosmos, and the steady reaching forward and upward of the course of evolution proclaim not the unconscious throbbing of a soulless engine, but the directing mind of an all-knowing spirit. The indwelling of God in the universe does not mean the identity of God with the universe. According to the latter view God is so immanent in everything that we have only to open our eyes to see God in it, but also there is nothing of God left outside the whole of things. God lies spread out before us. The world is not only a revelation, but an exhaustive revelation of God. Hindu thought takes care to emphasise the transcendent character of the Supreme. 'He bears the world but is by no means lost in it.' The world is in God and not God in the world. In the universe we have the separate existence of the individuals. Whether the divine spark burns dimly or brightly in the individual, the sparks are distinct from the central fire from which they issue.

European thinkers

Ernst Cassirer describes how new ways of thinking in the fifteenth century called in question the traditional Christian belief:

All this is suddenly called into question by the new cosmology. Man's claim to being the centre of the universe has lost its foundation. Man is placed in an infinite space in which his being seems to be a single and vanishing point. He is surrounded by a mute universe, by a world that is silent to his religious feelings and to his deepest moral demands.

He quotes some words of *Montaigne* which, he says, give the clue to the whole subsequent development of the modern theory of man.

'Let man . . . make me understand by the force of his reason, upon what foundation he has built those great advantages he thinks he has over other creatures. Who has made him believe that this admirable notion of the celestial arch, the eternal light of those luminaries that roll so high over his head, the wondrous and fearful motions of that infinite ocean, should be established and continue so many ages for his service and convenience? Can anything be imagined so ridiculous, that this miserable and wretched creature, who is not so much as master of himself, but subject to the injuries of all things, should call himself master and emperor of the world, of which he has not power to know the least part, much less to command the whole?

'Whoever shall represent to his fancy, as in a picture, the great image of our mother nature, portrayed in her full majesty and lustre; whoever in her face shall read so general and so constant a variety, whoever shall observe himself in that figure, and not himself but a whole kingdom, no bigger than the least touch of a pencil, in comparison of the whole, that man alone is able to value things according to their true estimate and grandeur.'

Montaigne's words give us the clue to the whole subsequent development of the modern theory of man. Modern philosophy and modern science had to accept the challenge contained in these words. They had to prove that the new cosmology, far from enfeebling or obstructing the power of human reason, establishes and confirms this power. Such was the task of the combined efforts of the metaphysical systems of the sixteenth and seventeenth centuries. These systems go different ways, but they are all directed toward one and the same end. They strive, so to speak, to turn the apparent curse of the new cosmology into a blessing.

Julian Huxley:

In the evolutionary pattern of thought there is no longer either need or room for the supernatural. The earth was not created: it evolved. So did all the animals and plants that inhabit it, including our human selves, mind and soul as well as brain and body. So did religion.

All aspects of reality are subject to evolution, from atoms and stars to fish and flowers, from fish and flowers to human societies and values—indeed . . . all reality is a single process of evolution.

A. J. Ayer:

While I believe that there can be an explanation in mundane terms for anything that happens within the world, I do not think it makes sense or ask for an explanation of the existence to characteristics of the world as a whole.

Jacob Bronowski indicates some of the assumptions of much scientific thinking today:

We have to accept the subtle but closely woven evidence that man is not different in kind from other forms of life; that living matter is not different in kind from dead matter; and therefore that a man is an assembly of atoms that obeys natural laws of the same kind that a star does . . .

The atoms in the brain as much as those in the body constitute a mechanism, which ticks with the same orderly regularity, and abides by similar laws, as any other interlocking constellation of atoms. Men have uneasily pushed this thought out of their heads because they wanted to avoid the conflict with their rooted conviction that man is a free agent who follows only the promptings of his own will. But we cannot hide this contradiction for ever.

My fundamental assumption . . . is that man is a part of nature.

This simple proposition seems innocent enough, and neutral. Nearly all educated men accept it now . . . In the latter half of the twentieth century, it seems self-evident to say that man is a part of nature, in the same sense that a stone is, or a cactus, or a camel . . . Yet this bland proposition contains the explosive charge which in this century has split open the self-assurance of western man.

We sense that there is no break in the continuity of nature. At one end of her range, the star has been linked with the stone; and at the other end, man has been put among the animals . . . An unbroken line runs from the stone to the cactus and on to the camel, and there is no supernatural leap in it. No special act of creation, no spark of life was needed to turn dead matter into living things.

D. H. Lawrence expresses his dissatisfaction with an arid naturalism:

Give me the mystery! And let the world live again for me!

The universe is dead for us, and how is it to come alive again? 'Knowledge' has killed the sun, making it a ball of gas with spots; 'Knowledge' has killed the moon—it is a dead little earth fretted with extinct craters as with smallpox; the machine has killed the earth for us . . . How, out of all this, are we to get back the grand orbs of the soul's heavens, that fill us with unspeakable joy? How are we to get back Apollo, and Attis, Demeter, Persephone, and the halls of Dis? We've got to get them back, for they are the world our soul, our great consciousness, lives in. The world of reason and science . . . this is the dry and sterile little world the abstracted mind inhabits . . . Two ways of knowing, for man, are knowing in terms of apartness, which is mental, rational, scientific, and knowing in terms of togetherness, which is religious and poetic.

Albert Camus, especially in his earlier works, writes freely of his sensations in enjoying nature:

The world is beautiful and, outside it, there is no salvation.

There is but one love in this world. To embrace a woman's body is also to retain, close to one, that strange joy which descends from the sky to the sea . . . I love this life with abandon and I want to speak of it freely; it fills me with pride at my human fate.

Some modern theologians

Teilhard de Chardin's thought is completely dominated by the concept of evolution, which he regards not simply as a biological principle, but as an all-inclusive philosophy. Although he speaks of God as Creator, it would seem that even God is in a sense subject to this same law of evolution.

One might well become impatient or lose heart at the sight of so many minds (and not mediocre ones either) remaining today still closed to the idea of evolution, if the whole of history were not there to pledge to us that a truth once seen, even by a single mind, always ends up by imposing itself on the totality of human consciousness. For many, evolution is still only transformism, and transformism is only an old Darwinian hypothesis as local and dated as Laplace's conception of the solar system or Wegener's Theory of Continental Drift. Blind indeed are those who do not see the sweep of a movement whose orbit infinitely transcends the natural sciences and has successively invaded and conquered the surrounding territory—chemistry, physics, sociology and even mathematics and the history of religions. One after the other all the fields of human knowledge have been shaken and carried away by the same under-water current in the direction of the study of some *development*. Is evolution a theory, a system or a hypothesis? It is much more: it is a general condition to which all theories, all hypotheses, all systems must bow and which they must satisfy henceforward if they are to be thinkable and true. Evolution is a light illuminating all facts, a curve that all lines must follow.

If as a result of some interior revolution, I were successively to lose my faith in Christ, my faith in a personal God, my faith in the Spirit, I think I would continue to believe in the World. The World (the value, the infallibility, the goodness of the World); that, in the final analysis, is the first and last thing in which I believe.

John Robinson seems to reject not only popular distortions of Christian beliefs, but the whole supernaturalism of historic Christianity:

A dualist model of the universe is out. Whether looked at from the outside or the inside, reality for us is all of a piece. As Van Peursen puts it, 'There is no supernatural reality, high and lofty, above us. There is only that reality which concerns us directly concretely.' There is no second storey to the universe, no realm of the divine over and above or behind the processes of nature and history which perforates this world or breaks it up by supernatural intervention.

What he puts in place of the historic Christian belief is the concept of a 'personalizing' universe:

The doctrine of creation *ex nihilo* does not exist to assert that there was a time or a state in which a Being called God was there alone and that 'out of nothing' he made the world—though he might not have done. That is to indulge in a tissue of mythopoeic speculation. What it asserts is that there is nothing in the whole range of experience which cannot be interpreted in terms of God or which requires any other ground. That is to say, there is no aspect of nature or history, however resistant to personal categories, that is not *ultimately* to be seen in terms of spirit, freedom, love. From the start, affirms the believer, this is a 'personalizing' universe, in the sense that the whole is to be understood as a process making for personality and beyond.

What essentially the Christian faith is asserting is that in and through all the processes of nature and history there is a personal outcome to be traced and a love to be met which nothing can finally defeat.

God is to be met in, with and under, not apart from, response to the world and the neighbour.

He vigorously rejects the accusation that he is propounding pantheism, or that he is seeking to abolish transcendence. But what he does, in effect, is simply to reinterpret the meaning of the word 'transcendence' in accordance with the belief he has outlined.

The implication of this is not the abolition of the transcendent in pure naturalism: it is an apprehension of the transcendent as given in, with and under the immanent. 'The beyond' is to be found always and only 'in the midst', as a function and dimension of it. This is a shot-silk universe, spirit and matter, inside and outside, divine and human, shimmering like aspects of one reality which cannot be separated or divided.

John Wren-Lewis:

The first thing to be said about this doctrine (of God as Creator of the world *ex nihilo*) is that it is in no sense . . . the starting-point of Christian belief . . .

   If . . . the idea of God originated from the experience of creative love in personal life (a con-clusion much more in line with the findings of modern anthropology) then Tennyson's question 'Are God and nature then at strife?' arises at once, for the system of nature as we ordinarily experience it has no place for such personal values as love, beauty or justice. Against this background, the assertion that nothing exists apart from God's creative action becomes *a supreme declaration of faith in man's ability to change the world if he acts upon it in the power of love:* there is no *thing*, no systematic order, apart from personal action—only potentiality.

THE ANSWER THIS APPROACH GIVES TO OTHER QUESTIONS ABOUT THE UNIVERSE

CAN WE BE SURE THE UNIVERSE IS REALLY THERE?

The eastern religions do not believe in a personal Creator God, and for them this is a very real question. Their general answer has been to say that we *cannot* be sure that there is anything there. We cannot be sure that our senses are not deceiving us.

Arthur Koestler:

The traditional Eastern way of looking at things is to deny that there *are* things independently from the act of looking. The objects of conscious-ness cannot be separated from the conscious subject; observer and observed are a single, indivisible, fluid reality, as they are at the dawn of consciousness in the child, and in the culture dominated by magic. The external world has no existence in its own right; it is a function of the senses; but that function exists only in so far as it is registered by consciousness, and consequently has no existence in its own right.

In *Sartre's* novel *Nausea*, Roquentin describes one aspect of his Nausea—the awareness of the bare existence of everything.

So this is the Nausea: this blinding revelation? To think how I've racked my brains over it! To think how much I've written about it! Now I know: I exist—the world exists—and I know that the world exists. That's all. But I don't care. It's strange that I should care so little about every-thing: it frightens me. It's since that day when I wanted to play ducks and drakes. I was going to throw that pebble, I looked at it and that was when it all began; I felt that it *existed*. And then, after that, there were other Nauseas; every now and then objects start existing in your hand.

But these things lose their names and their identity, and everything appears with a 'frightening, obscene nakedness':

Things have broken free from their names. They are there, grotesque, stubborn, gigantic, and it seems ridiculous to call them seats or say any-thing at all about them: I am in the midst of Things, which cannot be given names. Alone, wordless, defenceless, they surround me, under me, behind me, above me. They demand nothing, they don't impose themselves, they are there . . .

   All of a sudden, there it was, as clear as day: existence had suddenly unveiled itself . . . the diversity of things, their individuality, was only an appearance, a veneer. This veneer had melted, leaving soft, monstrous masses, in disorder—naked, with a frightening, obscene nakedness.

Lewis Carroll in *Through the Looking Glass* conveys the same frightening sense of things losing their identity in the account of Alice as she enters the wood where things lose their names.

'This must be the wood,' she said thoughtfully to herself, 'where things have no names. I wonder what'll become of *my* name when I go in? I shouldn't like to lose it at all . . . She was rambling on in this way when she reached the wood: it looked very cool and shady. 'Well, at any rate. it's a great comfort,' she said as she stepped under the trees, 'after being so hot, to get into the—into the—into *what*?' she went on, rather surprised at not being able to think of the word. 'I mean to get under the—under the—under *this*, you know!' putting her hand on the trunk of the tree. 'What *does* it call itself? I do believe it's got no name—why, to be sure it hasn't!'

She stood silent for a minute, thinking: then she suddenly began again. 'Then it really *has* happened, after all! And now, who am I? I *will* remember, if I can! I'm determined to do it!' But being determined didn't help her much, and all she could say, after a great deal of puzzling, was 'L, I *know* it begins with L!'

Just then a Fawn came wandering by: it looked at Alice with its large gentle eyes, but didn't seem at all frightened. 'Here then! Here then!' Alice said, as she held out her hand and tried to stroke it; but it only started back a little, and then stood looking at her again.

'What do you call yourself?' the Fawn said at last. Such a soft, sweet voice it had!

'I wish I knew!' thought poor Alice. She answered, rather sadly, 'Nothing just now.'

'Think again,' it said: 'that won't do.'

Alice thought, but nothing came of it. 'Please, would you tell me what *you* call yourself?' she said timidly. 'I think that might help a little.'

'I'll tell you, if you'll come a little further on,' the Fawn said. 'I can't remember here.'

So they walked on together through the wood, Alice with her arms clasped lovingly round the soft neck of the Fawn, till they came out into another open field, and here the Fawn gave a sudden bound into the air, and shook itself free from Alice's arms. 'I'm a Fawn!' it cried out in a voice of delight. 'And, dear me, you're a human child!' . . .

Alice Through the Looking Glass ends with Alice trying to discuss a vital question with the kitten. For many this is not mere fantasy; it is a very real and serious question: how can we be sure that we are not dreaming all the time? How can we be sure that we are not a part of someone else's dream?

'So I wasn't dreaming, after all,' she said to herself, 'unless—unless we're all part of the same dream. Only I do hope it's *my* dream, and not the Red King's. I don't like belonging to another person's dream,' she went on in a rather complaining tone. . .

'Now, Kitty, let's consider who it was that dreamed it all. This is a serious question, my dear, and you should *not* go on licking your paw like that—as if Dinah hadn't washed you this morning! You see, Kitty, it *must* have been either me or the Red King. He was part of my dream, of course—but then I was part of his dream, too! *Was* it the Red King, Kitty? You were his wife, my dear, so you ought to know—Oh, Kitty, *do* help me to settle it! I'm sure your paw can wait!' But the provoking kitten only began on the other paw, and pretended it hadn't heard the question.

Which do *you* think it was?

Life, what is it but a dream?

Francis Schaeffer describes the following conversation with an atheist who realized he had no reason for believing that anything is there outside of himself:

He was an atheist, and when he found out I was a pastor he anticipated an evening's entertainment, so he started in. But it did not go quite that way. Our conversation showed me that he understood the implications of his position and tried to be consistent concerning them. After about an hour I saw that he wanted to draw the discussion to a close, so I made one last point which I hoped he would never forget, not because I hated him, but because I cared for him as a fellow human being. I noticed that he had his lovely little Jewish wife with him. She was very beautiful and full of life and it was easy to see, by the attention he paid to her, that he really loved her.

Just as they were about to go to their cabin, in the romantic setting of the boat sailing across the Mediterranean and a beautiful full moon shining outside, I finally said to him, 'When you take your wife into your arms at night, can you be sure she is there?'

I hated to do it to him, but I did it knowing that he was a man who would really understand the implications of the question and not forget. His eyes turned, like a fox caught in a trap, and he shouted at me, 'No, I am not always sure she is there', and walked into his cabin.

COSMOS OR CHAOS? DESIGN OR CHANCE?

If there is no Creator God who gives order to the universe, it is far from self-evident that the universe is an ordered system.

Bertrand Russell.

Academic philosophers, ever since the time of Parmenides, have believed that the world is a unity . . . The most fundamental of my beliefs is that this is rubbish . . . I think the universe is all spots and jumps, without unity, without continuity, without coherence or orderliness.

Jules Romanes:

I find it difficult to say anything certain or even plausible on the subject (of God). It can at most be suggested that the God of traditional metaphysics, perfect, infinite, creator, and all-powerful ruler of the universe, is highly improbable. The probability continues to decrease as our knowledge of the universe grows and becomes richer. The crude, fortuitous, elements of the universe, its intolerable contradictions, the frightful, gratuitous waste inherent in it—to cite only a few shortcomings among many—scarcely make it seem possible that an intelligence has from the beginning been in perfect control of the cosmos in all its respects.

Colin Wilson:

For the bourgeois, the world is fundamentally an orderly place, with a disturbing element of the irrational, the terrifying, which his preoccupation with the present usually permits him to ignore. For the Outsider, the world is not rational, not orderly. When he asserts his sense of anarchy in the face of the bourgeois' complacent acceptance, it is not simply the need to cock a snook at respectability that provokes him; it is a distressing sense *that truth must be told at all costs*, otherwise there can be no hope for an ultimate restoration of order. Even if there seems no room for hope, the truth must be told.

Jacob Bronowski believes that modern science has gone beyond the concept of a thoroughly ordered cosmos. But he believes that the concept of chance may provide the clue which will deliver us from despair:

The statistical concept of chance may come . . . to unify the scattered pieces of science in the future . . . We are on the threshold of another scientific revolution. The concept of natural law is changing. The laws of chance seem at first glance to be lawless. But I have shown . . . that they can be formulated with as much rigour as the laws of cause. Certainly they can be seen already to cover an infinitely wider field of human experience in nature and in society . . . Chance has a helpless ring in our ears. But the laws of chance are lively, vigorous, and human, and they may give us again that forward look which in the last half century has so tragically lowered its eyes.

Von Weizacker points out the strange irony in the fact that modern science, while it owes its existence partly to Christian beliefs about the universe, has now discarded some of these beliefs.

I called modern science a legacy, I might even have said a child of Christianity. But then I had to show how science lost contact with its parental home. Children can experience the death of their parents.

It is one thing to speak of chance as a theory in science. It is quite different when chance invades the life of the individual.

In *Sartre*'s *Nausea*, Roquentin experiences the feeling that there are no fixed natural laws: 'anything could happen'.

It is out of laziness, I suppose, that the world looks the same day after day. Today it seemed to want to change. And in that case, *anything, anything* could happen.

The idiots. It horrifies me to think that I am going to see their thick, self-satisfied faces again. They make laws, they write Populist novels, they get married, they commit the supreme folly of having children. And meanwhile, vast, vague Nature has slipped into their town, it has infiltrated everywhere, into their houses, into their offices, into themselves. It doesn't move, it lies low, and they are right inside it, they breathe it, and they don't see it, they imagine that it is outside, fifty miles away. I *see* it, that Nature, I *see* it . . . I know that its submissiveness is laziness, I know that it has no laws, that what they consider its constancy doesn't exist. It has nothing but habits and it may change those tomorrow.

An absolute panic took hold of me. I no longer knew where I was going. I ran along the docks, I turned into the deserted streets of the Beauvoisis district: the houses watched by flight with their mournful eyes. I kept saying to myself in anguish: 'Where shall I go? Where shall I go? *Anything* can happen.' . . .

Martin Esslin speaks of the 'terrible stability of the world' as seen in *Samuel Beckett*'s plays, where time loses all meaning.

Waiting is to experience the action of time, which is constant change. And yet, as nothing real ever happens, that change is in itself an illusion. The ceaseless activity of time is self-defeating, purposeless, and therefore null and void. The more things change, the more they are the same. That is the terrible stability of the world. 'The tears of the world are a constant quantity. For each one who begins to weep, somewhere else another stops.' One day is like another, and when we die, we might never have existed.

IS THERE SUCH A THING AS BEAUTY?

Many are not conscious of any problem here simply because they are still living off the legacy of Christian beliefs.

C. E. M. Joad, writing in the days when he was still an agnostic, speaks of how he thinks of beauty and its significance.

If . : . beauty means something, yet we must not seek to interpret the meaning. If we glimpse the unutterable, it is unwise to try to utter it, nor should we seek to invest with significance that which we cannot grasp. Beauty in terms of our human meanings *is* meaningless. It does not mean that the universe is good, that life has a purpose, that God is in heaven, or even that the human and the friendly conditions and underlies the alien and the brutal . . .

But we still look for meaning in life and above all for meaning in beauty, meaning that we can somehow relate to ourselves . . . To realize . . . the vast indifference of the universe to man, is the beginning of the wisdom of an adult mind.

Somerset Maugham for some years believed that it is beauty alone which gives meaning to life, but later came to reject this belief:

The work of art, I decided, was the crowning product of human activity, and the final justification for all the misery, the endless toil, and the frustrated strivings of humanity. So that Michelangelo might paint certain figures on the ceiling of the Sistine Chapel, so that Shakespeare might write certain speeches and Keats his odes, it seemed to me worth while that untold millions should have lived and suffered and died. And though I modified this extravagance later by including the beautiful life among the works of art that alone gave a meaning to life, it was still beauty that I valued. All these notions I have long since abandoned.

He sees beauty not as something objective and lasting, but as relative and temporary.

The only conclusion is that beauty is relative to the needs of a particular generation, and that to examine the things we consider beautiful for qualities of absolute beauty is futile. If beauty is one of the values that give life significance it is something that is constantly changing and thus cannot be analysed, for we can as little feel the beauty our ancestors felt as we can smell the rose they smelt.

For many today, however, there is no longer any such thing as beauty. In *Sartre*'s *Nausea* Roquentin has repeated experiences of nausea. He cannot speak about 'beauty', since for him there is **no** such thing as 'beauty'; there can only be things which produce a pleasant sensation in him.

I went out and walked along the streets as usual . . . And then, all of a sudden, as I was pushing open the gate of the municipal park, I had the impression that something was signalling me. The park was bare and empty. But . . . how shall I put it? It didn't have its usual look, it was smiling at me. I stayed for a moment leaning against the gate, and then, suddenly, I realized it

was Sunday. It was there in the trees, on the lawns, like a faint smile.

Henry Moore's conception of his work is summed up in this way by *Herbert Read*. The old ideal of beauty is rejected.

The modern artist has dared—and no one has been more explicit than Moore about his intentions in this respect—to abandon the ideal of beauty and to establish in its place the ideal of vitality. But vitality is but a provisional word which serves to disguise the fact that we do not know and cannot measure the nature of life. Beauty is no mystery: it can be presented in geometrical formulas, by calculated proportions. But the vital process is intangible, and can be represented only in symbolic forms—forms symbolic of the essential nature of living organisms and forms symbolic of the racial experiences that have left an impress on our mental condition—the archetypal patterns of birth and death, of social conflict and tragic drama.

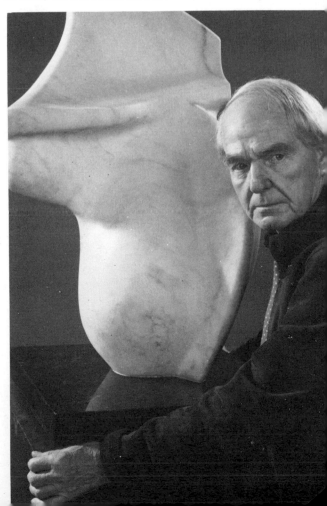

Sir Henry Moore, British sculptor.

Marc:

I found man to be ugly—animals are much more beautiful . . . but in them too I discovered so much that I felt to be appalling and ugly that my representations of them instinctively, out of inner necessity, became increasingly more schematic, more abstract. Each year trees, flowers, the earth, everything showed me aspects that were more hateful, more repulsive, until I came at last to a full realization of the ugliness, the uncleanness of nature.

Karel Appel:

I do not paint, I hit.
Painting is destruction.

Lucebert, the Dutch poet:

Beauty has burned its face.

Professor H. R. Rookmaaker, an art historian, speaks of the consensus in much modern art and the way in which it is interpreted by many critics.

Modern art, in a very direct and special way, speaks of the same things as Existentialist Philosophy. It is antinomian or gnostic and often preaches an anarchistic mysticism. Its expressions are often strange and not understandable at first encounter. In a way this is fortunate, for then at least a number of people just pass by. On the other hand it is not so fortunate; for if men turn all laws upside-down, beauty and the possibility of communication fall out. But we must not deceive ourselves. The strange situation in which art says 'A' and its critic says it means 'B'— a diluted, detached, euphemistic rendering of the actual message—still does not make it impotent. Quite the contrary. Because the spiritual struggle is avoided, a great many of the real issues are blurred. Nevertheless this art communicates something, even if it is only that there is nothing beautiful or sensible to say.

According to Eastern ways of thinking about the universe, beauty is something that is purely relative.

Rabindranath Tagore writes of the tradition in Hinduism which believes that ultimately there is no difference between beauty and its opposite:

According to some interpretations of the Vedanta doctrine Brahman is the absolute Truth, the impersonal It, in which there can be no distinction of this and that, the good and the evil, the beautiful and its opposite, having no other quality except its ineffable blissfulness in the eternal solitude of its consciousness utterly devoid of all things and all thoughts.

D. T. Suzuki in his book on *Mysticism, Christian and Buddhist* speaks of the difference in the understanding of art between the West and the East. This difference springs from a different way of thinking about the natural universe and its beauty.

I often hear Chinese or Japanese art critics declare that Oriental art consists in depicting spirit and not form. For they say that when the spirit is understood the form creates itself; the main thing is to get into the spirit of an object which the painter chooses for his subject. The west on the other hand, emphasizes form, endeavours to reach the spirit by means of form. The East is just the opposite: the spirit is all in all. And it thinks that when the artist grasps the spirit, his work reveals something more than colours and lines can convey. A real artist is a creator and not a copyist. He has visited God's workshop and has learned the secrets of creation—creating something beautiful out of nothing . . .

How does the painter get into the spirit of the plant, for instance, if he wants to paint a hibiscus as Mokkei (Mu-chi) of the thirteenth century did in his famous picture, which is now preserved as a national treasure in Daitokuji temple in Kyoto? The secret is to become the plant itself. But how can a human being turn himself into a plant? Inasmuch as he aspires to paint a plant or an animal, there must be in him something which corresponds to it in one way or another. If so, he ought to be able to become the object he desires to paint.

The discipline consists in studying the plant inwardly with his mind thoroughly purified of its subjective, self-centred contents. This means to keep the mind in unison with the 'Emptiness' or Suchness, whereby one who stands against the object ceases to be the one outside that object but transforms himself into the object himself. This identification enables the painter to feel the pulsation of one and the same life animating both him and the object. This is what is meant when it is said that the subject is lost in the object, and that when the painter begins his work it is not he but the object itself that is working and it is then that his brush, as well as his arm and his fingers, become obedient servants to the spirit of the objects. The object makes its own picture. The spirit sees itself as reflected in itself. This is also a case of self-identity.

It is said that Henri Matisse looked at an object which he intended to paint for weeks, even for months, until its spirit began to move him, to urge him, even to threaten him, to give it an expression.

BACK TO ANSWER ONE

"The universe was created and is sustained by God— God of the Bible"

PROBLEMS AND QUESTIONS

Having examined other possible answers to the basic question 'What kind of universe do we live in?' we return to option one, the Biblical Christian answer, to look at some of the questions and objections raised.

 How are we to reconcile cruelty in the animal kingdom and natural disasters with belief in a loving Creator?

Cruelty. Many animals prey on each other, and it is not very realistic to imagine that animals do not feel pain. It is probably true that they do not have the same horror and dread of death as most human beings do. But this does not remove the problem: were things always like this in the universe of which we are told, 'And God saw everything that he had made, and behold, it was very good' (Genesis 1 : 31)?

Natural disasters. Here again we are bound to ask: could earthquakes and tornados which can take such a toll of human life really be part of a universe which is 'very good'?

In answering these questions we need to look for clues in several different parts of the Bible:

▷ After the fall of Adam, God tells him some of the results of his disobedience, and some of these affect the physical world:

And to Adam he said,
'Because you have listened to the voice of your wife,
    and have eaten of the tree of which I commanded you,
        'You shall not eat of it,'
cursed is the ground because of you;
    in toil you shall eat of it all the days of your life;
thorns and thistles it shall bring forth to you;
    and you shall eat the plants of the field . . .'

▷ The Bible does not give us a clear picture of the state of the natural world before the fall. But some of the prophets speak about a future restoration of nature.

Isaiah:

The wolf shall dwell with the lamb,
    and the leopard shall lie down with the kid,
and the calf and the lion and the fatling together,
    and a little child shall lead them.
The cow and the bear shall feed;
    their young shall lie down together;
and the lion shall eat straw like the ox.
The sucking child shall play over the hole of
        the asp,
    and the weaned child shall put his hand on the
        adder's den.
They shall not hurt or destroy
    in all my holy mountain;
for the earth shall be full of the knowledge of the
        Lord
    as the waters cover the sea.

If this is a picture of how things will be in a restored universe, it may also give some idea of how things were before sin entered into the world.

▷ Paul speaks of 'the whole creation' being caught up in the bondage and futility to which man is subject. Similarly, 'the whole creation' will be affected when God's plan for the human race is brought to completion:

The creation waits with eager longing for the revealing of the sons of God; for the creation was subjected to futility, not of its own will but by the will of him who subjected it in hope; because the creation itself will be set free from its bondage to decay and obtain the glorious liberty of the children of God. We know that the whole creation has been groaning in travail together until now; and not only the creation, but we ourselves, who have the first fruits of the Spirit, groan inwardly as we wait for adoption as sons, the redemption of our bodies.

In the light of these different aspects of the Bible's teaching, the Christian should feel the full force of the objection and admit that these features of the universe as it is now do *not* seem to be marks of the creation of a good and loving God. They must be seen as evidence of the abnormal state of the universe resulting from man's sin, and they are not likely to be present in the 'new heavens and the new earth' to which we look forward.

⚠ How original is the Genesis account of creation?

How is the Genesis story of creation related to the many other creation stories and myths of the ancient Near East? Is there not some evidence to suggest that the Hebrews may have borrowed their story from their neighbours—for example in Babylon?

Alan Millard, a lecturer on the languages of the ancient Near East writes:

Genesis 1 and 2 consist of a general account of the creation of the heavens and the earth, followed by a more detailed description of the making of man. Stories of cosmic and of human creation, either separately or as unities, are numerous, and many have several points in common: pre-existent deity; creation by divine command; man the ultimate creature; man formed from the earth as a pot is made; man in some way a reflection of deity. Almost all polytheistic faiths possess family-trees of their gods which can figure in creation stories. A primal pair or even a single self-created and self-propagating god heads the divine family, all of whose members represent or control natural elements and forces.

Beautiful 'Messier 13', composed of a million suns, in the constellation 'Hercules'. It is about 22,000 light years from earth, in our own Milky Way.

For some peoples, the physical universe or a basic element such as water or earth always existed, and the gods arose from it. For others it was the handiwork of a god or gods. These are simple concepts based on observation and elementary logic. For example, man as 'dust' is easily deduced from the cycle of death and decay.

However, common ideas need not share a common origin; it is misleading to reduce differing stories from all over the world to their common factors in order to claim that they do. A single source for all, or large numbers, of different stories is improbable.

Nevertheless, it is quite in order to set Genesis beside other accounts from the world of the Old Testament. When we do so, we find that few of the ancient creation stories share more than one or two basic concepts—such as the separation of heaven and earth, and the creation of man from clay. The Babylonian literature, however, affords some striking resemblances. In the century since one was first translated into English, the Babylonian accounts have been cited as the ultimate source of the Hebrew's beliefs. Recently, the recovery of more texts and the re-assessment of those long known has shown that many of the accepted similarities are in fact illusory.

The famous *Babylonian Genesis*, usually linked with the Hebrew creation story, is one of several, and was neither the oldest nor the most popular. Written late in the 2nd millennium BC to honour Marduk, god of Babylon, who is its hero, it begins with a watery mother-figure, Tiamat, from whom the gods are born. (The name is related to the Hebrew word for 'the deep' through the pre-historic linguistic connections between Babylonian and Hebrew.) She is killed by Marduk in a battle with her children whose noise had angered her, and her corpse is formed into the world. Man is made to relieve the gods of the toil of keeping the earth in order, so the gods have rest.

There are clear indications that this story was made up from older ones, and earlier compositions have been found which contain some of these features. Only one theme recurs often, the relief of the gods from their labour by the making of man with a divine ingredient. The battle of the gods in the *Babylonian Genesis* has no Old Testament equivalent, despite attempts by many scholars to discover underlying references to it in the text of Genesis 1 : 2 and other passages which speak of God's power over the waters.

WHERE DO WE GO FROM HERE?

If the question for you now is the evidence for the person of Jesus himself, the meaning of his death and the evidence of his resurrection, turn to BOOK THREE.

If you still question the whole approach underlying this presentation of Christian beliefs about God, man and the universe, turn to BOOK ONE — How can I know if Christianity is true?

REFERENCES

PAGE 9
George Harrison, *Beatles* Magazine, February 1968
Alasdair MacIntyre; in *The Listener*, 15 February 1968, p. 194
John Robinson, *Exploration into God*, SCM Press 1967, p. 46

PAGE 11
Exodus 3: 14–15; Isaiah 55: 8–9; Psalm 135: 5–6

PAGE 12
Hosea 11: 8; Isaiah 57: 15; Psalm 25: 14; Isaiah 43: 10; Psalm
  90: 2; Jeremiah 23: 23–24; Psalm 139: 1–2; Isaiah 46: 9–10

PAGE 13
Job 23: 13–14; Habakkuk 1: 12; Genesis 1: 1; Psalms 148: 3–5;
  33: 6–9; Hebrews 11: 3

PAGE 14
Isaiah 40: 28–31; Psalms 104: 1–2, 14, 20; 147: 8–9; Nehemiah
  9: 6; Jeremiah 31: 3; Ezekiel 33: 11; Isaiah 55: 6–7; Lamentations 3: 22–23; John 3: 16; Romans 5: 8; John 5: 20; 17:24;
  Habakkuk 1: 13; Psalm 5: 4

PAGE 15
Jeremiah 9: 23–24; Genesis 17: 1; Leviticus 19: 2; Psalm 11: 7;
  Deuteronomy 13: 4–5; Psalm 7: 9, 11; Jeremiah 5: 7–9;
  5: 26–30; Exodus 34: 6–7; Isaiah 54: 7–8; Deuteronomy
  6: 4–5; Isaiah 45: 5–6, 22–23

PAGE 16
Matthew 11: 27; John 17: 5

PAGE 17
John 15: 26; Acts 1: 8; 2: 1–4; Galatians 5: 22–23; Psalms
  95: 6; 5: 7; 9: 1–2; 84: 1–2; 18: 1; 28: 7

PAGE 19
John Mbiti, *African Religions and Philosophy*, Heinemann 1969,
  pp. 29 and 35

PAGE 21
Robert Brow, *Religion, Origins and Ideas*, Tyndale Press 1966,
  pp. 10–11
Roy A. Stewart, *Rabbinic Theology*, Oliver and Boyd 1961, p. 20

PAGE 22
The Koran, tr. N. J. Dawood, Penguin 1964, Sura 2: 255, p. 349;.
  59: 23–24, p. 263
Al-Junayd, in S. M. Zwemer, *A Moslem Seeker After God
  (Al-Ghazzali)*, Revell 1920, p. 182
Reynold Nicholson, *The Mystics of Islam*, Khayyats 1966 Reprint,
  pp. 21–22 and pp. 22–23
Ahmad A. Galwash, *The Religion of Islam*, The Supreme Council
  for Islamic Affairs, Cairo 1966, Vol. 2, pp. 341–342

PAGE 23
Joseph Joubert, *Les Cahiers de Joseph Joubert*, in Hazard,
  European Thought in the Eighteenth Century, p. 288
Voltaire, Letter of 1741, in Colin Brown, *Philosophy and the
  Christian Faith*, IVF 1969, p. 85
Voltaire; in G. R. Cragg, *The Church And the Age of Reason
  (1648–1789)*, Penguin 1960, p. 237
Paul Hazard, *European Thought in the Eighteenth Century*, p. 128

PAGE 25
Basil Willey, *The Seventeenth Century Background*, Penguin 1967,
  pp. 106–107
Thomas Carlyle; in Froude, *Carlyle's Life in London (1884)*; in
  Basil Willey, *The Seventeenth Century Background*, p. 134
Radhakrishnan, *The Hindu View of Life*, Allen and Unwin 1960,
  p. 20

PAGE 26
Christmas Humphreys, *Buddhism*, Penguin 1967, pp. 79–80
Meister Eckhart, tr. C. de B. Evans; in D. T. Suzuki, *Mysticism,
  Christian and Buddhist*, Collier Books, New York 1962, pp.
  43–44
The Cloud of Unknowing, tr. Clifton Wolters, Penguin 1971,
  pp. 55 and 57–58

PAGE 27
Jack Kerouac, *The Dharma Bums*, Granada Panther 1972
Tom Wolfe, *The Electric Kool-Aid Acid Test*, Bantam 1971

PAGE 28
The Beatles' Illustrated Lyrics, Macdonalds 1969

PAGE 29
Albert Camus, *Cahiers du Sud*, April 1943; in *Camus, A Collection
  of Critical Essays*, ed. Germaine Brée, Prentice-Hall 1965,
  p. 70
Jean-Paul Sartre, *Nausea*, tr. Robert Baldick, Penguin 1965, p. 26
Baron von Hugel; in Michael de la Bedoyère, *Baron von Hugel*,
  Dent 1951, p. 291
Somerset Maugham, *The Summing Up*, Penguin 1963, p. 179

PAGE 30
Nietzsche, *The Joyful Wisdom*; in Robert Adolphs, *The Grave of
  God*, Burns and Oates 1967, pp. 13–14
Matthew Arnold, *Letters*; in Basil Willey, *The Nineteenth Century
  Background*, pp. 275–276
Martin Esslin, *The Theatre of the Absurd*, Penguin 1968, p. 389
Arthur Adamov, *L'Aveu*; in Martin Esslin, *The Theatre of the
  Absurd*, p. 90
A. J. Ayer, Essay in *What I Believe*, Allen and Unwin 1966, p. 14

PAGE 31
Jean-Paul Sartre, *Words*, Penguin 1967, pp. 62–65

PAGE 32
Albert Camus, *The Rebel*, Penguin 1967, pp. 59–60
Nietzsche, *The Joyful Wisdom* No. 343; in Colin Brown, *Philosophy
  and the Christian Faith*, p. 139
Michael Harrington, *The Accidental Century*, Penguin 1965, p. 115
Jean-Paul Sartre, *Existentialism and Humanism*, tr. Philip Mairet,
  Methuen 1968, pp. 32–33

PAGE 33
Robert Brow, *Religion, Origins and Ideas*, Tyndale Press 1966,
  pp. 37 and 13–14

PAGE 34
Robert Brow, *Religion, Origins and Ideas*, p. 84
K. M. Sen, *Hinduism*, Penguin 1969, p. 53
The Bhagavad Gita, tr. Juan Mascaro, Penguin 1965, pp. 85–88

PAGE 35
H. D. Lewis, *The Study of Religions*, Penguin 1966, p. 56
Professor Zaehner, *Foolishness to the Greeks*; in H. D. Lewis
  and R. L. Slater, *The Study of Religions*, Penguin 1969, p. 145
Paul Hazard, *The European Mind 1680–1715*, pp. 170–171
Hegel, in *The Philosophy of Religion*, Vol. 2, ed. N. Smart, SCM
  Press, p. 327

PAGE 36
Julian Huxley, 'The New Divinity', in *Essays of a Humanist*,
  Penguin 1966, p. 227
Julian Huxley, 'The Humanist Frame', in *Essays of a Humanist*,
  p. 117
Paul Tillich, *Biblical Religion and the Search for Ultimate Reality*,
  pp. 82–83
Paul Tillich, *Systematic Theology*, Vol. 1, 1953, p. 227
Paul Tillich, *The Shaking of the Foundations*, Penguin 1962,
  pp. 63–64
Teilhard de Chardin, *The Phenomenon of Man*, Collins Fontana
  1966, pp. 322 and 338

PAGE 37
John Robinson, *Honest to God*, SCM Press 1963, p. 7
John Robinson, *Exploration into God*, SCM Press 1967, pp. 36,
  39 and 41
Julian Huxley, *Essays of a Humanist*, p. 223
John Robinson, *Exploration into God*, pp. 23, 83–84, 127 and 15

PAGE 38
John Robinson, *Exploration into God*, p. 58
John Robinson, *Honest to God*, p. 53
John Robinson, *Exploration into God*, pp. 134 and 72
John Wren-Lewis, *They Became Anglicans*; in *Honest to God*,
  pp. 42–43
F. C. Happold, *Religious Faith for Twentieth Century Man*,
  Penguin 1966, p. 51
T. J. J. Altizer, *Radical Theology and the Death of God*, Penguin
  1968, p. 102
William Hamilton, *The New Essence of Christianity*, New York
  1961, pp. 58–59
William Hamilton, *Radical Theology and the Death of God*, p. 40
T. J. J. Altizer, *Radical Theology and the Death of God*, p. 30

PAGE 39
T. J. J. Altizer, *The Gospel of Christian Atheism*, Collins 1967, pp. 103, 106 and 136
William Hamilton, *Radical Theology and the Death of God*, p. 53
William Hamilton, *Radical Theology and the Death of God*, p. 58
Peter Dumitriu, *Incognito*; in *Exploration into God*, p. 89

PAGE 40
Y. Takeuchi, Essay 'Buddhism and Existentialism'; in *Religion and Culture, Essays in Honour of Paul Tillich*, ed. Walter Leibricht 1959, p. 304
Walter Kaufmann, *Critique of Philosophy and Religion*, Faber and Faber 1959, p. 128
Julian Huxley, *Essays of a Humanist*, Penguin 1964, pp. 225–226
Alasdair MacIntyre, 'God and the Theologians'; in *The Honest to God Debate*, ed. David L. Edwards, SCM Press 1963, pp. 215–216
Alasdair MacIntyre; in *The Listener*, 15 February 1968

PAGE 41
Alasdair MacIntyre, 'God and the Theologians'; in *The Honest to God Debate*, p. 220
Barbara Wooton; in *What I Believe*, pp. 205–206
T. J. J. Altizer, *Radical Theology and the Death of God*, p. 131
Professor Peter Beyerhaus, Paper for Islington Clerical Conference, June 1972, *Bulletin of EFAC* (Evangelical Fellowship in the Anglican Communion) July 1972
Radhakrishnan, *The Hindu View of Life*, p. 28
Arnold Toynbee; in Ved Mehta, *Fly and Fly-Bottle*, Penguin 1965, p. 124

PAGE 42
Exodus 33: 18–23; 34: 5–7; Isaiah 6: 1–5; Ezekiel 1: 26–28; Jeremiah 9: 23–24

PAGE 43
John 1: 18; 14: 8–10; Revelation 1: 12–17; 1 Peter 1: 8
Thomas Merton, 'New Seeds of Contemplation'; in H. A. Williams, in *Objections to Christian Belief*, Constable 1963, p. 32
James Mitchell, *The god I Want*, Constable 1967, pp. 1 and 9
Aldous Huxley, *Do What You Will*, Watts and Co. 1937, pp. 54–55
Albert Einstein; in *I Believe*, Allen and Unwin 1965, pp. 28–29
Ernst Cassirer, *An Essay on Man*, Yale University Press 1963, pp. 98–99

PAGE 44
Jean-Paul Sartre, *Nausea*, p. 26
Ronald Hepburn, *Objections to Christian Belief*, p. 31

PAGE 46
Genesis 4: 14, 16; 6: 5; Proverbs 6: 16–19
Stephen C. Neill, 'The Wrath of God and the Peace of God'; in Max Warren, *Interpreting the Cross*, SCM Press 1966, pp. 22–23
Jeremiah 31: 3; Isaiah 54: 7–8; 49: 15–16

PAGE 47
Luke 19: 41–44; Matthew 25: 41–43, 46; Romans 5: 8 9; 1 John 4: 10 (Revised Version); Revelation 6: 15–17

PAGE 48
Harold Pinter; in John Russell Taylor, *Anger and After*, Penguin 1968, p. 308
Jacob Bronowski, *The Identity of Man*, Penguin 1967, pp. 7–9

PAGE 49
Thomas Mann; in *I Believe*, p. 88
Aldous Huxley, *Brave New World Revisited*, Chatto and Windus 1966, p. 156
Somerset Maugham, *The Summing Up*, Penguin 1963, pp. 181–182
Tolstoy, *Memoirs of a Madman*; in Colin Wilson, *The Outsider*, Pan 1967, p. 164
Adam Schaff, *A Philosophy of Man*, Lawrence and Wishart, London 1963, p. 34

PAGE 50
Nietzsche, *The Will to Power*; in H. J. Blackham, *Six Existentialist Thinkers*, Routledge 1952, p. 31
Arthur Koestler, 'What the Modern World is Doing to the Soul of Man', Essay in *The Challenge of Our Time*, Percival, Marshall, London 1948, pp. 15–17
Albert Camus, *The Rebel*, p. 57
Jean-Paul Sartre, *Saint-Genet*; in *Sartre, A Collection of Critical Essays*, ed. Edith Kern, Prentice Hall 1962, p. 87
Jean-Paul Sartre; in *Sartre, A Collection of Critical Essays*, p. 211
John Russell Taylor, *Anger and After*, p. 287

Bertrand Russell, *The Impact of Science on Society*, Allen and Unwin 1952, p. 114
Thomas Mann, *The Magic Mountain*, Penguin 1967, p. 716

PAGE 51
Eugene Ionesco, 'L'orsque j'écris . . .'; in Martin Esslin, *The Theatre of the Absurd*, p. 132
Aldous Huxley, *Do What You Will*, p. 189
Adam Schaff, *A Philosophy of Man*, p. 35
Albert Camus, *The Myth of Sisyphus*; in Martin Esslin, *The Theatre of the Absurd*, p. 416
Albert Camus, *The Rebel*, p. 267

PAGE 53
Genesis 1: 26–27; 5: 1–3; 1: 31

PAGE 54
Psalm 8: 3–8; Isaiah 45: 9–10; Psalms 139: 13–17; 119: 73; Genesis 2: 16–17; Romans 5: 12; 1 John 3: 4; Romans 1: 18–21

PAGE 55
Romans 2: 1–3; 3: 9; 3: 23; Isaiah 65: 1–7; Ephesians 2: 3; 2 Thessalonians 1: 9; Isaiah 1: 18; Romans 5: 6–11; John 1: 12–13;

PAGE 56
2 Peter 1: 3–4; Job 7: 17–21; 23: 10; Ezekiel 18: 1–4, 20

PAGE 57
Luke 12: 6–7
Leslie Newbiggin, *Honest Religion for Secular Man*, SCM Press 1966, p. 62

PAGE 58
Exodus 6: 6–7; Jeremiah 1: 5; Ephesians 1: 3–10; Genesis 17: 1; 1 Peter 1: 15–16; Exodus 20: 3–17; Isaiah 61: 8; Malachi 3: 5; Matthew 22: 37–40

PAGE 59
Colossians 3: 5–14; Ephesians 5: 10, 17–18; Jeremiah 17: 9–10; Psalm 139: 1–4; 1 John 1: 7; Ephesians 4: 25; 4: 31–5: 2; Ephesians 5: 22, 25; Song of Solomon 6: 3; Psalm 22: 1–2; Habakkuk 1: 13

PAGE 60
Jeremiah 12: 1–2; Genesis 1: 31; 3: 16; 3: 19; Luke 13: 16; Deuteronomy 28: 2–4, 58–59; John 5: 14; Psalm 119: 71, 75–76

PAGE 63
Job 42: 2–6; 42: 7; Luke 4: 18–19; 11: 20–22; John 11: 33; Luke 13: 1–5; 12: 4–5

PAGE 64
Matthew 8: 17; Hebrews 2: 14–18, New English Bible; Psalm 96: 11–13; Isaiah 42: 1, 4; 58: 6–7; Revelation 21: 1–4
Michel Quoist *Prayers of Life*, Gill 1965, p. 66

PAGE 65
C. E. M. Joad, *Recovery of Belief*, Faber and Faber 1952, p. 63
S. Neill, *The Wrath of God and the Peace of God*; in Max Warren, *Interpreting the Cross*, pp. 22–23

PAGE 66
Leopold Senghor, *On African Socialism*, tr. Mercer Cook, Praeger 1964, p. 72

PAGE 67
Leopold Senghor, *On African Socialism*, p. vii footnote
Dr Isidore Epstein, *Judaism*, Epworth Press 1939, p. 80; in J. N. D. Anderson, *The World's Religions*, IVF 1965, p. 32
Dr Isidore Epstein, *Judaism*, p. 82
Dr Hertz, *The Pentateuch and the Haftorahs*; in J. N. D. Anderson, p. 32
Dr Hertz, *The Pentateuch and the Haftorahs*, pp. 523–524
Sura 38: 71–72, p. 280; 2: 30, p. 326
H. A. R. Gibb, *Mohammedanism*, OUP 1964, p. 70
C. C. Adams, *Islam and Modernism in Egypt*, A Study of the Modern Reform Movement Inaugurated by Mohammad Abduh, OUP 1933, p. 147
Sura 20: 117–122, p. 225

PAGE 68
Carl Becker, *The Heavenly City of the Eighteenth Century Philosophers*; in H. J. Blackham, *Objections to Humanism*, Penguin 1967, p. 10
Paul Hazard, *The European Mind 1680–1715*, pp. 295–296

PAGE 69
Sura 81: 27–29, p. 17
Mohammad Abduh; in C. C. Adams, *Islam and Modernism in Egypt*, p. 153 (two quotations)
Sura 19: 93–95, p. 37; 28: 88, p. 81
Nicholson, *The Mystics of Islam*, Khayyats, Beirut Reprint 1966, pp. 167–168
Norman Hampson, *The Enlightenment*, Penguin 1968, pp. 94–95

PAGE 70
Charles Darwin, *Autobiography*, chapter 3
J. Mbiti, *African Religions and Philosophy*, pp. 165 and 99
Sura 51: 56, p. 118; 76: 4–22, p. 18

PAGE 71
Sura 51: 56, p. 118; 76: 4–22, p. 18
Diderot; in Hampson, *The Enlightenment*, pp. 95–96
Martin Esslin, *The Theatre of the Absurd*, p. 55
John Mbiti, *African Religions and Philosophy*, pp. 213–214
Roy A. Stewart, *Rabbinic Theology, An Introductory Study*, Oliver and Boyd 1961, pp. 173–174
Herbert Danby, *The Jew and Christianity*, Sheldon Press 1927, pp. 83–85

PAGE 72
Sura 59: 23, p. 263
Beidhawi; in S. Zwemer, *The Moslem Doctrine of God*, American Tract Society 1905, pp. 58–59
Al-Ghazzali; in S. Zwemer, *The Moslem Doctrine of God*, pp. 55–56
J. N. D. Anderson, *The World's Religions*, p. 85

PAGE 73
John Locke, *On Civil Government*, Book II, chapter 11; in Paul Hazard, *The European Mind 1680–1715*, p. 325
Hooke; in Hampson, *The Enlightenment*, p. 155
Basil Willey, *The Eighteenth Century Background*, p. 254
John Mbiti, *African Religions and Philosophy*, pp. 209 and 38

PAGE 74
Sura 42: 23, p. 152; 30: 20–21, p. 188; 60: 7–9, p. 260
John Mbiti, *African Religions and Philosophy*, pp. 214–215 and 169–170
Sura 13: 11, p. 140; 4: 79, p. 363

PAGE 75
Albert Camus, *The Rebel*, p. 47
Jean-Paul Sartre, *The Rebel*, p. 269
Christopher Dawson, 'Christianity and the New Age', in *Essays in Order*, 1931; in Basil Willey, *The Seventeenth Century Background*, p. 16
Hannah Arendt, *The Human Condition*, Anchor Books 1959, pp. 12–13
Ernst Cassirer, *An Essay on Man*, pp. 21–22

PAGE 76
Glossary of Humanism, under Humanism
H. J. Blackham, *Humanism*, Penguin 1968, pp. 13 and 19
Edmund Leach; in *The Listener*, 16 November 1967
Lord Willis; in *An Inquiry into Humanism*, BBC 1966, p. 21
Geoffrey Scott, *The Architecture of Humanism*; in *Objections to Humanism*, p. 8
A. J. Ayer; in *An Inquiry into Humanism*, p. 2

PAGE 77
H. J. Blackham, *Objections to Humanism*, p. 11
Julian Huxley, 'The Humanist Frame', in *Essays of a Humanist*, pp. 77 and 107
E. L. Allen, *Existentialism from Within*; in Brown, *Philosophy   d the Christian Faith*, pp. 181–182
    Heim; in Alec Vidler, *The Church in an Age of Revolution*,   nguin 1961, p. 211
    nanist Glossary, under Existentialism
    a-Paul Sartre, *Existentialism and Humanism*, pp. 56, 27–28
    nd 29
    J. Blackham, *Six Existentialist Thinkers*, pp. 151–152

AGE 78
 hn Lewis, *Marxism and the Open Mind*, 1957, pp. 33–34, 161 and 144–146; in Lester DeKoster, 'Pretence of Humanism: The New Face of Marxism' in *Christianity Today*, October 26 1962

PAGE 79
Guy Wint, *Spotlight on Asia*, Penguin 1955, pp. 211–212
Richard Crossman, *The God That Failed, Six Studies in Communism*, Hamish Hamilton 1950, pp. 9–10

K. M. Sen, *Hinduism*, Penguin 1969, p. 19
W. Cantwell-Smith, *The Faith of Other Men*, Mentor 1965, pp. 25–26
Christmas Humphreys, *Buddism*, pp. 85 and 157

PAGE 80
Pearl Buck; in *I Believe*, pp. 24–25
E. M. Forster; in *I Believe*, p. 50
Colin Wilson, *The Outsider*, pp. 71–72

PAGE 81
Eugene Ionesco, *Le Point du Départ*; in M. Esslin, *The Theatre of the Absurd*, p. 155
Harold Pinter; in John Russell Taylor, *Anger and After*, p. 308
Aldous Huxley, *Brave New World Revisited*, p. 164
Virginia Woolf; in C. E. M. Joad, *The Book of Joad*, Faber and Faber 1944, p. 112
C. E. M. Joad, *The Book of Joad*, p. 116
Jean-Paul Sartre, *Nausea*, p. 241

PAGE 82
H. G. Wells; in *I Believe*, pp. 170–171
Julian Huxley, *Essays of a Humanist*, p. 89
Aldous Huxley, *Ends and Means*, pp. 290–291
Christmas Humphreys, *Buddhism*, p. 128
D. T. Suzuki, *Mysticism, Christian and Buddhist*, pp. 35–36

PAGE 83
Arthur Koestler, *The Sleepwalkers*, Penguin 1968, p. 540
Albert Camus; in *Camus, A Collection of Critical Essays*, p. 116
S. Maugham, *The Summing Up*, Penguin 1963, pp. 181–182
Bertrand Russell, 'A Free Man's Worship'; in *Why I am Not a Christian*, Simon and Shuster 1966, p. 107
H. J. Blackham, *Humanism*, p. 116
Francis Bacon; in John Russell, *Francis Bacon*, Methuen 1965, pl; in H. Rookmaaker, *Modern Art and the Death of a Culture*, IVP 1970, p. 174
Martin Esslin, *The Theatre of the Absurd*, pp. 22–23
Eugene Ionesco; in M. Esslin, *The Theatre of the Absurd*, p. 23

PAGE 84
Martin Esslin, *The Theatre of the Absurd*, p. 85
Jean-Paul Sartre, *Nausea*, pp. 123–124 and 162
Allen Ginsberg; in Steve Turner, Some Notes from the Underground', *Voice* Magazine, IVF 1972, p. 6

PAGE 85
George Eliot, *Cross's Life*; in Basil Willey, *Nineteenth Century Studies*, p. 247
Bertrand Russell, 'A Free Man's Worship', in *Why I am Not a Christian*, pp. 115–116
Nietzsche, *The Will to Power 1041*; in Blackham, *Six Existentialist Thinkers*, p. 33
Nikos Kazantzakis; in Helen Kazantzakis, *A Biography based on his letters*, Simon and Shuster 1970
Maurice Friedman, *The Problematic Rebel*
Jean-Paul Sartre, *Words*, pp. 61–62
André Malraux, 'The Walnut Trees of Altenberg'; in Maurice Friedman, *To Deny Our Nothingness*, Gollancz 1967
Arthur Adamov, *L'Aveu;* in Martin Esslin, *The Theatre of the Absurd*, pp. 89–90
Jean-Paul Sartre, *Words*, p. 157
Colin Wilson, *The Outsider*, p. 38

PAGE 86
Rebecca West, in *I Believe*, p. 189
Santayana, *Three Philosophical Poets;* in *Objections to Humanism*, ed. H. J. Blackham, pp. 111–112
Lin Yutang, in *I Believe*, p. 76
Albert Camus, *The Rebel*, p. 14
Albert Camus, *The Plague*, tr. Stuart Gilbert, Penguin 1966
H. J. Blackham, *Humanism*, pp. 211–212
Julian Huxley, *Essays of a Humanist*, pp. 91–92

PAGE 87
Colin Wilson, *Beyond the Outsider*, Baker 1965, p. 62 and p. 165
Henry Miller, *Tropic of Cancer;* in H. R. Rookmaaker, *Modern Art and the Death of a Culture*, p. 146
Rabindranath Tagore, *Fruit Gathering*, Macmillan 1922, pp. 82–83
Pete Townshend, *The Seeker;* in Steve Turner, 'Some Notes from the Underground', *Voice*, p. 7
Jean-Paul Sartre, *Existentialism and Humanism*, p. 54

PAGE 88
Proust; in Michael Harrington, *The Accidental Century*, p. 154
Arthur Koestler, *What the Modern World is Doing to the Soul of Man*, p. 15

Donald Kalish, 'What (If Anything) To Expect from Today's Philosophers', *Time*, January 7 1966, p. 20; in Leslie Paul, *Alternatives to Christian Belief*, Hodder 1967, p. 159
McLuhan Hot and Cold, ed. Gerald Emanuel Stern, Penguin 1968, p. 18
George Eliot; in *McLuhan Hot and Cold*, p. 90
Edmund Leach; in *The Listener*, 7 December 1967
Jean-Paul Sartre, *Existentialism and Humanism*, p. 33
Arthur Koestler, *What the Modern World is Doing to the Soul of Man*, pp. 16–19

PAGE 89
J. B. Priestley, *Literature and Western Man;* in Arthur Calder-Marshall, Essay in *I Believe*, p. 68
Lin Yutang, Essay in *I Believe*, p. 83
Somerset Maugham, *The Summing Up*, p. 203
T. H. Huxley, *Evolution and Ethics and Other Essays*, Romanes Lecture 1893, D. Appleton, New York 1905, p. 80
H. J. Blackham, *Humanism*, pp. 58–59
Adam Schaff, *A Philosophy of Man*, p. 60

PAGE 90
J. S. Mill, *Autobiography*, 1873
John Wren-Lewis, *Fact, Faith and Fantasy*, Collins Fontana 1964, p. 32
John Robinson, *Honest to God*, pp. 114–115

PAGE 91
Jacob Bronowski, *Science and Human Values*, Penguin 1964, pp. 66, 77, 80, 68 and 70, 75, 63

PAGE 92
Arthur Koestler, *The Ghost in the Machine*, Hutchinson 1967, pp. 153–154
Jacob Bronowski, *Science and Human Values*, p. 8
Arthur Koestler, *The Sleepwalkers*, Penguin, pp. 552 and 553
Radhakrishnan, *The Hindu View of Life*, Allen and Unwin 1960, pp. 56 and 55

PAGE 93
D. T. Suzuki, *Mysticism, Christian and Buddhist*, p. 58
Christmas Humphreys, *Buddhism*, p. 122
Francis Schaeffer, *The God Who is There*, Hodder 1968, p. 101
Rousseau; in Norman Hampson, *The Enlightenment*, p. 195
Charles Darwin, *The Descent of Man*
Albert Camus, *The Rebel*, pp. 27–28

PAGE 94
Albert Camus, *The Rebel*, pp. 258–260
Jean-Paul Sartre, *Existentialism and Humanism*, pp. 33-34
Jean-Paul Sartre; in Sartre, *A Collection of Critical Essays*, p. 167
Jean-Paul Sartre, *Existentialism and Humanism*, pp. 47–49
Colin Wilson, *The Outsider*, p. 39
John D. Wild; in Sartre, *A Collection of Critical Essays*, p. 145
Jean-Paul Sartre, *Existentialism and Humanism*, pp. 36 and 31

PAGE 95
Adam Schaff, *A Philosophy of Man*, pp. 24 and 26
H. J. Blackham, *Objections to Humanism*, pp. 13–18
Edmund Leach; in *The Listener*. 11 January 1968
Alasdair MacIntyre; in *The Listener*, 11 January 1968
Norman Hampson, *The Enlightenment*, pp. 124 and 127
Dostoievsky; in Michael Harrington, *The Accidental Century*, p. 123

PAGE 96
C. S. Lewis, *The Abolition of Man*, OUP 1944, p. 30
C. E. M. Joad, *Is Christianity True?*
Leslie Paul, *Alternatives to Christian Belief*, Hodder 1967, pp. 60 and 66

PAGE 97
Harold Pinter, in *The Theatre of the Absurd*, p. 274
Martin Esslin, *The Theatre of the Absurd*, pp. 69 and 84
John D. Wild; in *Sartre, A Collection of Critical Essays*, p. 146
Cyril Connolly and Jonathan Miller; in *The Listener*, 3 November 1966
Albert Camus, *The Plague*, p. 249
Jean-Paul Sartre, *Nausea*, pp. 160–161

PAGE 98
Francis Schaeffer, *The God who is There*, p. 29
D. R. Davies, *On to Orthodoxy*, 1939, p. 61
W. E. Hocking, 'Tentative Outlook for the State and Church', in *This is My Philosophy*, ed. W. Burnett, Allen and Unwin 1958, pp. 304–305
Aldous Huxley, *Do What you Will*, p. 180

Radhakrishnan, *The Hindu View of Life*, p. 88
Christmas Humphreys, *Buddhism*, p. 123

PAGE 99
John Robinson, *Exploration into God*, pp. 89, 88 and 110
G. T. Manley; in *The World's Religions*, ed. J. N. D. Anderson, p. 65
Leslie Newbiggin, *Honest Religion for Secular Man*, p. 27
H. W. Van Loon; in *I Believe*, pp. 153–154
Bertrand Russell, *Has Man a Future?*, Penguin 1961, pp. 126–127

PAGE 100
Franz Fanon, *The Wretched of the Earth*, Penguin 1967, pp. 251–255
Arthur Koestler, *The Ghost in the Machine*, pp. 267, 336, 335 and 335–336
Julian Huxley, *Essays of a Humanist*, pp. 130, 117 and 252

PAGE 101
John Wren-Lewis, *Fact, Faith and Fantasy*, p. 44
Thomas Mann; in *I Believe*, pp. 89–90
Michael Harrington, *The Accidental Century*, pp. 35–36
Bertrand Russell, in *Fly and Fly-Bottle*, p. 41
Arthur Koestler, *Darkness at Noon*, Jonathan Cape 1940, pp. 253–254
Albert Camus, 'Actuelles'; in *Camus, Collected Essays*, p. 56

PAGE 102
Albert Camus, *The Rebel*, pp. 266–267
Albert Camus, *The Plague*, pp. 107–108 and 214

PAGE 103
Albert Camus, *The Plague*, pp. 170–171, 251–252
Dostoievsky; in Colin Wilson, *The Outsider*, p. 175
Aldous Huxley, *Do What you Will*, p. 50
Aldous Huxley, *Ends and Means*, p. 298
C. E. M. Joad, *Recovery of Belief*, p. 174
Christmas Humphreys, *Buddhism*, p. 123
Aldous Huxley, *Ends and Means*

PAGE 104
Nietzsche; in *Six Existentialist Thinkers*, ed. H. J. Blackham, p.40
Colin Wilson, *The Outsider*, p. 119
Albert Camus, *The Rebel*, p. 16
Aldous Huxley, *Ends and Means*, pp. 274–275

PAGE 105
Lewis Carroll, *Alice in Wonderland*, Macmillan 1964, pp. 127–128
Nietzsche, *Twilight of the Idols*, tr. R. J. Hollingdale, Penguin 1968, pp. 69–70

PAGE 106
C. E. M. Joad, *Is Christianity True?*, pp. ix–xx
Jean-Paul Sartre, *Existentialism and Humanism*, pp. 32–33

PAGE 107
Colin Wilson, *Beyond the Outsider*, p. 164
Lord Willis, *Inquiry into Humanism*, BBC, p. 24

PAGE 108
Jacob Bronowski, *The Identity of Man*, Penguin 1967, pp. 14–15 and 82–83
Professor Donald Mackay, *Freedom of Action in a Mechanistic Universe*, Cambridge University Press, 1967, pp. 11–12

PAGE 109
Professor Donald Mackay, *Freedom of Action in a Mechanistic Universe*, pp. 36–37, 30–33 and 33–34

PAGE 110
Matthew 19: 3–5; Luke 3: 23, 38; Romans 5: 12–19

PAGE 111
John Habgood, *Religion and Science*, Mills and Boon 1964, pp. 69–70

PAGE 112
Professor W. R. Thompson, *Introduction to The Origin of Species*, Everyman Library No. 811, 1956

PAGE 113
Julian Huxley, *Essays of a Humanist*

PAGE 114
Derek Kidner, *Genesis*, Tyndale Press 1967, p. 30
Julian Huxley, *Evolution in Action*, Penguin 1963
A. S. Romer, *Man and the Vertebrates*, Penguin 1963, Vol. 2, p. 236
David Lack, *Evolutionary Theory and Christian Belief: The Unresolved Conflict*, Methuen 1957
Professor W. R. Thompson, *Introduction to The Origin of Species*

PAGE 115
Julian Huxley, *Essays of a Humanist*, pp. 24–25
Professor D. S. M. Watson; in C. E. M. Joad, *Recovery of Belief*
John Stott; in *The Church of England Newspaper*, 7 June 1968

PAGE 116
Fred Hoyle, *The Nature of the Universe*, Blackwell 1960, p. 90
Julian Huxley, *Essays of a Humanist*, p. 112
Bertrand Russell, *The Problems of Philosophy*, Home University Library, Thornton Butterworth 1932, pp. 26–27
C. E. M. Joad, *The Book of Joad*, p. 213
H. R. Rookmaaker, *Art and the Public Today*, L'Abri Fellowship 1968, pp.13–14

PAGE 118
Genesis 1: 1–4; Hebrews 11: 1–3; Psalm 104: 10–15

PAGE 119
Jeremiah 51: 15–16; Colossians 1: 15–17; 1 Corinthians 8: 6; John 1: 1–3; Genesis 1: 31; 3: 17–18; Psalm 104: 1–2
Professor Donald Mackay, *Science and Christian Faith Today*, CPAS 1970, pp. 9–10 and 14

PAGE 120
Psalm 148: 3–6; Genesis 8: 22; Psalm 104: 5–9

PAGE 121
R. Hooykaas, *Religion and the Rise of Modern Science*, Scottish Academic Press 1972, pp. 161–162
C. F. Von Weizacker, *The Relevance of Science*, Collins 1964, p. 163
Donald Mackay, *Science and Christian Faith Today*, CPAS, pp. 18–19 and 20

PAGE 122
H. R. Rookmaaker, *Art and the Public Today*, pp. 50–51 and 19–20

PAGE 123
John Mbiti, *African Religions and Philosophy*, pp. 56–57
Sura 50: 7–11, p. 119; 15: 16–22, p. 236

PAGE 124
R. Hooykaas, *Religion and the Rise of Modern Science*, pp. 7–9 and 12–13
Lallemant; in Colin Wilson, *The Outsider*, p. 149
Basil Willey, *The Seventeenth Century Background*, pp. 35 and 37–39

PAGE 125
Shaftesbury; in Basil Willey, *The Eighteenth Century Background*, pp. 65–66
Basil Willey, *The Eighteenth Century Background*, pp. 67 and 267
Mark Rutherford, *Autobiography*; in Basil Willey, *The Eighteenth Century Background*, pp. 275–276
Charles Darwin, *Life and Letters of Charles Darwin*, John Murray 1888, Vol. 3, pp. 312–313
Charles Darwin, *Life and Letters*, p. 313

PAGE 126
Charles Darwin, Letter to D. Hooker 1870; *More Letters*, Vol. 1, p.85

Basil Willey, *The Eighteenth Century Background*, p. 277
Charles Darwin, *Autobiography*, chapters 2 and 3

PAGE 127
Radhakrishnan, *The Hindu View of Life*, pp. 48–49 and 51
Ernst Cassirer, *An Essay on Man*, pp. 13–14

PAGE 128
Ernst Cassirer, *An Essay on Man*, pp. 14–15
Julian Huxley, *Essays of a Humanist*, pp. 82–83 and 78
A. J. Ayer; in *What I Believe*, Allen and Unwin 1966, p. 14
Jacob Bronowski, *The Identity of Man*, pp. 8 and 2–4
D. H. Lawrence, *A Propos of Lady Chatterly's Lover*; in Basil Willey, *Nineteenth Century Studies*, p. 36

PAGE 129
Albert Camus, 'Noces'; in *Camus, A Collection of Critical Essays*, p. 66
Teilhard de Chardin, *Phenomenon of Man*, Collins Fontana 1965, p. 241
Teilhard de Chardin; in H. de Lubac, *The Faith of Teilhard de Chardin*, Collins 1967, p. 136
John Robinson, *Exploration into God*, pp. 78, 97, 107, 127 and 79

PAGE 130
John Wren-Lewis, *Fact, Faith and Fantasy*, p. 40
Arthur Koestler, *The Lotus and the Robot*; in Leopold Senghor, *On African Socialism*, p. 73
Jean-Paul Sartre, *Nausea*, pp. 176 and 180–183
Lewis Carroll, *Through the Looking Glass*, pp. 180–182

PAGE 131
Lewis Carroll, *Through the Looking Glass*, pp. 284–285
Francis Schaeffer, *The God who is There*, p. 64
Bertrand Russell, *The Scientific Outlook*; in Abel Jones, *In Search of Truth*, Nelson 1945, p. 150
Jules Romanes, Essay in *I Believe*, p. 113

PAGE 132
Colin Wilson, *The Outsider*, pp. 13–14
Jacob Bronowski, *The Common Sense of Science*, Penguin 1966, p. 101
Von Weizacker, *The Relevance of Science*, p. 163
Jean-Paul Sartre, *Nausea*, pp. 113–114, 225 and 115
Martin Esslin, *The Theatre of the Absurd*, p. 51
C. E. M. Joad, *The Book of Joad*, pp. 218–219

PAGE 133
Somerset Maugham, *The Summing Up*, pp. 195, 196
Jean-Paul Sartre, *Nausea*, p. 63
Henry Moore, *A Study of His Life and Work*, Thames and Hudson 1965, p. 257
Marc; in H. R. Rookmaaker, *Modern Art and the Death of a Culture*, p. 110
Karl Appel; in H. R. Rookmaaker, *Modern Art and the Death of a Culture*, p. 160
Lucebert; in H. R. Rookmaaker, *Art and the Public Today*, p. 44
Rookmaaker, *Art and the Public Today*, p. 18

PAGE 134
Rabindranath Tagore, *The Religion of Man*, Allen and Unwin 1931, p. 127
D. T. Suzuki, *Mysticism, Christian and Buddhist*, pp. 30–31

PAGE 135
Genesis 3: 17–18; Isaiah 11: 6–9; Romans 8: 19–23

PAGE 136
Alan Millard, *Lion Handbook to the Bible*, Lion Publishing 1973, pp. 129–130

INDEX

Abduh, M., 69
Adam, historicity of, 110
Adamov, A., 30, 76, 85
Adams, C. C., 147
Agnosticism, 25, 29
Al-Ghazzali, 72
Alice in Wonderland, 104f.
Alice through the Looking Glass, 131
Al-Junayd, 22
Allen, E. L., 77
Altizer, T. J. J., 38, 39, 41
Anderson, J. N. D., 72
Appel, K., 133
Arendt, H., 75
Arnold, M., 30
Atheism, 30ff.
Ayer, A. J., 30, 128

Babylonian Genesis, 137
Bacon, F., 83
Beat movement, 27
Beatles, 28
Becker, C., 68
Beckett, S., 71, 97, 132
Beidhawi, 72
Beyerhaus, P., 41
Bhagavad Gita, 34
Blackham, H. J., 76, 77, 83, 86, 89, 95
Bronowski, J., 48, 91, 92, 108, 128, 132
Brow, R., 21, 33
Buck, P., 80
Buddhism, 26, 79, 93, 103

Cain, 46
Camus, A., 29, 32, 50, 51, 75, 83, 86, 93, 97, 101ff., 104, 129
Cantwell Smith, W., 79
Carlyle, T., 25
Carroll, L., 130f.
Cassirer, E., 43, 75, 127
Chardin, Teilhard de, 36, 41, 129
Cloud of Unknowing, 26
Communism, 78
Conolly, C., 97
Creation, 111, 136
Crossman, R., 79

Danby, H., 71
Darwin, C., 70, 93, 112, 125, 126
Davies, D. R., 98
Dawson, C., 75
'Death of God' theologies, 38
Deism, 23, 68, 69, 71, 73, 124ff.
Descartes, 125f.
Dharma, 92
Diderot, 71
Dostoievsky, 94, 95, 103
Dumitriu, P., 39, 99

Eckhart, 26
Einstein, A., 43
Eliot, G., 85
Eliot, G., 88
Epstein, I., 67
Esslin, M., 30, 71, 83, 84, 97, 132
Evolution, 86, 100, 111
Existentialism, 77
Ezekiel, 42, 56

Fanon, F., 100
Forster, E. M., 80
Friedman, M., 85

Galwash, A., 22
Gibb, H. A. R., 67
Ginsberg, A., 84
Glossary of Humanism, 76

Habakkuk, 13
Habgood, J., 111
Hair, 29
Hamilton, W., 38, 39
Hampson, N., 69, 95

Happold, F. C., 38
Harrington, M., 32, 101
Harrison, G., 9
Hazard, P., 23, 25, 35, 68, 124
Hegel, 35
Heim, K., 77
Hepburn, R., 44
Hertz, 67
Hinduism, 25, 33ff., 79, 92, 99, 127
Hobbes, T., 25
Hocking, W. E., 98
Holy Spirit, 17
Hooke, 73
Hooykaas, 121, 124
Hoyle, F., 116
Humanism, 75f., 101
Humphreys, C., 79, 82, 93, 98, 103
Huxley, A., 43, 49, 51, 81, 82, 98, 103, 104
Huxley, J., 36, 40, 77, 82, 86, 100, 113, 114, 115, 116, 128
Huxley, T. H., 89

Individual, the, 48, 56, 69, 80, 103
Ionesco, 51, 80f., 83
Isaiah, 15, 42, 46, 135
Islam, 22, 67, 68, 70, 72, 74, 123

Jeremiah, 42, 46, 58
Jesus Christ, quotations from, 14, 16, 17, 47, 57, 58, 60, 110
Joad, C. E. M., 64f., 81, 96, 103, 116, 132
Job, 56, 60, 63
John, 43, 47, 54
Joubert, J., 23
Judaism, 21, 67, 71, 123

Kalish, D., 88
Kaufmann, W., 40
Kazantzakis, N., 85
Kerouac, J., 27
Kidner, D., 114
Koestler, A., 50, 83, 88, 92, 100, 101, 130
Koran, see Qur'an

Lack, D., 114
Lallemant, 124
Lawrence, D. H., 128
Leach, E., 76, 88, 95
Lewis, C. S., 96
Lewis, H. D., 35
Lewis, J., 78
Locke, J., 73, 124
Lucebert, 133
Luke, 110

MacIntyre, A., 9, 40, 95
Mackay, D., 108ff., 119, 121
Malraux, A., 85
Manley, G. T., 99
Mann, T., 49, 50, 101
Marc, 133
Maugham, S., 29, 49, 83, 89, 133
Mbiti, J., 19, 70, 73, 123
McLuhan, 88
Merton, T., 43
Mill, J. S., 89, 90
Millard, A. R., 136
Miller, H., 87
Miller, J., 97
Mitchell, J., 43
Mohammad Abduh, L., 67, 68
Montaigne, 127
Moore, H., 133
Moses, 15, 42, 60
Mysticism, 26

Nehemiah, 14
Neill, S., 46, 65
Newbiggin, L., 57, 99
Nicholson, R., 22, 69
Nietzsche, 30, 32, 50, 85, 104, 105

Origin of Species, 113, 125

Pantheism, 33ff.
Paul, 47, 54, 55, 58, 119, 135
Paul, L., 96, 110
Peter, 43, 56
Pinter, H., 48, 50, 81, 97
Priestley, J. B., 89
Primal religion, 19, 66, 70, 71, 73, 74, 123
Proust, 87

Quoist, M., 64
Qur'an, 22, 67, 69, 70, 72, 74, 123

Radhakrishnan, 25, 41, 92, 98, 127
Read, H., 133
Robinson, J., 9, 37, 40, 90, 99, 129
Romanes, J., 131
Romer, 114
Rookmaaker, H. R., 116, 122, 133
Rousseau, 93
Russell, B., 50, 83, 85, 99, 101, 131
Rutherford, M., 125

Santayana, 86
Sartre, J.-P., 29, 31, 32, 50, 75, 77, 81, 84, 85, 87, 88, 94, 97, 106, 130, 132, 133
Satan, 15, 63, 67
Schaeffer, F., 93, 98, 131
Schaff, A., 49, 51, 89, 95
Scheler, M., 75
Science, values of, 91
Science and revelation, 113ff.
Scott, G., 76
Sen, K., 79
Senghor, L., 66
Shaftesbury, 125
Spinoza, 35
Stern, G. E., 88
Stewart, R. A., 21, 71
Stott, J., 115
Suffering and evil, 51, 59–65, 74, 98
Suzuki, D. T., 26, 82, 93, 134

Tagore, R., 87, 134
Takeuchi, Y., 40
Taylor, J. R., 50
Ten Commandments, 58
Thompson, W. R., 112, 114
Tillich, P., 36, 41
Tolstoy, 49
Townshend, P., 87
Toynbee, A., 41

Upanishads, 34, 79

Values, 50, 58, 87
Van Loon, H. W., 99
Voltaire, 23
Von Hugel, Baron, 29
Von Weizacker, C. F., 121, 132

Waiting for Godot, 71
Watson, D. S. M., 115
Wells, H. G., 82
West, R., 86
Westminster Shorter Catechism, 58
Wild, J. D., 94, 97
Willey, B., 73, 124, 125, 126
Willis, Lord, 76, 107
Wilson, C., 80, 85, 87, 94, 104, 107, 132
Wint, G., 79
Wolfe, T., 27
Woolf, V., 81
Wooton, B., 41
Wordsworth, W., 125, 126
Wren-Lewis, J., 38, 90, 101, 130

Yutang, L., 86, 89

Zaehner, 35
Zarathustra, 30